The Scottish Moralists

ON HUMAN NATURE

AND SOCIETY

Edited and with an Introduction by

LOUIS SCHNEIDER

THE UNIVERSITY OF CHICAGO PRESS

CHICAGO AND LONDON

Library of Congress Catalog Card Number: 67–15316

THE UNIVERSITY OF CHICAGO PRESS, CHICAGO & LONDON
The University of Toronto Press, Toronto 5, Canada

Printed in the United States of America

Designed by Andor Braun

Acknowledgments

I AM MUCH INDEBTED to Friedrich A. Hayek, who directed my particular attention to the Scottish moralists. I also owe a debt to the Center for Advanced Study at the University of Illinois. During the fall-winter semester of 1965–66, the Center supported work on my part undertaken for objects somewhat different from those pursued in this volume but in connection with which I gathered materials necessary for its making. Responsibility for any shortcomings the volume may have is mine alone.

Note on the Readings

Numerous minor changes have been made in the readings, primarily in the way of modernizing punctuation and spelling, although occasionally on other lines—as in the case of omission of now meaningless or trivial references. It has seemed pointless to record these changes in detail.

Contents

INTRODUCTION *by Louis Schneider*   *xi*

I. ASPECTS OF HUMAN PSYCHOLOGY

1. David Hume. "On Feeling and Association"   3
2. David Hume. "Some Limitations of Reason"   7
3. David Hume. "Of the Idea of Necessary Connection"   9
4. Thomas Reid. "Instinct and the Inductive Principle"   24
5. Adam Smith. "Of Wonder, or of the Effects of Novelty"   27

II. THE UNIFORMITY OF HUMAN NATURE

6. Francis Hutcheson. "Sensational Anthropology"   39
7. Francis Hutcheson. "Agreement and Disagreement among Men"   41
8. David Hume. "Human Uniformity and Predictability"   44
9. Dugald Stewart. "Of the Moral Faculty"   52

III.   SOCIAL PSYCHOLOGY AND THE SOCIAL BOND

10.   Adam Smith.   "Self-Approbation, Self-Disapprobation and the Man within the Breast"   69

11.   Adam Ferguson. "Of the Principles of Union among Mankind"   77

12.   Adam Ferguson. "Of the Principles of Society in Human Nature"   81

13.   Dugald Stewart. "The Desire of Society"   90

IV.   INDIVIDUAL ACTIONS AND UNINTENDED SOCIAL OUTCOMES

14.   Thomas Reid. "Bees and Men: Instinct and the Limitations of Reason"   99

15.   Adam Smith. "The Invisible Hand"   106

16.   Adam Ferguson. "Unintended Establishments"   108

17.   Dugald Stewart. "Government, Unintended Developments, Expediency, Innovation"   112

V.   ANTICIPATIONS OF FUNCTIONALISM

18.   Adam Smith. "Of the Influence of Fortune upon the Sentiments of Mankind, with Regard to the Merit or Demerit of Actions"   123

19. Dugald Stewart. "Of the Speculation concerning Final Causes"   *143*

20. David Hume. "Marriage of Relatives"   *166*

21. Francis Hutcheson. "Relationship and Marriage" *168*

VI. HISTORY AND SOCIOLOGY

22. David Hume. "Of Superstition and Enthusiasm"   *173*

23. David Hume. "Remarks on Reform, Puritanism, and Liberty"   *178*

24. Adam Smith. "How the Commerce of the Towns Contributed to the Improvement of the Country" *191*

25. Adam Ferguson. "Of the Political Arts"   *200*

VII. THE RANGE OF SOCIOLOGICAL CONCERN

26. Adam Ferguson. "Of Contract or the Principle of Conventional Obligation"   *211*

27. Thomas Reid. "Rights and Duties"   *220*

28. Adam Smith. "Of the Origin of Ambition and of the Distinction of Ranks"   *223*

29. Adam Smith. "The Three Great Orders of Society" *235*

30. David Hume. "Of the Populousness of Ancient Nations"   *238*

31. Henry Home, Lord Kames. "A Great City Considered in Physical, Moral, and Political Views"   *243*

VIII.   THE ANTHROPOLOGICAL IMPULSE

32.   Henry Home, Lord Kames. "The Development of Religious Belief"   255
33.   James Burnet, Lord Monboddo. "Examples from Ancient and Modern History of Men Living in the Brutish State, without Arts or Civility"   271

BIBLIOGRAPHICAL NOTE   287

Introduction

THE SCOTTISH MORALISTS are men whose work in a variety
of areas included much that today we would unhesitatingly call
"sociological." They constituted a more or less distinctive group
that has long since achieved recognition as such, although there
might not be instant scholarly consensus on every name one or
another student of the Scots might wish to include or exclude. The
choice made in the present volume has been to follow Gladys
Bryson in her choice of Ferguson, Hume, Hutcheson, Kames,
Monboddo, Reid, Adam Smith, and Dugald Stewart as representatives of the eighteenth-century Scottish attempt to establish
foundations for "the study of man and society."[1] These men are
accordingly the "Scottish moralists" here dealt with. If there is an
element of arbitrariness in choosing these particular eight, it is
slight, and it is probably conservative to say that a great deal of
what is important in the emergent Scottish sociology of the eighteenth century may be found in their work. Aside from the matter
of the choice of the eight, it has often been contended that the
Scottish moralists are in general a genuinely significant group in
the development of sociological thought. Part of the object of this
volume is to lend support to this bias.

Although the names of some of the Scottish moralists are certainly well known, those of others are less generally familiar, and
it may be useful in any case to afford a brief identification of each
of our men. Francis Hutcheson (1694–1746) is often regarded

[1]   Gladys Bryson, *Man and Society: The Scottish Inquiry of the Eighteenth Century,* pp. 1–2.

as the "originator" in some sense of the work of the Scots.[2] He was elected to the chair of moral philosophy at the University of Glasgow in 1729 and began his lectures there in 1730. He evidently exercised great influence as a teacher, but by the testimony of his writings was not of the intellectual stature of the most able of the Scottish moralists. His work shows a strong interest in questions of ethics, psychology, and some aspects of law and social organization. The person elected to succeed him in his professorship was Thomas Craigie, but, upon the latter's death, Adam Smith (1723–90) took the chair in 1752. Smith is of course the famous economist, whose work on *The Theory of Moral Sentiments* is, for its significance in regard to sociology, as worth attending to now as is the later work on *The Wealth of Nations*. He held his chair at Glasgow until 1764, when he was succeeded by Thomas Reid (1710–96), who had previously professed philosophy at King's College, Aberdeen. Reid's interest in sociological and historical questions is quite incidental to his predominating philosophical-psychological concerns, but he is unmistakably a member of the "school" of Scottish moralists (with all its internal disagreements as well as agreements), was particularly influenced by David Hume and has at least at few things to say that are worth noting for a treatment and presentation of the Scots directed to their sociological achievement.

Two others of our eight men were also professors. Adam Ferguson (1723–1816) was originally appointed at the University of Edinburgh in 1759 to teach natural philosophy or physics, but in 1764 received another appointment there that enabled him thenceforth to devote his attention to moral philosophy. (Actually, he became professor of pneumatics and moral philosophy.) His work shows strong preoccupation with political philosophy and history, but he is also very much a sociologist in a modern

2   Thus, Dugald Stewart writes: "The metaphysical philosophy of Scotland, and, indeed, the literary taste which so remarkably distinguished this country during the last century, may be dated from the lectures of Dr. Francis Hutcheson, in the University of Glasgow. Strong indication of the same speculative spirit may be traced in earlier writers; but it was from this period that Scotland, after a long slumber, began again to attract general notice in the world of letters." *Collected Works*, I, 428. Cf., however, William R. Scott, *Francis Hutcheson*, chap. 13, for pertinent cautions.

sense. When he retired in 1785 he was succeeded by Dugald Stewart (1753–1828), who performed the duties of professor for approximately a quarter of a century. Stewart's thought ranges through psychology, economics, and the history of thought and often presents features of interest to the sociologist. He has a certain relative prominence in this volume more for his flair for "summing up" than for any conspicuous originality or depth.

Of the three men who were not professors, David Hume (1711–76) is, to be sure, the best known, as he is, with the possible exception of Adam Smith, the best known of the entire group. Hume was famous in his time both as philosopher and as historian. His work is often sociologically relevant and indeed presents much more that is to the point than can be utilized in a relatively brief anthology. Henry Home (1696–1782) was trained in the law and functioned from 1752 as a judge (a so-called ordinary lord of session), with the title of Lord Kames. He was a versatile writer but will figure in the following pages mainly as an anthropologist. James Burnet (1714–99) was also a lawyer by training and also became an ordinary lord of session (in 1767), assuming the title of Lord Monboddo. Even in his work as a judge he was very much his own man—"generally in the minority and sometimes alone," as his biographer in the *Dictionary of National Biography* puts the matter. It is a certainty that he was his own man in his positions on the anthropological problems with which we shall find him preoccupied.

The eight men thus briefly, almost perfunctorily, identified to begin with "stand as a connected group of scholars, mutually influencing one another."[3] The mutual influence appears plainly in their printed works. One vivid, concrete indication of the tendency for "connection" among them is afforded by Graham's imaginary but realistic construction of a street scene in the Edinburgh of about 1771, in which appear David Hume, Lord Kames, Adam Smith, and Lord Monboddo, to be followed by Adam Ferguson within a page.[4] The fact of connection and mutual influence is not lessened by the circumstance that the interests of all or virtually

3 Bryson, *Man and Society*, p. 2.
4 Henry G. Graham, *The Social Life of Scotland in the Eighteenth Century*, pp. 115–17.

all were so far-flung that they could scarcely have avoided touch-
ing upon one another's provinces. But it is worth stressing that
breadth of the subject of "moral philosophy," which has already
inevitably been intimated. Bryson observes quite correctly that
the opening of volumes of moral philosophy will show preoccupation with matters of psychology, family, economics, government,
religion, jurisprudence, primitive custom, ethics, aesthetics, and
more.[5] Hume's biographer, Mossner, similarly remarks of moral
philosophy that in the eighteenth century it "still included, not
only ethics and psychology, but also politics and government,
history, all the social studies, and aesthetics and criticism."[6] And
a recent writer on Hume notes that the latter intended by "moral
subjects" what we might call "historical subjects," treating, that is
to say, "of subject matter in which the changes that take place,
and that are described in histories, are traced not to physical
causes, but to human causes." The same writer then suggests that
we would now call the moral subjects the humanities and the
social sciences.[7]

   This volume must be restricted to a range of materials narrower
than that of the old moral philosophy. It represents an effort to
analyze and present the sociological thought of the Scottish moralists, and it has already been suggested that the sociological com-
ponent in their work is considerable enough. It will help to clarify
the objectives of the volume to note some things it is not designed
to do. For one, it is not designed to consider the Scotland (or,
indeed, the Europe) of the eighteenth century insofar as that
constituted a significant background for the work of our eight
men; nor is it designed to relate their work to that of contemporaries in other fields of endeavor. The work of any group of
thinkers will presumably have been influenced in some sense by
their environment and will have fed back into it, but this is not
taken up here as a matter of special interest in the case of the Scots.
Also, there is little concern with the work of the Scots as showing

5   Bryson, *Man and Society*, p. 4.
6   Ernest C. Mossner, *The Life of David Hume*, p. 72.
7   John B. Stewart, *The Moral and Political Philosophy of David Hume*,
p. 10.

their place in the history of thought. Montesquieu may have had a profound influence on Adam Ferguson, but this kind of circumstance will be entirely incidental. In her recent volume on early anthropology, Hodgen remarks that even those who have followed the antecedents of sociology and anthropology back to the eighteenth century, to "the Encyclopedists and the Scottish moral philosophers," have in fact "reached back only part of the way."[8] So be it. The object here is not to "reach back" or trace the sources of a variety of ideas.[9] The Scottish moralists were clearly not self-created, but the point need not be pursued. Not even the history of the Scots' own thought, in the sense of a painstaking delineation of how they affected one another or changed their views over time, is of especial interest. What is of interest, however, is to draw from the work of our eight men sociological analyses, conceptions, and descriptions that are of ongoing significance in the work that sociologists do. Other interests are quite subordinate to this one.[10]

The treatment of the Scottish moralists afforded has accordingly been much influenced by present-day sociological concerns that do, however, reach into the past and therefore have had a certain duration already, but that also appear likely to have a certain tenacity in the future. Judgment must play a role in this. That is quite inevitable. Different emphases would certainly be possible. A representative of another generation might be alert —and impervious—to other things. But a conscientious effort has been made to give due weight to at least some elements in sociological thought on whose significance there would be wide agreement—and to avoid antiquarianism. It will be seen that even Lord Monboddo's work is not without its relation to main streams of

8   Margaret T. Hodgen, *Early Anthropology in the Sixteenth and Seventeenth Centuries* (Philadelphia: University of Pennsylvania Press, 1964), p. 7.
9   Among the most interesting historical connections of the Scottish moralists are those with Bernard Mandeville. The work of Hutcheson, Hume (however rarely he mentions Mandeville by name), and Adam Smith, in particular, can profitably be related to Mandeville's. Some mention of Mandeville is made below, but it is not pretended that his significance to the Scots is adequately indicated.
10   Occasionally, it is necessary to refer to philosophical matters, but this is done with the primary sociological interest in view.

anthropological-sociological concern. The term sociological is understood in a fairly strict sense, yet not, it may be allowed, in an unduly cramping one. At the same time, space has been allowed for psychological views held by the Scots, partly because of the intrinsic interest of these but more importantly because the Scots' ideas of human nature are closely related to their sociological notions; and more strictly "anthropological" material is both discussed and presented.

The eight section headings that follow afford convenient rubrics under which to discuss the work of the Scottish moralists. They have also been used as titles to organize the readings from the Scots that make up the bulk of this volume.[11]

I. *Aspects of Human Psychology*

The Scottish moralists were in general shrewd psychologists. They frequently engaged in what one may call gifted social-psychologizing, talented if not very systematic reflection about man as a being endowed with certain traits who is constrained to operate within a social order. In the course of a discussion of gallantry, David Hume is prompted to reflect that there are situa-

---

[11]   It may be well to note here that both for the readings and for purposes of citation it has seemed a sensible rule to utilize late (or latest) editions in order to make sure that a man's thought would be represented in its final published form. (This is obviously not to deny that for certain objects it might be important to trace changes in a man's thought.) Thus, the reprint of Smith's *Theory of Moral Sentiments* which has been used is in all essentials the same as the sixth edition of that work which appeared in 1790, the last year of Smith's life. In the case of Hume's *History of England*, T. E. Jessop (*A Bibliography of David Hume and of Scottish Philosophy*, p. 30) lists for 1778 a "New edition, with the author's last corrections and improvements. To which is prefixed a short account of his life by himself." The 1879 six-volume edition published by Harper's, which has been used as a matter of convenience, carries precisely the same legend. But the Scottish moralists were prolific writers and their works, all told, went through numerous editions: it was simply not feasible in all cases to obtain a sufficiently late (or a latest) edition, and it was not even possible to obtain any copy of a few works. Fortunately, this is of minor importance for the purposes of this volume. The reader who wishes more information about various editions of particular works may find guidance in the *Bibliographical Note* at the end of the volume.

tions in which we are tempted to "vice" and to "passion disagree-able to others," but in which, nevertheless, "refined breeding has taught men to throw the bias on the opposite side, and to preserve, in all their behavior, the appearance of sentiments different from those to which they naturally incline." Thus, where pride and self-ishness may prompt us to assume precedence over others, polite-ness exacts deference toward them. Old men aware of their shortcomings might expect depreciation from the young, who, however, when appropriately educated, show their elders intensi-fied regard. Strangers and foreigners, unprotected as they are, may be shown the highest courtesies.[12]

But not even all the social psychology the Scots have to offer is quite so casual. Adam Smith could present the beginnings, at any rate, of an analysis that has clear affinities with relatively well-developed notions in social psychology today. Aside from this par-ticular field, a drive toward system in psychology generally is well exemplified in Hume's analytically respectable concern with the "laws" of mental association and the movement of the passions. In the readings that follow, two short passages from Hume have been connected to afford a statement "on feeling and association." The "hard" and "scientific" bent in the psychological thought of one of the two leading figures in our group is evident in these passages.

One of the most striking aspects of the psychological analysis of the Scots consists in their keen awareness (in an "Age of Rea-son") of the limitations of human reason. There is a strong vein of insistence in Hutcheson on the point that reason judges about means or subordinate ends, while "about the ultimate ends there is no reasoning," for we pursue the latter "by some immediate dis-position or determination of soul, which in the order of action is prior to all reasoning; as no opinion or judgment can move to action where there is no prior desire of some end."[13] Reason is not of the stuff of the passions. It may adjust means to ends or perhaps

---

12 David Hume, *Essays*, I, 191–93.
13 Francis Hutcheson, *A System of Moral Philosophy*, I, 38. Hutcheson had also written before this that "no reason can excite to action previously to some end" and that "no end can be proposed without some instinct or affec-tion." *An Essay on the Nature and Conduct of the Passions and Affections* 3d ed.; London, 1742), p. 291.

seek a certain harmony among ends already in existence and de-
riving their existence from non-rational sources, but it cannot of
itself supply motivation or "passion," and when the passions take a
new turn, it must follow them in their wanderings if it is to be
of any service. Particularly in the second of two concise para-
graphs (in "Some Limitations of Reason") drawn on in the following anthology Hume suggests these restrictions: "reason alone can
never produce any action, or give rise to volition"; "nothing can
oppose or retard the impulse of passion, but a contrary impulse";
"reason has no original influence." Hume further writes forth-
rightly: "We speak not strictly and philosophically when we talk
of the combat of passion and of reason. Reason is, and ought only
to be the slave of the passions and can never pretend to any other
office than to serve and obey them."[14] A fundamental point is thus
made clear.[15] But there are also other ways in which the Scots are
aware of the limitations of reason.

   Hume's famous analysis of the idea of causation still makes both
interesting and important reading today for a variety of reasons to
which no reference need me made here. It is not to slight other
features of that analysis to stress what is most pertinent for us,
namely, Hume's own strong sense of "the weakness and narrow

[14]   *A Treatise of Human Nature*, II, 194, 195.
[15]   To be sure, it can be argued that Hume states it in such fashion as
to create unnecessary difficulty. He writes, again in the *Treatise* (II, 195–96):
" 'Tis not contrary to reason to prefer the destruction of the whole world to
the scratching of my finger. 'Tis not contrary to reason for me to choose my
total ruin, to prevent the least uneasiness of an Indian or person wholly unknown to me." The difficulty is not with Hume's meaning, which seems clear
enough. The scratching of my finger might conceivably appear to me as a
calamity to be avoided at all costs and the prospect of my total ruin as something of very slight significance—and if such is my disposition, such it is.
But it is hard to eliminate from the concept of reason an element of frank
valuation that leads us to recognize, for example, that there may be a highly
rational organization of means for the attainments of ends that are entirely
"irrational," say, as in the case of an army superbly organized to destroy the
world, including itself. Properly developed, the sense of the term reason thus
suggested would involve the further notion of a hierarchy of ends, explicit
or implicit, cherished by the same human(s). But the development possible
must be foregone here. It is enough to allude to the relative importance in
human psychological and social life of the phenomenon of highly rational
organization for ends that may in some significant sense be regarded as quite
mad. See footnote eighteen below.

limits of human reason and capacity" (to use his words) when we note how "imperfect" are our ideas about cause and effect, and that it is "impossible to give any just definition of cause, except . . . from something extraneous and foreign to it."[16] At the same time, the compact and brief form of the argument about causation in the following readings (taken from the *Enquiry concerning Human Understanding*) reveals much of Hume's power as a psychologist beyond the point regarding limitations of reason.

Hume was not alone in taking his analysis of the notion of causation as revealing of the limitations of reason. Thomas Reid adopts a great deal of Hume's outlook in this matter, although he insists that our "belief of the continuance of the laws of nature" was an "original principle of the mind," which he labels the inductive principle for obvious reasons. He was explicit on the point that "*antecedently to all reasoning, we have, by our constitution,* an anticipation that there is a fixed and steady course of nature."[17] This and other pertinent statements will be found in the brief commentary on "Instinct and the Inductive Principle," here reproduced from his *Inquiry into the Human Mind*. Reid was sensitively aware of limitations upon reason in a number of directions. He could write that "it is the intention of nature that we should be carried in arms before we are able to walk upon our legs; and it is likewise the intention of nature that our belief should be guided by the authority and reason of others before it can be guided by our own reason." Most men, he also commented, "continue all their days to be just what nature and human education made them," for they are molded by "habit, limitation, and instruction; and reason has little or no share in forming them."[18] There will be occasion later to turn to Reid again in connection with the theme of the limitations of reason.

The influence of the mode of analysis of causation that Hume had presented also appears elsewhere among the Scots, as in the case of Smith's pages on "Wonder," reproduced in this volume from his *Essays on Philosophical Subjects*. Smith is not directly

16   *Essays*, II, 63.
17   Thomas Reid, *Works*, I, 199; italics supplied.
18   *Ibid.*, I, 197, 201.

or greatly concerned with the theme of the limitations of reason in these pages, to be sure, although what he has to say is not unconnected with that theme. Rather, he is concerned with "how we think." His passage shows a characteristic clarity and penetration, and since Hume and Reid will have already given us a certain background for an understanding of what the latter called the inductive principle, it is well to present this statement of Smith's as a further instance of the talent of the Scottish moralists in psychological matters. Consideration of Smith as a social phychologist in particular will be afforded under the rubric of social psychology and the social bond.

If the Scots are keenly aware of the limitations of reason, this is plainly connected with their strong sense of its non-rational foundations.[19] Reid's comment that it is "the intention of nature" that we be carried in arms before we walk has already been noted, as it has been suggested that reason may introduce a certain system or order into that which is itself not rational. It does not seem incompatible with Reid's view of the inductive principle to say that, once there exists what he considered the instinctive yield of the latter (in the form of suppositions arrived at by a kind of "constitutionally" determined inductive process), reason may build a variety of structures on the non-rational foundations represented by that yield; nor does this appear incompatible with Hume's remarks on causation. There is an analogy in the social sphere. The Scottish moralists tended to look on custom and tradition as presenting "materials," again—materials that reason might process with caution; not materials to be rejected out of hand by a "reason" that, if indeed it acted in unqualifiedly rejecting fashion, would become self-consuming and self-destructive. Reason thus must

---

[19]   Non-rational is used simply in the sense of having nothing immediately to do with reason. Passions, appetites, drives, and impulses are not, as such, either rational or irrational. They are non-rational "materials" on which reason may, and indeed must, work. (They may stand in the way of, or interfere with, other passions which possess the same humans, and then they may be regarded as irrational if the other passions are given higher value than they.) A custom, such as that of shaking hands under certain circumstances, is also as such neither rational nor irrational, but non-rational, although when, say, shaking hands is done for reasons of expediency it takes on a rational aspect.

operate in the social sphere with materials in the form, say, of already existing institutions (roughly, "established," more or less widely agreed upon patterns for action relating to important areas of social life) that antedate it. The point will come up again, in connection with Ferguson's work. In the interim, it is worth remembering that the Scottish moralists were hardly socially or politically radical or revolutionary. No doubt, their rather conservative stance helped them to "see" the value of non-rational (for instance traditional or customary) elements in social life with greater ease than they might have done otherwise. But even if one should be quite averse toward their political orientation, a perception of the limitations of reason is not in itself illiberal and is indeed an indispensable prerequisite for the realization or release of as much reason as there may be. The significance of the Scots' perception of these limitations becomes very considerable with the subsequent discussion of individual actions and unintended social outcomes.

If the limitations of reason, in the Scottish view, have been stressed as they have, this need not obscure the circumstance that one can also find in the Scots (as notably, and inconsistently, in the case of David Hume)[20] instances of the exaggeration of the role of reason in human affairs.

II. *The Uniformity of Human Nature*

The view of human nature entertained by the Scottish moralists is marked in general by an emphasis on uniformity in that nature. The idea of the constancy of man's psychic makeup was indeed a familiar notion of the Enlightenment. The Scots might have gotten it from a variety of sources, for example, from Mandeville, who writes in what were virtually commonplace terms that "manners and customs may change, but human nature is much the same in all ages."[21] Francis Hutcheson was particularly interested in urging uniformity in human nature arising from what

[20]   See below, pp. lv–lvi.
[21]   *Free Thoughts on Religion, the Church, and National Happiness* (2d ed.; London, 1729), p. 159.

he took to be a certain unstated, sometimes elusive, but still ascertainable moral consensus of mankind. He was critical of that kind of superficial and mindlessly dramatic anthropology that bids us, as he put it in a passage reproduced in the readings, "stare" in astonishment at the ways of various peoples, too hastily supposed to be unqualifiedly "different." He sought to reinforce the thesis of uniformity in his *System of Moral Philosophy,* from which some pertinent statements have also been drawn. David Hume gave one of the ablest statements of the thesis in his *Enquiry concerning the Human Understanding.* This, too, is reproduced in the present volume under the title of "Human Uniformity and Predictability." Hume may be said actually to be interested here in two things, the discussion of which he has interwoven. He evidently wishes to press the thesis that the Greeks and Romans, say, were once much as the French and English are now. Over time and through space men resemble one another considerably. For Hume this coalesces easily with the view that there exists a certain "necessity" in the characters of men and the affairs of society that makes for predictability and stability of conduct. Without the strong probability of the occurrence of various events, the existence of human society would become precarious. "The poorest artificer, who labors alone, expects at least the protection of the magistrate. . . . He also expects that, when he carries his goods to market, and offers them at a reasonable price, he shall find purchasers."[22] But the presumption of this predictability, again, is tied in with the notion of widespread or universal human sameness. Hume is sophisticated enough to allow for a margin of the "unexpected" that may have to be accounted for by factors not otherwise reckoned with, but he stays with his position that the ways of man and events in society are in principle predictable and that men always and everywhere tend to resemble one another profoundly.

The Enlightenment stress on the uniformity of human nature could and did sometimes go to the point where the representation of men and women, as in historical writings, involved a sameness of portrayal that was certainly challengeable. The historian J. B. Black asserts with regard to Voltaire that "it seems never to have

[22]   *Essays,* II, 73.

crossed his mind that the medieval man, for instance, differs from the modern by the whole heaven. . . . The whole structure of his mind, the circle of ideas, beliefs, illusions, prejudices within which he lives, is different." One might well argue that Black exaggerates here in his turn and refuse to follow him without some reservations when he asserts that "what the modern mind craves is not the reduction of all events and characters to a common denominator, but their *differentiation*."[23] Yet Black has a point. He suggests that Hume was "dominated" by "the belief that human nature was uniformly the same at all times and places" and that history accordingly became for him "a repeating decimal." Black asserts further with regard to Hume's historical work: "The great drama is transacted on a flat and uniform level; each age or group working up into forms that are already familiar the common stock of attributes." In discussing a passage from Hume's *History* on Luther, Black will remark that "in accordance with Hume's philosophical theory the universal is emphasized, the local and particular are suppressed, and all sense of perspective is obliterated"; or, as regards Hume's passages on Joan of Arc, he will comment that Hume's description is so generalized that one does not realize that Joan lived in the fifteenth century.[24]

[23]   J. B. Black, *The Art of History: A study of Four Great Historians of the Eighteenth Century*, p. 58. (Black's four historians are Voltaire, Hume, Robertson, and Gibbon).

[24]   *Ibid.*, pp. 86, 98, 100–01. See also Thomas P. Peardon, *The Transition in English Historical Writing: 1760–1830* (New York: Columbia University Press, 1933), p. 22; Bryson, *Man and Society*, pp. 106–7. Meinecke has criticisms similar to Black's. He regards it as "the typical mistake" of Enlightenment historiography to be "overhasty to generalize and to construct causal laws." Meinecke, too, refers to Hume's psychology in connection with his historiography and avers that in virtue of that psychology Hume could only discern psychological "parts" or fragments and their mechanical interplay but could not grasp psychological wholes evolving from an inner, individual center. By and large, in Hume's representation of development one can see only the play of human affects and drives that are eternally the same. Friedrich Meinecke, *Die Entstehung des Historismus*, I, 215, 223–24. It may be remarked that the word mechanical, or mechanistic, is critically applied to Hume's psychology with some frequency. The language of a statement such as the following may appear to give some warrant to the critical reaction. (Hume is at the end of his "Dissertation on the Passions," *Essays*, II, 166). "I pretend not to have exhausted this subject. It is sufficient for my purpose if I have made it appear that in the production or conduct of the passions there

A subtler view of human nature than he had might well have helped Hume as a historian. By allowing for an appreciable internalization of cultural norms and meanings, he could have created historical actors who would have been more differentiated, more full-bodied, more believably within their special centuries. Trivial differences in outer garments would then have been paralleled by significant differences in the inner cultural-moral furniture of the psyche. And while thus doing more justice to human diversity, Hume need not have given up his very valuable stress on uniformity. He and others who thought like him in the relevant respects have been accused of superficiality.[25] But he was penetrating enough to see, at least, that the mere observation of cultural differences, of diversity of customs and manners does not "prove" a diversity of underlying human nature, but merely presents a problem for analysis. It may be granted that it is all too easy to get involved in rather purely verbal issues in these matters. One might acknowledge in the abstract that men are the same and also different and thereby achieve very little aside from a vague feeling that such a stance is somehow "correct." Evidently much more than this is needed. The doing of some sort of justice to both universal and non-universal elements in human nature (including the job of considering what the universal and non-universal "mean" in processes of social change) is a tremendous task of analysis and investigation. But the Scots were at least beyond mere verbalism in this field.

Dugald Stewart is allowed a last word on the theme of uniformity of human nature in our anthology. As is his wont, Stewart performs well in summarizing for his "school." His arguments are hardly definitive, but they are marked above all by the feature

---

is a certain regular mechanism which is susceptible of as accurate a disquisition as the laws of motion, optics, hydrostatics or any part of natural philosophy." If it should be granted that this is vulnerably mechanistic it is also of course still significant as an indication of Hume's faith that the passions are subject to law, are regularly evoked or restrained by phenomena in principle subject to human generalization.

25   For example, Peardon, *The Transition in English Historical Writing*, p. 37, writes of the "brilliant superficiality" of Hume as a historian.

that he will not relinquish the notion of uniformity in an easy capitulation to the mere circumstance of cultural difference. Stewart was well aware that situations shape motives and that consequently, let us say, a people exposing or abandoning old persons to death might be as fundamentally humane or benevolent as one not doing so, given the harsher physical conditions under which the former lived. He might even have argued that the very fact of cultural differences is itself evidence for a certain sameness of human nature, since different peoples have indeed faced different situations; and that there should be a difference of cultural outcome is precisely what we would then expect on the assumption of a common human nature: identity of cultural outcome in the face of differing situations would, paradoxically, suggest a differing underlying human material.[26]

The problems in this whole field suggested by Hume, Hutcheson, Stewart, and others remain very much with us today. They are not necessarily "sociological" problems alone, but interest philosophers, psychologists, and anthropologists. The Scots approached them with a realization of their importance and with genuine sophistication, if not always with the greatest possible subtlety. Their unwillingness to subscribe to a moral philosophy that might deny human moral consensus as soon as some overt differences of judgment and custom appeared or to embrace radically relativistic anthropological doctrine may be regarded as a valuable heritage to sociology among other disciplines. Although they leave this entire subject in too "general" and unsystematic a state, their statements on it are still to the point and worth recalling.[27]

26   Ferguson is another of the Scots who may well be pointed to in connection with the thesis of a common human nature. (It will be noted that Stewart relies on him.) He was most alert to evidences of moral consensus where differences in other respects might easily persuade one to presume the existence of dissensus. See his *Principles of Moral and Political Science*, II, 135–48.

27   Kames and Monboddo, because of their special anthropological concern, are of peculiar interest in regard to the thesis of a uniform human nature, and pertinent views of theirs are touched upon under the last heading of this Introduction.

III. *Social Psychology and the Social Bond*

The prior discussion of uniformity in human nature might well have been preceded by or combined with the comments now to be made. The separation of themes in these sections is to some extent simply a matter of convenience. Adam Smith could well have argued that his "rules" of social psychology applied to human beings in general, and it would have been entirely in the spirit of his thought to do so. In any case, his outlook in the sphere of social psychology is one of two main matters to be considered at this point, the other being the social bond or bond of union among men, as conceived more particularly by Ferguson.

Smith's treatment of the individual's attitude toward, and evaluation of, himself is one of the more striking achievements in social psychology on the part of the Scots. This work has evident affinities with that of much later social psychologists, such as Cooley and George H. Mead, and it is also likely to suggest some aspects of the Freudian notion of the superego. Smith writes in a passage reproduced in our readings that man in society is provided with a "mirror" by which he may look upon his own character, his own sentiments, his own "beauty or deformity" of mind or body. The mirror is "placed in the countenance and behavior of those he lives with." When we imagine ourselves the spectators of our own comportment, we are afforded "a looking-glass by which we can, in some measure, with the eyes of other people, scrutinize the propriety of our own conduct."[28] And Smith also refers, in particularly well-known phrases, to the impartial spectator, to that man within the breast who may be said broadly to be the representative within ourselves of *others* in the society about us—of others who make our judgments of our own conduct and sentiments less partial or self-interested than they would be if we had not effected precisely that internalization whereby the others come to be represented within us.

This most promising notion of society within us, of the impartial spectator, of the man within the breast, was susceptible of

[28]   See *The Theory of Moral Sentiments*, pp. 161–65.

much development that Smith did not yet afford. Smith writes that our judgments of our own sentiments and motives "must always bear some secret reference, either to what are, or to what, upon a certain condition, would be, or to what, we imagine, ought to be the judgment of others." The ways and means of this "secret reference," however, are given little clarification. Smith will make apt comments, as when he avers that "the man within the breast, the abstract and ideal spectator of our sentiments and conduct, requires often to be awakened and put in mind of his duty, by the presence of the real spectator," by a friend or stranger who may be seen and conversed with in person.[29] But he proposes no theory of the impartial spectator on the line, for example, of inquiry into divergent or conflicting moral norms or directives coming to the individual from different "others." Smith is still far from the subtlety in these matters achieved by sophisticated Meadians or Freudians (although his ideas foreshadow theirs.) Also, there is a certain evident indeterminateness in the notion of the impartial spectator, indicated plainly by Smith's own reference to what "are" and to what "ought to be" the judgments of others. What others' judgments are in fact and what they ought to be are quite clearly different things.

It is not surprising that criticism of Smith in regard to the matter just mentioned should have been forthcoming soon. Ferguson, for example, contended that in Smith's reference to "a supposed well-informed and impartial spectator" there is "an implied confession that there is some previous standard of estimation, by which to select the judge of our actions." Ferguson makes it quite clear that he is not raising "merely a question of fact," but has in view ethical standards by which the judgments of any "others" might be challenged.[30] So Dugald Stewart, too, asserts that "the metaphysical problem concerning the primary sources of our moral ideas and emotions will be found in the same obscurity as before" when we have gone through Smith's *Moral Sentiments*. The man within the breast, social product that he is, may in principle be morally wrong at any time. Stewart regrets that Smith

29   *Ibid.*, pp. 161–62, 216.
30   *Principles of Moral and Political Science*, II, 126.

did not use, instead of "the man within the breast," more familiar terms such as reason and conscience.[31] Smith actually writes at one point of "reason, principle, conscience, the inhabitant of the breast, the man within, the great judge and arbiter of our conduct," as if these were all the same.[32] Yet Stewart and Ferguson were justified in their view that the judgments of the man within, as nearly as one could understand what Smith meant in referring to him, were not necessarily ethically ideal ones. Smith, however, was far too acute to be misled in such a matter. Undoubtedly, he knew very well that his contribution was not in the strict sense an ethical one: it was rather in the line of social psychology, and for this purpose the peculiar vocabulary he employed was appropriately suggestive. The gain for social psychology represented by his work is not destroyed because he did not resolve certain associated ethical problems.[33]

The social bond itself was of interest to all the Scottish moralists. Some of the more significant statements regarding it were made by Ferguson. Two of them are reproduced herein. In these Ferguson writes in his wonted rather discursive way and throws out a number of points he does not develop. In the first statement, "Of the Principles of Union among Mankind," from his *Essay on the History of Civil Society,* several features stand out. Ferguson's insight frequently stated (and which will be encountered again) that men constantly but inadvertently achieve results in their conduct that seem as if they must have been projected and sought for beforehand is there suggested with the observation that "a great work, like that of forming society, must in our apprehension arise from deep reflections, and be carried on with a view to the advantages which mankind derives from commerce and mutual support." As always, Ferguson is skeptical of such "apprehension." For him, the foundations of the social bond lie in considerable measure in man's spontaneous, "instinctive" reaching out for others. And it is from the union with his species that man derives "not only the

---

31   *Collected Works,* VI, 331, 333.
32   *Ibid.,* p. 194.
33   See Leslie Stephen, *History of English Thought in the Eighteenth Century,* II, 62–65, for other pertinent comments on *The Theory of Moral Sentiments,* in which dissatisfaction with Smith as an ethical philosopher perhaps also tends to obscure his merit as a social psychologist.

force, but the very existence of his happiest emotions; not only the better part, but almost the whole of his rational character"— an interesting view likely enough to remind us of Durkheim on society and man. There is finally the suggestion that it is not in relatively little developed social conditions but rather in "a commercial state" and in the prevalence of modern competition that man is "sometimes found a detached and a solitary being."[34]

The second of the passages reproduced from Ferguson in our anthology, on "Principles of Society in Human Nature," from the treatise on moral and political science, it will be noted, is a wide-ranging essay on the social bond. It needs no comment. Its various affirmations are well complemented by the following statement not reproduced in our readings: "We are apt to treat the origin of language, as we treat that of society itself, by supposing a time when neither existed; but . . . we may venture to infer that, since mankind were fairly entered on this scene of human life, there never was any such time; that both associating and speaking, in however rude a form, are coeval with the species of man."[35]

The mere assertion, so very clearly made, that society or the social bond coexists with man is important even if by Ferguson's time it was hardly novel. All this could not possibly have pleased Lord Monboddo, who held very different views,[36] but, although Monboddo, in his way, was more elaborately argumentative than Ferguson, the latter unquestionably had the better case in these matters.

Dugald Sewart's piece on "The Desire of Society" does not add much to what will already have been afforded. But it is a statement whose clarity, brevity, and apt insistence that "man has always been found in a social state" warrant its inclusion in this volume.

IV. *Individual Actions and Unintended Social Outcomes*

By now the Scottish moralists may be said to have brought man fully onto the social scene. But even when he is conceived as

---

34   *Essay on the History of Civil Society*, pp. 30–31, 33, 34.
35   *Principles of Moral and Political Science*, I, 43.
36   See below, pp. lxxv–lxxviii.

being fully on that scene, psychological considerations remain relevant for the comprehension of what he does. And the limitations of reason previously referred to are particularly relevant. It is one of the most insistent themes in the work of the Scots that men frequently act with certain restricted objects in view and have not the capacity to contemplate larger "objects," while at the same time it is in some sense important or indispensable for social or political or economic systems that those larger "objects" (or special "results" of action) be realized.[37] In accordance with this theme, too, it is frequently the aim of the Scots' analysis to show how the larger "objects" are brought about indirectly but effectively through the pursuit of more restricted goals that men can and do set for themselves. In the development of the theme it is argued repeatedly that human reason is too frail a reed to rely upon to bring about a variety of "results."

[37]   A number of things need noting here in the interest of clarity. It has been quite usual for sociological theorists to contrast intention or purposiveness in the "social action" of individuals with the unintended character of the results of some or much of that action. Accordingly, such phrases as Robert K. Merton's "unanticipated consequences of purposive social action" have had considerable currency. (See Robert K. Merton's *Social Theory and Social Structure* (Glencoe, Ill.: The Free Press, 1957), for example, at p. 51, note.) The Scottish moralists very often also mean to contrast intention on the part of the individual and the unintended character of certain outcomes of individual action. But they are not invariably insistent that the individual action be clearly "purposive." It may shade off into the traditional, the ceremonial (or what is somewhat indeterminately called the instinctive"), while still having important uncontemplated social results. Again, in the present contrast between individual actions and unintended social outcomes, there is the object of stressing individual actions in the sense of actions which are unconcerted, not engaged in by a number of individuals working out a design together. Yet individual actions in this sense can in another way still be social actions and should be understood as such: no matter how unconcerted individual actions, they are "social" insofar as they occur in a context in which individuals are oriented to one another and in which choices are made and meanings prevail. Finally, in the contrast made, a word about "social outcomes" is in order. Insofar as consequences of individual actions are not the product of design, they are evidently not strictly "goals," "aims," "objects," or the like. This freedom from intention seems well enough conveyed by words like outcome, result, and terminus. But also, the term social in *this* connection is intended to suggest outcomes that either are in a loose, intuitive sense "socially important" or that refer to social system "needs" rather than direct individual ones—and this last reference will be clarified in the course of the present section.

Some interesting notions bearing on this theme were entertained by Thomas Reid.[38] Reid writes of instinct in a way that may have been broadly commonplace in the theology of his time, but it is eminently worth recalling today for its connection with the notion of unintended social outcomes of individual actions. Reid asserts that by instinct he means "a natural blind impulse to certain actions, without having any end in view, without deliberation, and very often without any conception of what we do." In an eloquent discussion of the instinctive activity of bees in constructing their honeycombs, he comments that bees, as if acquainted with solid geometry, follow the principles of that discipline most accurately and indeed resolve a problem calling for "fluxionary calculation" on the part of mere humans. Yet if bees "work most geometrically," they do so "without any knowledge." The knowledge is in the possession of "that great Geometrician who made the bee."[39] Individually working bees, then, have their own small "purposes" in view, to speak most anthropomorphically, but only "the great Geometer" has in view the important end (which, of course, to the bees is not an end in the sense of a contemplated and endeavor-motivating object)—the construction of a proper honeycomb on accurate mathematical principles. An analogy with human actions that lead to results that are also quite uncontemplated and may in various particular cases go quite beyond men's mental horizons suggests itself readily, and Reid is quick to take it up.

By instinct and habit, Reid argues, man is led to "many actions necessary for his preservation and well being" which, without instinct and habit, "all his skill and wisdom would not have been able to accomplish." There are at work in man "inferior principles

[38]   Appropriate passages from Reid's *Essays on the Active Powers of Man* are quoted in this volume. It may be noted that section D of the anthology devoted to the present theme of individual actions and unintended social outcomes comprises only four items of modest length, although the theme is of great importance both for the Scots and more generally. This is partly because much that is pertinent to the theme is also presented in sections E and F of the anthology. (There are in any case close connections among D, E, and F). It is also partly due to the desire to avoid a large number of very short statements in the anthology itself, for some of the most effective and illuminating assertions of the Scots having to do with the theme are skilfully brief.
[39]   *Essays on the Active Powers of Man*, in *Works*, II, 545, 546, 547.

of action," and these "with little or no aid of reason or virtue, preserve the species." Hence the case of man is appreciably like that
of the bee. Human "inferior principles of action," too, are divinely
summed or integrated and guided to good outcomes on earth.
Were reason perfect, it would induce men to preserve themselves
and to reproduce their kind. But "the Author of our being" did
not entrust this sort of endeavor to the suggestions of reason alone,
but gave men appropriate appetites ("inferior principles") whereby they effected self-preservation and reproduction, even without
cognizance that this was what they were doing.[40]

Lord Monboddo refers to the bee in terms very much like those
of Reid. He too argues that no one will contend that "this animal
knows the rules of geometry, by which it makes its hexagons, and
joins them together in such a way that . . . it makes its cells contain the greatest quantity of honey possible." It is accordingly admitted that "the bee is no geometer." Nor does the bee possess
intelligence; yet it acts by divine intelligence. Monboddo also sees
a significant human analogy, for he adds that "it often happens,
even among us who have intelligence, that we act by an intelligence superior to our own, doing what we are directed to do by
men wiser than we without knowing for what purpose we act."
He thinks that this is "the case of every well-governed society,
where by far the greater part of the subjects act by rules of which
they do not understand the reason."[41] A bridge from bee to man
is also constructed by a contemporary sociologist, who writes,
possibly in reminiscence of the older Scots: "The purposive actions
of men . . . bring unpurposed results that are no less remarkable
than, say, the hexagons of the hive of the honey bee."[42]

The theological language employed by Reid and Monboddo
should not for a moment be allowed to obscure the basic insight
that men may aim at quite limited objects that work indirectly or

---

[40]   *Ibid.*, p. 558.
[41]   *Antient Metaphysics* (London, 1782), II, 299–300. The theme is
stated in other places in Monboddo, as in his *Origin and Progress of Language*
(2d ed.; Edinburgh, 1774), I, 412, where he writes succinctly: "The bee . . .
forms her hexagon cells as accurately as if she had been instructed by Euclid."
[42]   Robert M. MacIver, *Social Causation* (Boston: Ginn and Co., 1942),
p. 314.

intermediately to realize larger and very important results or termini never sought as objects.[43] One might almost have expected Reid to go on to suggest that, just as "marvelous" results could be achieved by bees not intending them, so "marvelous" results might sometimes be achieved in human institutions by men also not intending them. But, as has been noted, a human analogy in these matters did not escape Reid. It will have been remarked that he referred to appetites that would insure reproduction of the human species. The situation involved was also of interest to others. Thus, in a passage presented in the third section of our anthology Ferguson writes that "the increase of numbers is procured without consulting the mind or the intention of the parties" in families. This "effect"—that is, increase of numbers or reproduction—he adds, is "too necessary to the preservation of nature's work to be entrusted to the precarious will or intention of those most nearly concerned."[44] "Inferior principles of action" are thereby again called into play. It is well to set out here a rudimentary distinction previously merely alluded to. Men and women engage in sexual activity by reason of what Smith called "the passion

---

43   Actually, neither Reid nor Monboddo exploited the insight as he might have, and as Adam Smith and Adam Ferguson, in particular, did. Reid once more stopped short of a serious systematic concern with sociological matters. The insight was, disappointingly, left undeveloped by Monboddo in his work on language, where it is clear that he did not realize its implications, although they would have helped his work greatly. Ferguson, who presumably could not have matched Monboddo's knowledge of numerous aspects of language, could nevertheless note how in the field of language the effect of the actions of numerous individuals over time was to produce something impressively complex and orderly (without concert among individuals and without the proposing beforehand of such results)—developed even *beyond* what one might think deliberate and concerted human contrivances likely to achieve. Ferguson wrote, a bit ecstatically, that when the language of a people has reached a certain fullness of development, then "the speculative mind is apt to look back with amazement from the height it has gained; as a traveler might do, who, rising insensibly on the slope of a hill, should come to look from a precipice of an almost unfathomable depth, to the summit of which he could scarcely believe himself to have ascended without supernatural aid." And some lines farther on Ferguson referred to "this amazing fabric of language, which, when raised to its height, appears so much above what could be ascribed to any simultaneous effort of the most sublime and comprehensive abilities." *Principles of Moral and Political Science*, I, 43.
44   See *ibid*. I, 28.

which unites the two sexes." They may "intend" the gratification of this passion if they intend nothing else, although they may also (depending on their knowledge and motivation) intend to have offspring—their own particular offspring. This is all at the "level" of individual aim or motivation. Beyond this, there is a second level of abstract functional requisites ("needs," "imperatives") of a society or social system. The passion that unites the two sexes being operative and acted upon in a sufficient number of cases, and other things being equal, the human community is continued from one generation to another. This continuation may be understood as distinctively social outcome in that it involves reference beyond individuals to the more or less strong "need" of a society for replenishment of its personnel by reproduction if it is to survive the generations—a "need" that individuals cannot be said to have in any direct sense and one that they *can* fulfill altogether unintentionally.

It is of interest that Mandeville has his character, Horatio, aver that "the end of love between the different sexes in all animals is the preservation of their species." To which Cleomenes replies: "But . . . the savage is not prompted to love from that consideration. He propagates before he knows the consequences of it; and I much question whether the most civilized pair, in the most chaste of their embraces, ever acted from the care of their species, as an active principle."[45] The shrewdness of Mandeville's psychology here may be granted. Still, a "most civilized pair" might in some sense be desirous of having their own offspring; but they clearly could not reproduce the species. That reproduction would occur as conjoint effect of the activity of numerous human couples.[46]

---

[45]   *The Fable of the Bees,* II, 228.

[46]   The distinction of levels—that of individual aim or motivation and that of abstract functional requisites or social system needs—is of course relevant beyond the sex-reproduction case. (This is plainly not the place for an effort at a critical and systematic presentation of the terms or logic of functional analysis. All that need be asked of such a phrase as "abstract functional requisites" in the present context is that it have a certain minimum clarity.) Broadly "important" social outcomes and system needs are of constant concern to the Scottish moralists—and unintended ones especially so. Sometimes it is true that there is considerable human awareness of these requisites and even desire that they be met, but it may also be true that they can still be

Aside from the hints of Reid and Monboddo, the entire matter of individual actions and unintended social outcomes is important for Hume, Adam Smith, Ferguson, and Dugald Stewart. Hume was not always clear on some essentials involved in the matter, as will appear below.[47] But the concern at this point is with his relevant clarities rather than with ambiguities. There is an interesting passage in his *Treatise* in which he considers the "laws of justice" rules by which "properties, rights, and obligations" are determined. He clearly implies that had men been directly endowed with a strong regard for public welfare they could have been expected to seek it directly. But, instead, they have sought limited, piecemeal adjustments of their interests designed to render social relations tolerable amid uncertainty, dispute, and competition. These adjustments rear the laws of justice, and "it is self-love which is [the] real origin" of those laws. The self-love of one interacting with that of another rears a system that is "of course advantageous to the public; though it be not intended for that purpose by the inventors."[48] The theme so developed might be described as that of the invisible hand in politics.[49] If this kind of reflection be found in

---

achieved "best," or even exclusively, through the performance of individual actions which conjointly fulfill them. Various complications easily suggest themselves. Central planning, say of population levels by a state authority, may be allowed to raise new questions about "intention." It would have been excessively clumsy to entitle this section "Individual actions and unintended social outcomes and nearly unintended outcomes and ambiguously intended outcomes and outcomes that are known and desired but still achieved quite as if they were not." The language of abstract functional requisites is not designed to obscure the circumstance that second-level phenomena—let us say here simply unintended social outcomes of conjoint individual actions—may not be "good" or beneficent. Finally, "unintended outcomes" are in any case inclusive of far more than is suggested by the particular phrase, abstract functional requisites. Certain contemporary interests and the interests of the Scottish moralists have shaped the present statement.

47   See pp. lv–lvi.
48   See Hume's *Treatise of Human Nature,* II, 295–96.
49   Compare the following from Adam Ferguson, which plainly pursues the same general theme: "The public interest is often secure, not because individuals are disposed to regard it as the end of their conduct, but because each, in his place, is determined to preserve his own. Liberty is maintained by the continued differences and opposition of members, not by their concurring zeal in behalf of equitable government. In free states, therefore, the wisest laws are never, perhaps, dictated by the interest and spirit of any

the *Treatise,* it can certainly be found in other work of Hume's. In his *History of England,* in the course of one discussion of English liberty and government, he refers—not lightly or casually, one may feel sure—to "the great mixture of accident which commonly occurs with a small ingredient of wisdom and foresight in erecting the complicated fabric of the most perfect government." He writes in the same passage of "the remote, and commonly faint and disfigured, originals of the most finished and most noble institutions," suggesting by his phraseology that those who developed "the originals" were as far as possible from being capable of conceiving the "finished" and "noble" institutions.[50]

Sometimes Hume looks at the matter of unintended social outcomes from the point of view of a "practically" motivated observer who might wish to ascertain the "best" way to get human beings to bring about certain things. In his essay on commerce, he argues that if in his day one could immediately infuse into men sentiments of the type of "a passion for public good," such sentiment "might now, as in ancient times, prove alone a sufficient spur to industry, and support the community." But this is not feasible; and the argument touches familiar ground when Hume avers that it is "requisite to govern men by other passions, and animate them with a spirit of avarice and industry, art and Luxury" to get the same results that might otherwise have been obtained through direct concern for public welfare.[51] (Adam Smith was later to make the famous addition: "I have never known much good done by those who affected to trade for the public good."[52]) Inevitably, questions are suggested about the relative merits of alternative ways of achieving goals or outcomes, with a range through indirection and no intention or foresight of outcomes to direct onslaught on goals and "maximization" of intention or foresight. Some of Hume's attitudes in such matters today are apt to strike

---

order of men; they are moved, they are opposed, or amended by different hands; and come at last to express that medium and composition which contending parties have forced one another to adopt." *Essay on the History of Civil Society,* p. 233.

50   *History of England,* II, 513.
51   *Essays,* I, 294–95.
52   *The Wealth of Nations,* p. 199.

us as decidedly dated and marked by an excessive optimism about the ways of indirection.[53] It is, however, worthy of note in passing that his stimulating views with regard to indirection had wider range than the above suggests.[54]

Adam Smith is a figure of major importance in the present

[53]   Thus, consider the following: "When the interests of one country interfere with those of another, we estimate the merits of a statesman by the good or ill which results to his own country from his measures and councils, without regard to the prejudice which he brings on his enemies and rivals. His fellow citizens are the objects, which lie nearest the eye, while we determine his character. And as nature has implanted in every one a superior affection to his own country, we never expect any regard to distant nations, where a competition arises. Not to mention that, while every man consults the good of his own community, we are sensible that the general interest of mankind is better promoted than by loose indeterminate views to the good of a species, whence no beneficial action could ever result, for want of a duly limited object on which they could exert themselves." Hume, *Essays*, II, 212, note.

[54]   He was interestingly aware that a created or "manufactured" object showing real ingenuity of form and function need not be the direct product of the work of an intelligent artificer who had the entire design in mind at once. So, he implies, the world might be a most ingenious structure while yet great ingenuity need not be imputed to a designer who had deliberately so made it: "If we survey a ship, what an exalted idea must we form of the ingenuity of the carpenter, who framed so complicated, useful, and beautiful a machine? And what surprise must we entertain when we find him a stupid mechanic, who imitated others and copied an art which, through a long succession of ages . . . had been gradually improving. Many worlds might have been botched and bungled, throughout an eternity, ere this system was struck out." Thus Philo speaks in the *Dialogues concerning Natural Religion*, N. K. Smith, ed. (Indianapolis, n.d. [Thomas Nelson & Sons, 1947], p. 167). And when, later, Demea asks how order can spring from anything "which perceives not that order which it bestows" (*ibid.*, p. 179), part of Philo's reply is that "a tree bestows order and organization on that tree which springs from it, without knowing the order;" and Philo rejects as question-begging the general assumption that order implies design. Hume's reference to a ship is inevitably reminiscent of Mandeville, who had already argued briefly but brilliantly that arts may be raised to prodigious heights, over time, by the labor and experience of ordinary men, and who had specifically referred to ships as final products undreamed of by their "first inventors" or by those who had made "improvements" in them. See *The Fable of the Bees*, II, 141, 143. It may be added that since absence of design or purpose is sometimes followed by a relative excellence of "results," one might occasionally be led to speculate, most paradoxically, that it is "poor results" rather than excellent ones that suggest the existence of design or purpose in the first place. (How important such a speculation might be in view of empirical realities is another matter.)

context. His *Theory of Moral Sentiments* presents some fundamentally significant argument. Smith writes:

> With regard to all those ends which, upon account of their peculiar importance, may be regarded . . . as the favorite ends of nature, she has constantly . . . not only endowed mankind with an appetite for the end which she proposes, but likewise with an appetite for the means by which alone this end can be brought about, for their own sakes and independent of their tendency to produce it.[55]

Smith goes on to mention "self-preservation and the propagation of the species" as "the great ends which nature seems to have proposed in the formation of all animals." As regards men's being endowed with an appetite for nature's ends in such cases, it might have been well for Smith to explain precisely what he intended. (In just what sense do men have an appetite for the end of propagation of the *species?*) It is a crucial point, however, that Smith argues that although we strongly desire such ends as self-preservation and propagation of the species, nevertheless

> it has not been entrusted to the slow and uncertain determinations of our reason to find out the proper means of bringing [these ends] about. Nature has directed us to the greater part of these by original and immediate instincts. Hunger, thirst, the passion which unites the two sexes, the love of pleasure and the dread of pain prompt us to apply those means for their own sakes, and without any consideration to those beneficent ends which the great Director of nature intended by them.[56]

Here again, at the conclusion of Smith's statement, "the great ends" are put beyond the consideration of human actors. The notion that reason is not to be relied on for the attainment of certain important things is once more plainly evident. "Nature" or its "Director" takes no chances, as it were, and provides instrumentalities in the form of "instincts" that move men powerfully to the performance of what abstract reason might much too faintly suggest as "desirable." These instrumentalities thus operate indirectly to bring about the larger outcomes or "results."[57]

55   *Theory of Moral Sentiments*, p. 110.
56   *Ibid.*, p. 110.
57   Even where "instinct" is apparently not involved but where "great ends" still exist, nature or deity will not employ overfrail instruments. Thus,

In another statement, which Dugald Stewart quotes in full in one of the following readings[58] and whose substance must be resumed here, Smith achieves thorough clarity on the distinction between individual-level motivations and the abstract functional requisites of a social system. He writes that digestion of food, circulation of the blood, and so on are "operations all of them necessary for the great purposes of animal life." Yet, he adds in effect, we never seek to account for digestion and circulation as immediately occasioned by some kind of "aim" of fulfilling "the great purposes of animal life." We do not "imagine that the blood circulates, or that the food digests of its own accord, and with a view or intention to the purposes of circulation or digestion." The larger outcomes—the "great purposes"—are achieved, but not by way of a direct "determination" to achieve them—and the analogy intended for the social realm cannot be missed. Smith's language now takes a new turn. The wheels of the watch point the hour and "their various motions conspire in the nicest manner to produce this effect." Smith avers that "if they were endowed with a desire and intention" to produce the effect, "they could not do it better," although "we never ascribe any such desire or intention to them, but to the watchmaker." The immediate impulses and aims that move humans ("efficient causes") are not to be confused with the perhaps very important larger social system-level outcomes or functional requisites ("final causes") that emerge from them. There are numerous situations in which the final causes are even quite unknown to human agents, and we are not "to imagine that to be the wisdom of man, which in reality is the wisdom of God."[59] There is a tendency not to reflect at all upon at least some of the functional requisites. "All men," Smith writes a little farther on, "even the most stupid and unthinking, abhor

---

Smith contends that "religion even in its rudest form gave a sanction to the rules of morality, long before the age of artificial reasoning and philosophy." He adds at once: "That the terrors of religion should thus enforce the natural sense of deity was of too much importance to the happiness of mankind for nature to leave it dependent upon the slowness and uncertainty of philosophical researches." *Ibid.*, p. 233.

58   See below, p. 159.
59   *Theory of Moral Sentiments*, pp. 126–27.

fraud, perfidy, and injustice and delight to see them punished. But few men have reflected upon the necessity of justice to the existence of society, how obvious soever that necessity may appear to be."[60]

The second selection in this volume, under the present rubric, consists of Smith's two statements, from his two major works, about the invisible hand—an inevitable choice, surely. Smith is now on ground that is entirely familiar to those who know anything of his work. It is still worth remembering his stresses that men may advance social interest without intending or knowing it and that they can, in seeking the gratification of individual selfishness, fail to grasp the connection between that gratification and the achievement of general welfare. The author of *The Wealth of Nations* who could write that the individual in pursuit of his own interest "frequently promotes that of the society more effectually than when he really intends to promote it"[61] readily recalls the author of *The Theory of Moral Sentiments* who wrote that the wheels of the watch could not achieve the effect of pointing the hour better than they do "if they were endowed with a desire and intention" to do it. Smith's relevance to the present theme is hardly hereby exhausted, but for immediate purposes it may suffice to point to only one additional passage in *The Wealth of Nations,* to ensure something like adequate documentation of crucial and germane points in his thought. The passage refers to the division of labor, and its argument, though also quite familiar, is perhaps slightly less well known than that of the invisible hand passage in the same volume. Smith notes that the division of labor ("from which so many advantages are derived") is itself "not originally the effect of any human wisdom, which foresees and intends that general opulence to which it gave occasion." Rather, "it is the necessary, though very slow and gradual, consequence of a certain propensity in human nature, which has in view no such extensive utility; the propensity to truck, barter, and exchange one thing for another." In this case once again Smith quite plainly contends that

60   *Ibid.*, p. 129.
61   *The Wealth of Nations,* p. 199.

something eminently advantageous for a society as a whole grows out of individual activities that do not foresee or intend it.[62]

Adam Ferguson could write with clarity and power on unintended social outcomes, as is indicated by the selection in our anthology under the title "Unintended Establishments," from Ferguson's *Essay on the History of Civil Society*. Friedrich Meinecke, whom the whole conception of unintended outcomes interested greatly and who was particularly impressed with Vico's contribution thereto, summarizes some of Ferguson's pertinent views appreciatively:

> As if in the dark, men grope toward institutions which are not intended, but the result of their activity. . . . The doctrine of the rise of the state through a contract . . . also fell to the ground for Ferguson without further ado. The constitution of Rome and Sparta . . . rested . . . not on the planning of single persons but on the situation and genius of the people. Vico had once led a lonely way with ideas such as these.[63]

Ferguson's relevant perception is again exemplified in the following passage, among others:

> The artifices of the beaver, the ant, and the bee are ascribed to the wisdom of nature. Those of polished nations are ascribed to themselves, and are supposed to indicate a capacity superior to that of rude minds. But the establishments of men, like those of every animal, are suggested by nature, and are the result of instinct, directed by the variety of situations in which mankind are placed. Those establishments arose from successive improvements that were made, without any sense of their general effect; and they bring human affairs to a state of com-

---

62   *Ibid.*, p. 13. Smith also asserts elsewhere that "we cannot imagine" the division of labor to be "an effect of human prudence." *Lectures on Justice, Police, Revenue and Arms*, E. Cannan, ed. (Oxford: Clarendon Press, 1896), p. 168. See also Hermann Huth, *Soziale und Individualistische Auffassung im 18. Jahrhundert*, p. 34. Huth is generally excellent on unintended social outcomes of individual actions.

63   *Die Entstehung des Historismus*, I, 283. Something of the drift of Meinecke's comments on Vico may be gained from this statement: "Vico's notion that men themselves did not know what they accomplished when they created civil orders and culture but only followed their narrow egoistic—sensual interest of the movement—this notion had a further liberating effect for historical thought." *Ibid.*, I, 63.

plication, which the greatest reach of capacity with which human nature was ever adorned, could not have projected; nor even when the whole is carried into execution can it be comprehended in its full extent.[64]

Clearly, there are only limited possibilities in the statement of the notion of unintended social outcomes, but the resemblance between some of Ferguson's pertinent assertions and others made generations later is rather striking.[65]

Dugald Stewart once more summarizes well the outlook of a number of the other Scottish moralists without making any distinctive contribution of his own. Some germane passages from his work have been collated and are presented in the selection

[64]   *Essay on the History of Civil Society*, pp. 327, 328.

[65]   Another of Ferguson's germane commentaries, published in 1792, may be compared with one on the same general theme published by an outstanding philosopher in 1927. Ferguson: "Among the circumstances which lead in the progress or decline of nations that of political situation may be reckoned among the first or most important. And in this the most favorable conjuncture is sometimes attained, or the reverse is incurred with perfect blindness to the future or ignorance of the consequences which are likely to follow. The parties would often better themselves: but they are often driving they know not whither. Thus the Barons of England, in times of high feudal aristocracy, knew not the charters, which they extorted from their sovereign, were to become foundations of freedom to the people over whom they themselves wished to tyrannize. No more did the Roman people foresee that the support they gave to Caesar, in reducing the Senate, was in effect to establish a military despotism, under which they themselves were to forfeit all the advantages of a free nation." *Principles of Moral and Political Science*, I, 313–14. Morris R. Cohen observed, nearly a century and a half later: "We must . . . draw a distinction between the microscopic and the macroscopic view of human purpose, between the little drops of human volition and the general social streams which result from them. Little does the respectable paterfamilias intend, when he begets and rears lusty children, to lay the basis of imperialistic wars or monastic institutions. The voyage of Columbus was undoubtedly one of the causes of the spread of English civilization to America. Yet Columbus no more intended to bring it about than the microscopic globigerinae could have planned the chalk cliffs of England which are the result of their life work." In W. F. Ogburn and A. A. Goldenweiser, eds., *The Social Sciences*. Boston: Houghton, Mifflin, 1927, p. 446. (The passage is reprinted in Cohen's *Reason and Nature* [Glencoe, Ill.: The Free Press, 1953], p. 342.) The juxtaposition of these two statements is not intended to gainsay the merit of the second one. And it is certainly possible that Cohen's statement was made quite independently of Ferguson's.

entitled "Government, Unintended Developments, Expediency, Innovation." Stewart is inclined to the view that social institutions represent a kind of deposit of wisdom, a heritage of the community that has put into them, over time, sagacity and reflection on much experience, transcending by far that of any individual. (One may think analogously of a ship, à la Mandeville, as an instance of a device that incorporates the sagacity of generations of workmen). But the wisdom so deposited in social institutions has been built piecemeal, to be sure, and is hardly the product of an intelligence that plans everything out at once in a total conception of the ends institutions are to fulfill. Excellence in institutions generally, as in language, is, in Stewart's words, "the gradual result of time and experience, and not of philosophical speculation."[66] This is by Stewart's time hardly greatly illuminating, and Stewart (among others) may have been in general somewhat reluctant to note cases in which the "wisdom" of old institutions seems rather to resemble foolishness (and in which the analogy of institutions and tools or technological devices, we may add, proves unreliable). It is only correct to say, as Hayek does, that "*sometimes* grown institutions which nobody had invented may provide a better framework for cultural growth than more sophisticated designs."[67]

Stewart also writes about "analogy" in the sense of the need for "fit" between existing institutional cumulations on the one hand and innovations on the other. This notion of "fit" or congruity and the readily forthcoming ideas of "packaging" or "storing" wisdom

---

66   *Collected Works*, IX, 423.
67   F. A. Hayek, "Kinds of Rationalism," *The Economic Studies Quarterly*, XV (March, 1965): 11, italics supplied. (It is particularly important to note that italics have been supplied here, in view of Hayek's own interest in the article cited.) It is only fair to add that Stewart could contend that while the danger of "sudden and rash innovations" could not be stressed enough, yet "it is possible also to fall into the opposite extreme, and to bring upon society the very evils we are anxious to prevent, by an obstinate opposition to those gradual and necessary reformations which the genius of the times demands." And he could write of "bigoted attachment to antiquated forms," "principles borrowed from less enlightened ages," and "reverence for abuses sanctioned by time." *Collected Works*, II, 228–29.

and of a certain comparability of institutions and technological devices (even if the comparability is limited), together with the conception of unintended outcomes, afford at least some elements of a speculative and theoretical conception of social evolution. This is a matter on which the Scottish moralists are interesting and even provocative, particularly in view of a certain contemporary sociological and anthropological revival of interest in evolution. It is indeed another of the numerous matters that one wishes they had developed more.[68]

The entire matter of individual actions (prominently including strictly purposive actions) and unintended social outcomes has been of considerable importance in modern sociology and in spheres of thought closely related to it. Some few indications of this may be noted, although they must be left undeveloped. In sociology itself, Pareto is a figure of some relevance. He found the formation of language by humans no less "marvelous" than instinctive behavior on the part of insects. The theory of grammar, he recognized, certainly did not precede the practice of speech, and

[68]   Mention should be made of the two remaining Scots in connection with unintended outcomes. Hutcheson seems not to have been influenced by this entire mode of thought, judging particularly from his synthetic *System of Moral Philosophy*. Possibly the following might even suggest an antipathy to the mode: "Men have some power, and make some changes: we can exert our force in making them two ways: one in which we have no intention of any particular form or effect; as when we throw carelessly any materials out of our hands; another, when we design some end, intend some form, and direct motives for that purpose. By the former manner scarce ever arises anything, regular, uniform, or wisely adapted to any purpose: by the other it is that we produce things regular and well adapted." *A System of Moral Philosophy*, I, 172–73. The notion of unintended outcomes was at least not unfamiliar to Kames. Setting forth what he regards as the "true and genuine principles of human action," Kames briefly discusses or mentions love of life, self-love, fidelity, gratitude, and benevolence; and then writes: "These several principles of action are ordered, with admirable wisdom, to promote the general good in the best and most effectual manner. We act for the general good when we act upon these principles, even when it is not our immediate aim. The general good is an object too sublime, and too remote, to be the sole impulsive motive to action. It is better ordered that, in most instances, individuals should have a limited aim, which they can readily accomplish. To every man is assigned his own task. And if every man do his duty, the general good will be promoted much more successfully than if it were the aim in every single action." *Essays of the Principles of Morality and Natural Religion*. Anonymous (Edinburgh, 1751), pp. 90–91.

yet without knowledge of that theory human beings have created very subtle grammatical structures.[69] Max Weber effectively distinguished the objects of conduct undertaken by individuals with limited aims in view from its consequences at a social system level.[70] In the United States, Robert M. MacIver, himself of Scottish origin and conceivably directly influenced by the Scottish moralists, shows much interest in their problem of unintended social outcomes.[71] Pitirim A. Sorokin has interested himself in consequences of action both unanticipated and, once they are present, likely to be widely unwanted since they work in the direction of "weakening and destroying" the socio-cultural context in which they arise.[72] Robert K. Merton has frequently concerned himself with problems suggested by his apt phrase, "the unanticipated consequences of purposive social action."[73]

In the field of history, the contrast between individual aims and general social resultants informed much of the work of Friedrich Meinecke previously referred to. The contrast appears in Meinecke's discussions of Vico, Adam Ferguson, Herder, Ranke, and in his inevitable awareness of notions such as Wundt's heterogony of ends and Hegel's cunning of reason.[74] Much the same

---

[69]   Vilfredo Pareto, *The Mind and Society* (New York: Harcourt, Brace, 1935), I, 84.
[70]   See *The Theory of Social and Economic Organization* (New York: Oxford University Press, 1947), for example, at pp. 184–86 and 211–12.
[71]   See his *Social Causation*, especially pp. 313–21.
[72]   *Social and Cultural Dynamics* (New York: Bedminster Press, 1962), for example, III, 222–24.
[73]   See for example, *Social Theory and Social Structure*, ch. I.
[74]   See *Die Entstehung des Historismus*, I and II. German historical thought has been much affected by such notions as these of Wundt and Hegel. It may be recalled that, in the case of heterogony of ends, human aims change as results of purposive action occur that are other than results originally contemplated and suggest new values (or as what was once instrumentally conceived or used becomes an end in itself.) In the case of the cunning of reason, historical actors are the instruments of "higher" objects that their own small, limited purposes inadvertently serve so that the historical process may be said to work at two levels—one of small, everyday human aims and another of uncontemplated "great results" that emerge from but in the end quite transcend the small aims. These notions bear some relation to the ideas of the Scottish moralists here reviewed. A full comparison of relevant Scottish and German points of view would be too much of a distraction, but it should be said that the two points of view share something of a tran-

general contrast has begun to find its way into semipopular writing
on history, if one may judge from one recent volume.[75] The special matter of institutions as incorporating "wisdom" has recently
been interestingly discussed by the historian, Pocock.[76]

In social philosophy, Popper gives stress to the "indirect," the
"unintended," and "often the unwanted" by-products of "conscious
and intentional human actions."[77] Much the same contrast has
been repeatedly emphasized by F. A. Hayek, who, for his part, has
without any doubt been directly influenced by the Scottish moralists and by Mandeville.[78] It is useful for our purposes to note
Hayek's insistence on the importance of the "not-of-human-design"
perspective in the field of law, where he employs this perspective in critical reaction to legal positivism. Law is taken by him as

scendence outlook. Once results or outcomes have gone beyond the intention
of actors, something "new" has arisen; an emergent exists. The attention of
actors (or of theorists of society) may then turn precisely to the new, the
emergent, and concentrate on that, while the sources out of which the new
has emerged fall into the background. But in the German case there has been
more of a propensity (although it has certainly not been unresisted) than in
the Scottish to develop a metaphysic of "higher" and "lower" (as just suggested in connection with the cunning of reason) in which the emergent has
a unique value while its sources are devalued. The Scots do tend to admire
what they take to be the frequent excellence of unintended outcomes and
can also view the "lower"-level phenomena as leading to or in some sense
instrumental to the "higher" results, but there their metaphysical inclination
is likely to end, at least in the eighteenth century.
[75]   See Edward H. Carr, *What Is History?* (New York: Knopf, 1962).
Carr begins a long, relevant paragraph (pp. 62–64) with the statement (p.
62): "Writers of many different schools of thought have concurred in remarking that the actions of individual human beings often have results which
were not intended or desired by the actors or indeed by any one else."
[76]   J. G. A. Pocock, *The Ancient Constitution and the Feudal Law* (Cambridge: Cambridge University Press, 1957), especially pp. 34–36, 173, 242–
43. See also Pocock, "Burke and the Ancient Constitution—A Problem in the
History of Ideas," *The Historical Journal* III, No. 2 (1960): 125–43.
[77]   Karl R. Popper, *The Open Society and Its Enemies* (Princeton, N.J.:
Princeton University Press, 1963), II, 93, 323–24.
[78]   See, for example, his "Kinds of Rationalism," and his "The Results of
Human Action but not of Human Design," in *Studies in Philosophy, Politics
and Economics* (London: Routledge and Kegan Paul, in press.) (The title
of the latter article is from a phrase of Adam Ferguson's.) Important in the
background of Hayek's thought on these lines, also, is Carl Menger. See the
latter's *Problems of Economics and Sociology* (Urbana: University of Illinois
Press, 1963), especially Book III, chap. 2.

at least in part an unintended resultant of an historical development in the light of which questions of justice cannot be decided by arbitrary fiat but must be resolved by reference to a grown system of rules, socially inherited even if not explicitly articulated. Hayek's view supports the notion of a justice that can be "found" and not simply "decreed by the will of a legislator."[79]

The contrast between individual action and unintended social outcomes was not developed by the Scottish moralists alone, but it was developed by them with considerable skill, and, in the case of a man like Adam Smith, in a fashion such as to challenge economic and social thought for generations afterward. Not all the persons who have since the days of the Scots given emphasis to the contrast and treated it significantly have been directly influenced by them. In a way, this bears witness the more strongly to the importance of their preoccupations in this area. The preoccupations are in any case inescapable when one deals with the Scots, and they will shortly be encountered again.

The matters taken up in this section easily lead on to other kinds of concerns. Some points significant for present-day functionalism have been suggested in the foregoing, and accordingly adumbrations of that functionalism in the work of the Scots may next be attended to. Also, we have nearly touched on some relations of history and sociology that merit subsequent attention for their part.

V. *Anticipations of Functionalism*

To think in terms of individual actions that are, let us say, bounded by quite limited aims, while recognizing that such aims can contribute to socially significant results or indirectly fulfill abstract functional requisites, is already to take a significant step toward what sociologists now call structural-functional analysis or, more briefly, functional analysis or functionalism. There are certainly anticipations of this mode of analysis or perspective in the work of the Scottish moralists. To help make it quite evident

[79] "The Results of Human Action but not of Human Design." See below, p. lxix.

that this is the case, four selections from the available body of written work have been afforded in our readings—selections by Smith, Dugald Stewart, Hume, and Hutcheson.[80]

Smith's awareness of the difference between level of individual aim or motivation and level of social outcome has already been noted, as in the case of the characteristic view that the individual's selfish motivation for gain is one thing, while the presumed outcome (at least under some circumstances) of the interaction of selfishly motivated men operating on the market, in the form of general economic welfare, is another, the latter being an emergent at a whole-system level. Also, Smith used the language of "efficient" and "final" causes to denote, respectively, the "forces" that operate at the level of individual motivation and at the level of abstract functional requisites for a society that the activities initiated at the first level so often unwittingly fulfill.

The Aristotelian terminology is significant. Adam Ferguson gives one of the simplest statements of the distinction of efficient and final cause: "The efficient cause is the energy or power producing an effect. The final cause is the end or purpose for which an effect is produced."[81] The terminology is helpful once there is a sense of the distinction between individual-goal-or-motivation and social-system levels. Again in the case of sexual activity, we might say that it is the passion which unites the two sexes which is the activity's efficient cause. If we then agreed to regard the "purpose" or final cause of the activity as the design of a couple to have their own children, where such a design existed in fact, and we then had nothing further to say about final cause, the way to functional

---

80   The arrangement of the selections is in this case somewhat peculiar. Smith's material on the influence of fortune on sentiments of merit or demerit, from *The Theory of Moral Sentiments*, is put first because it is so very plainly an authentic and somewhat developed anticipation of functionalism. Dugald Stewart's item on final causes, from his *Philosophy of the Human Mind*, is of outstanding importance in connection with functionalism and is placed immediately after Smith's work to stress its significance. Hume's and Hutcheson's statements on marriages and relatives (from the former's *History of England* and the latter's *System of Moral Philosophy*) are added to the larger statements by Smith and Stewart as examples of interesting gropings in the direction of functional analysis in a particular area.
81   *Institutes of Moral Philosophy* (Edinburgh, 1773), p. 5.

analysis as understood in sociology would hardly be opened. For that way to be effectively opened, if the same terminology is to be employed, it would be important to postulate another kind of final cause, on the order of propagation of the species, which could be argued to have reference to a social-system "need." Final causes need not always be so global, but some of the sociologist's "big" problems with analysis of societies should at least be suggested by a set of postulated "ends" or "purposes" or "final causes," if that indeed is the language that is going to be used. Here Adam Smith himself pointed to the "great ends of nature," as we know, and, characteristically, not to modest or minuscule final causes.

But this language has strong teleological and, indeed, theological overtones. "Nature" and its "director" or "author" and the "deity" figure prominently in connection with the Scots' discussions of efficient and final causes. The possibility that some central notions of modern social science should initially have had theological coloring need not especially surprise us. We are here concerned more particularly with ideas that prefigure functional analysis, but the suggestion of theological origin or influence has been made with regard to other significant ideas in social science also.[82] The language of Adam Smith, among others, is, to be sure, precisely the kind of language that points to the theological background. In the anthology material quoted from Smith under the rubric of functionalism, comprising his comments on "the influence of fortune upon the sentiments of mankind, with regard to the merit or demerit of actions," he is concerned with the circumstance that while men may agree to the notion that benevolent or malevolent intention on the part of an actor ought to occasion approval or disapproval of that action or its results, yet the actual consequences that ensue from action (*whatever* intention may be) in fact influence profoundly the judgment as to its merit or demerit. In the

---

82   An interesting case is presented by the suggestion that Mandeville's notion that society rests upon a machinery of self-seeking lusts that ultimately (under certain conditions) works out beneficially or harmoniously for a social whole (a notion of evident importance for Adam Smith also) goes back to religious (specifically, Calvinist-predestinationist) ideas. See Wilhelm Deckelmann, *Untersuchungen Zur Bienenfabel Mandevilles* (Hamburg: Friederichsen, de Gruyter & Co., 1933), p. 100.

l INTRODUCTION

discrepancy between the judgment that we would find if men judged actions strictly on the ground of intention and the judgment that they actually tend to make under the influence of observation of consequences, we have an "irregularity" of sentiment. Smith undertakes to explain this irregularity in point of its sources and the extent of its influence, but also in the light of "the end which it answers, or the purpose which the Author of nature seems to have intended by it."[83] He might have been asking himself, in currently encountered sociological language: How does this irregularity of sentiment function? What (if any) are the "adaptive" consequences of its existence for society? (And we have the more reason to put matters thus since the irregularity of sentiment as Smith conceived it could well be culturally patterned.) It would be foolishness, again, to allow theological language to make us lose sight of the merits of an analysis. Yet Smith's language *is* in part theological, and even perfunctory pieties may be suggestive of religious influences once actively operative. It is impossible to avoid the impression that the Scottish anticipations of functionalism are theologically influenced and in considerable degree theologically inspired. And the theological language blends with teleological: "Nature . . . when she implanted the seeds of this irregularity in the human breast, seems, as upon all other occasions, to have intended the happiness and perfection of the species."[84]

As Smith carries on his analysis of the irregularity of sentiment referred to, in terms of final cause, he argues that if men were to be adjudged thoroughly wicked, and treated accordingly, by reason of their harboring malevolent impulses, then "there would be no safety for the most innocent and circumspect conduct. Bad wishes, bad views, bad designs might still be suspected."[85] The "great Judge of Hearts"[86] reserves to himself the decision upon men's inward dispositions. On the other hand, not to allow the fullest possible rewards for action inspired by high ideals (or for good in-

83   *Theory of Moral Sentiments*, p. 135.
84   *Ibid.*, p. 152.
85   *Ibid.*, p. 153.
86   *Ibid.*

tentions, even if they are spectacularly good) but that fails to achieve its ends is to give valuable stress to the importance of actual results for human society. This is the barest outline of Smith's functional analysis of the irregularity of sentiment of his concern. The analysis is not inordinately complex or immensely subtle. It is "speculative" and not grounded in a convincing empirical demonstration, although it shares these features with at least a great deal of what currently goes under the name of functional analysis. But whatever it lacks, it has some evident merits. It is to some degree developed. Smith is well aware that men never "planned" that the irregularity of sentiment should function as he claims it does. He is once again cognizant of the difference of levels of individual aim or motivation and larger social results. An individual might simply have (culturally patterned) inclinations to leniency toward a person whose malevolence of design failed of concrete effects and to reserve toward one whose splendid ideals failed similarly, but these inclinations, found in one individual after another, have special consequences for society as a whole. They protect a certain inner freedom for men and they stimulate them to high-level performances. The functions that Smith thus imputes are hardly trivial.

In the long selection from Dugald Stewart on the subject of final causes, Stewart has been allowed sufficient space to make quite plain the background against which he discusses final causes in "the philosophy of the human mind."[87] He stresses once more the difference between matters having to do with motivation of actions by individuals, or with the latters' goals, and matters at the level of a society as a whole (and utilizes his sense of the difference in a discussion bearing on ethical questions). Stewart's vocabulary in this piece of work should be carefully attended to. He writes of understanding the structure of an animal body, of the conformation of its parts, of the functions of those parts and of their ends and uses; and he refers again to the functions "of the various organs in the human frame." Although there are some linguistic

---

[87]   Material very similar to, and in part identical with, that which has been reproduced here from volume III of Stewart's *Collected Works* will also be found in vol. VII, pp. 93–108.

usages that make him uneasy, he evidently believes that that general frame of mind in which an investigator is disposed to think on the line of final causes (whatever these are called) has great heuristic value. Particularly striking in this connection is the illustration of such value given in the case of Harvey's work on the circulation of the blood. The exceedingly close affinity of "function" (and "design") and "final cause" is once more very effectively suggested. Stewart's work is most pertinent for the theological and teleological backgrounds of final cause and function that have been alluded to.[88] It is of interest that there is still some current tendency to observe that functional analysis is teleological. The observation need not be assessed here. It is in no way affected by the historical origins of functional analysis. Yet, it would be an intriguing enterprise and a genuine service to the history of social thought (and conceivably to sociological theory) to go carefully over the development of social science that lies between the Scots and present-day sociology a century and a half to two centuries later, in an effort to ascertain with precision how functionalist ideas in particular may have gotten translated to us over the intervening period. It would clearly be pertinent to inquire about the changing fortunes of theological and teleological strains in functionalism. In the absence of the kind of careful historical work suggested there must remain an element of uncertainty about just what the relation of the functionalism of the Scots is to that of today. Until further evidence is available, however, it may be taken as a respectable guess that there have

[88]   Views very much like Stewart's are expressed by Alexander F. Tytler in his *Memoirs of the Life and Writings of the Honorable Henry Home of Kames*, III, 32–59 ("On Final Causes"). Tytler notes that Kames made much reference to final causes, and while he concedes that argument based on this notion can be "abused," he regards such argument as fundamentally defensible. He touches on anatomy, refers to structures and functions, and writes that in anatomy, which involves "accurate knowledge of the animal machine," we must hold in view "the proper functions of the several parts of that machine." Like Stewart, he stresses the heuristic value of thought in terms of final causes (which is "eminently serviceable in guiding or conducting our inquiries.") He also refers to Harvey's thinking in terms of "nature's design" when the latter scrutinized the structures that effected the circulation of the blood. ("The consideration of the final cause actually led to the discovery of the physical truth." 53–54.)

been definite (if at times indirect) and significant influences of the Scots on present-day thought in this as in other social science areas.

In the short passage from his *History of England* that appears in the following readings under the title "Marriage of Relatives," David Hume writes of problems suggested by the marriage of Henry VIII and Catherine of Aragon. Catherine had previously been married to Henry's deceased brother, Arthur, and Henry no longer wanted Catherine for his wife. Henry, following Aquinas and fortified by others, was disposed to throw doubt on the lawfulness of marriage to a brother's widow.[89] Hume is stimulated to suggest in effect that if love or marriage were allowed between those who are intimately associated from early years, then "the frequent opportunities of intimate conversation, especially during early youth, would introduce a universal dissoluteness and corruption."[90] Prohibition of marriage among those closely associated from early youth would prevent a situation in which foreknowledge that one could later cohabit with or marry a certain other would encourage an immediate intimacy. But if Hume certainly suggests this, it is also true that he writes that "the natural reason why marriage in certain degrees is prohibited . . . and condemned . . . is *derived from men's care to preserve purity of manners*," for men "reflect that if a commerce of love were authorized between near relations," the dissolution and corruptness referred to would ensue.[91] There is another passage in Hume's work in which he takes up the same matter more briefly and also sets out variations in the practice of peoples regarding the permission or disallowance of marriage of relatives. He comments significantly: "Public utility is the cause of all these variations."[92] The influence of "pragmatistic" thought, as Meinecke would call it, is plain. Here Hume gives reason rather too much credit. He does not quite know how to handle certain "functions" except by presuming that men somehow "see" and intend them. It is men's "care to preserve purity

---

89   Hume, *History of England,* III, 74.
90   *Ibid.,* III, 95.
91   *Ibid.,* italics supplied.
92   *Essays,* II, 199.

of manners" and their "reflection" that account for certain marriage prohibitions. Elsewhere, Hume seems to lean toward the view that "as justice evidently tends to promote public utility and to support civil society," the sentiment of justice derives from "our reflecting on that tendency."[93] There are occasions, then, when Hume's thought goes too far in the direction of presuming that what is socially useful is directly instituted by way of rational reflection that it *is* useful. Hume was not consistent or clear-headed in all this. There has already been occasion to note his awareness that men frequently acted with objects in view that did *not* coincide with various results of their actions supposed to be socially useful. But he could also confuse the levels of individual motivation or aim on the one hand and of unsought larger social outcomes on the other.[94]

Some germane remarks reprinted in our readings (from Hutcheson's *System of Moral Philosophy*) under the title "Relationship and Marriage" say much in few words. Hutcheson notes that the nearer degrees of consanguinity and affinity, especially among different age generations, have been widely regarded as impediments to marriage; he writes further that "not only the inequality of years, but the natural reverence" in the relations between older and younger generations "are very opposite to the equality produced

93   *Essays*, II, 194.
94   Hume at times makes highly suggestive remarks bearing on what we would often today call function, despite the limitation indicated. See, for example, *Essays*, II, 197–201. It is rather curious that he should so clearly have understood at times that in various crucial cases men's actions work without their intention, indirectly, to social outcomes that may be most useful, while at other times he faltered on this point and posited a rational envisagement of "ends" where it would have been correct to posit rather an indirect attainment of certain outcomes. It may be that one source of his inconsistencies in this matter lies in the circumstance that he was influenced by the idea previously noted that institutions incorporate wisdom, bits of human sagacity built into them over time. This idea had not (and has not) been developed as an instrument of refined analysis. It is conceivable that Hume could not adequately manage the tensions involved in doing justice to the notion of humans putting a certain overall sagacity into their institutions while at the same time doing justice to the insight that the sagacity they put in on particular occasions is perhaps quite limited. But this possibility cannot be pursued. And, in any case, the extent to which Hume exhibited inconsistency in all this and adhered ineptly to a pragmatistic or rationalistic outlook should not be exaggerated. He could write forcefully in a quite different sense.

by marriage."⁹⁵ He then introduces some qualifications of the latter assertion. But what is clear is that he has anticipated a fairly common functionalist argument of the present day. He specifically asserts that the relations of parents to children seem "inconsistent" with the marital relation. The matter might now be put thus: in order for a parent to do the usually necessary job of socializing a child, transmitting to it the values and outlook of a group in such fashion that they are securely made part of the child's psychic equipment, a certain authority and acknowledgment of right to discipline must be granted the parent by the larger society and the child must in its own way allow the authority and the right. All this may be difficult or impossible to reconcile with a certain ease and looseness of relations of partners in marriage. Hutcheson is suggesting what might now be called functional incompatibility between the role of parent and that of marriage partner, and he sounds, indeed, very much like a contemporary British anthropologist or a sociological theorist.⁹⁶ It is also worth noting that Hutcheson is quite aware of a crucial outcome of the prohibition and abhorrence of the marriages of close relatives. The prohibition and abhorrence make for exogamy, and thereby families are prevented from becoming closed little systems, for "multitudes of families are beautifully interwoven with each other in affection and interest, and friendly ties are much further diffused."⁹⁷ It is true of Hutcheson and Hume, as it is of Adam Smith, that when they engaged in their early forms of functional analysis their sense of what was significant stayed with them and the functions they chose to discuss were not minor or quite incidental things in the social life of man.

95 *A System of Moral Philosophy*, II, 170.
96 Adam Smith, too, may well be suggesting the kind of incompatibility noted when he writes that "it is unnatural that the father, the guardian, and instructor of the daughter, should turn her lover and marry her." *Lectures on Justice, Police, Revenue and Arms*, p. 87.
97 *A System of Moral Philosophy*, II, 172. It may be noticed also that Hutcheson appears to challenge a view that Hume had put forth in his "Marriage of Relatives." Hutcheson avers that it frequently happens that first cousins and other persons less closely related are "educated together in the same intimacy" and yet "we see no dismal effects from the permission of intermarriages among them." *Ibid.*, II, 171. This apparent discrepancy is merely noted in passing.

VI. *History and Sociology*

The sociology of the Scottish moralists has a strong historical bent. Classical history and the history of the modern world, in
particular, were never far from the minds of a number of the
Scots. And their vision of unintended social outcomes has a predictable relevance to their historical concerns. But concrete history cannot be written on the basis of this vision alone. There is
one field of concrete history, having to do with Puritanism and
liberty as treated by David Hume, that merits special attention for
its presentation of a number of historical matters that are also of
some sociological interest. This is accordingly taken up, while the
strategy of the present section is to allow the concrete field to lead
again to the consideration of unintended outcomes.

Hume confronted a very considerable problem when in the
course of his *History of England* he sought to deal with the relations of Puritanism on the one hand and civil and political liberty
on the other. His efforts bring to mind Max Weber's work on the
Protestant ethic and the spirit of capitalism, despite all the differences. Weber may be said to have been concerned with the congruity between certain value-attitudes that gave great stress to
rationality ("the spirit of capitalism") and other value-attitudes of
religious origin that at least at first blush might be thought to
have nothing in particular to do with rationality.[98] Hume, too, may
be said to have been concerned with congruities between rationality and dispositions of religious provenience.[99] But it must be
added immediately that rationality must be differently understood
in the two cases. Weber used the term to refer to such things as
methodical, constantly renewed work activity conducted in a non-
traditional spirit. He had reference, then, to a kind of instrumental
rationality. Hume, who did not himself use the term rationality as
a major descriptive one in his statements on Puritanism and liberty,
referred particularly to a "love of liberty," which, it may be argued,

---

[98]   See Talcott Parsons, *The Structure of Social Action* (New York:
McGraw-Hill, 1937), chap. 14.
[99]   It is not implied, incidentally, that Hume and Weber are entirely
unique in their preoccupations with the matters noted.

he himself appreciably shared and which was important in the English-language world for which he wrote. To significant portions of that world, at least, liberty as a broad value seemed in itself eminently "rational" or morally and politically defensible—a "final," not an instrumental matter. Thus, both Weber and Hume saw "rational" phenomena deeply valued by the modern world— the rational organization of economic enterprise; and civil and political liberty—as peculiarly connected with religious sources. In the case of Hume, indeed, there is ground for saying that the sources of the English liberty of his day, as he conceived matters, were specifically in something rationally indefensible as well as entirely uncongenial to him—the religious enthusiasm of the Puritans.[100]

It must be granted that Hume's caution and conservatism would constantly incline him to warn of the dangers of loosening certain political restraints, of "licentiousness," in the same breath with which he might extol liberty. But he is not without his sympathies with liberty and himself regards it as reasonable in men to pursue it unless one goes against the sense of some clear statements of his—even if he could express dislike of "democratical enthusiasm." "On the whole," he writes, "the English have no reason . . . to be in love with the picture of absolute monarchy, or to prefer the unlimited authority of the prince, and his unbounded prerogatives, to that noble liberty, that sweet equality, and that happy security by which they are at present distinguished above all nations in the universe."[101] He seems constrained, however, to stress again, and precisely, the close connection betwen Puritanism and liberty or love of liberty. He writes of the "noble principles of liberty" taking root and "spreading themselves under the shelter of Puritanical absurdities" and at another point once more connects Puritanism and liberty, now commenting that "these two characters of such unequal merit arose and advanced together."[102] There is no question of his depreciation of Puritanism, at any rate. It is not entirely surprising that someone quite out of sympathy with

100 Cf. Meinecke, *Die Entstehung des Historismus*, I, 217–18.
101 *History of England,* IV, 215.
102 *Ibid.,* IV, 213–14, 556.

him could, then, write of him as Macaulay did, that he "hated religion so much that he hated liberty for having been allied with religion, and has pleaded the cause of tyranny with the dexterity of an advocate, while affecting the impartiality of a judge."[103] Whatever Hume's own attitude toward liberty may have been, it would still be of interest that he considered this value, significantly adhered to in his own world, as having the religious roots he believed it did. To the extent that he himself valued liberty personally (and we do in fact believe that he did value it appreciably), the poignancy of the paradox that "noble liberty" should have emerged from that unlovely compound of theological rage and gloomy enthusiasm which he thought Puritanism to be is enhanced.

In the development of Hume's views in this matter, his early essay, published in 1741, on superstition and enthusiasm (the first item under the present rubric found in the following readings) is relevant. He comments that superstition is inimical to civil liberty, while enthusiasm is friendly to it. But he really has disappointingly little to say about these presumed connections. Superstition "grows under the dominion of priests," whereas enthusiasm destroys all ecclesiastical power. Enthusiasm, "being the infirmity of bold and ambitious tempers, is naturally accompanied with a spirit of liberty; as superstition renders men tame and abject and fits them for slavery."[104] Other observations in this brief early item do not substantially forward understanding of the linkages or connections Hume claims to see. Some four pertinent statements that Hume makes in his *History* appear together in the following readings, under the title "Reform, Puritanism, and Liberty." The statements are of genuine interest and of course afford some historical detail, but part of their interest comes simply from the circumstance that one must note that they mark no real advance over the essay of 1741. In the first of the four statements reproduced, Hume writes of the anticeremonial, antipriestly disposition that he considered strongly associated with Puritanism. He writes of "the same bold and daring spirit" as appearing in the Puritans' addresses to the

---

103   As quoted by Wilbur C. Abbott, *Adventures in Reputation* (Cambridge, Mass.: Harvard University Press, 1935), p. 128.
104   *Essays,* I, 149–50.

divinity and in their political speculaton, while also referring to
Puritan advocacy of civil rights. In a second statement, Hume re-
sumes a relevant parliamentary speech by the Puritan, Peter Wentworth. A third statement provides a significant initial background
for later remarks on Puritanism and liberty. And a final brief paragraph suggests that Hume would think what he regards as the generally adverse effects of enthusiasm likely to be mitigated if there
were some admixture in it of "superstitious" rites and ceremonies.[105]
It seems likely that a valid insight is half concealed in this last
paragraph, but Hume evidently remains firm on the point that to
"a philosophical mind" pious ceremonies must appear as matter
for "ridicule." And his analysis is not advanced by other passages
that have not been quoted. He obviously but reiterates what he has
said before when he asserts, for example, that James I found in the
case of the "Scottish brethren" of the Puritan clergy that "the same
lofty pretensions which attended them in their familiar addresses
to their Maker, of whom they believed themselves the peculiar
favorites, induced them to use the utmost freedoms with their
earthly sovereign."[106]

Perhaps Hume was even suggesting his own bafflement about
the linkage of Puritanism and liberty to which he recurred with
such considerable frequency when he wrote the following (in
which he refers to James I): "But it is an observation suggested by
all history, and by none more than that of James and his successor
that the religious spirit, when it mingles with faction, contains in
it something supernatural and unaccountable; and that, in its operations upon society, effects correspond less to their known causes
than is found in any other circumstance of government."[107]

It is of interest, too, that Hume classified Puritans as political
Puritans (strong for civil liberty), Puritans in discipline ("averse
to the ceremonies and episcopal government of the Church"), and
doctrinal Puritans ("who rigidly defended the speculative system
of the first reformers").[108] At a later point he writes: "Though the

105 *History of England*, III, 526–31, 591–94; IV, 575–77; V, 203–4.
106 *Ibid.*, IV, 243.
107 *Ibid.*, IV, 306.
108 *Ibid.*, IV, 468.

political and religious Puritans mutually lent assistance to each other, there were many who joined the former, yet declined all connection with the latter."[109] This should certainly have received elaboration in order to clarify the general theme of linkage of Puritanism and liberty. (Hume himself would presumably have had least sympathy with the doctrinal Puritans among the three types he identifies.) In the end, he is left with a valid insight in the form of the notion of (what seemed to him a paradoxical) linkage between Puritanism and liberty—but not with more. He may well have been defeated here by a refusal to give serious consideration to historical and theological particulars, by a preference for thinking in terms of a "superstition" and "enthusiasm" that might recur endlessly in history, never to be accorded that differentiation that would make them discernibly the *special* "superstition" and "enthusiasm" of special historical epochs. And the limitations thus suggested may be accounted for both by the inadequacies of Hume's view of man-in-history and by his plain lack of sympathy and impatience with manifestations of religion. As regards the latter, Dilthey expresses rather forcefully a view that a good many others have substantially shared: "For the dark religious motives that he [Hume] sees holding sway in the history of the seventeenth century, more powerful than all political interests, he has only hate and disdain, not understanding."[110]

109   *Ibid.*, V, 10.
110   Wilhelm Dilthey, *Gesammelte Schriften* (Leipzig and Berlin: B. G. Teubner, 1927, III, 245. Macaulay's previously quoted comment may be recalled. Note the following statement regarding Hume: "How could he sympathize with Puritans or Covenanters who staked their lives and their country on questions he laughed at? As little as Gibbon, who sneered both at Arian and Trinitarian, and wondered how churches and states should madly quarrel over the difference of a diphthong." Henry G. Graham, *Scottish Men of Letters in the Eighteenth Century*, pp. 43–44. Certain strong general tendencies of Hume's writing on religion (aside from the particular Protestant case) may be suggested by his description of auricular confession as "one of the most powerful engines that ever was contrived for degrading the laity and giving their spiritual guides an entire ascendant over them," to which he adds, in the same flattering vein, that "it may justly be said that, though the priest's absolution, which attends confession, serves somewhat to ease weak minds from the immediate agonies of superstitious terror, it operates only by enforcing superstition itself, and thereby preparing the mind for a more violent relapse into the same disorders." *History of England*, III, 275. Hume

For a variety of reasons, a comparison of the quality of the performances of Hume and Weber on their respective problems beyond a point quickly reached would be inept and unfair. Hume could not fare well in such a comparison. And he never launched such broad and imposing inquiries into world religion as Weber was capable of for reasons perhaps both of temperament and of availability of needed materials. Nevertheless, as has been remarked, Hume had a valid insight in regard to Puritanism and liberty and he touched on problems whose vitality is constantly attested in present-day scholarship. If modern research finds the linkage between Puritanism and liberty complex, Hume had an inkling of the complexity. In a carefully presented argument, one of the most recent students of the linkage construes the effect of Puritanism or liberalism as no simple matter and contends that Puritanism afforded a "historical preparation" for the liberal world but no direct "theoretical contribution" thereto.[111] Walzer's historical work in detail expectably shows talents which Hume could not exhibit and might not have understood. But he could surely have understood that the men of religion he dealt with laid the foundations for developments that went well beyond their own intentions. Walzer has contended that Calvinism is related "not with modernity but with modernization . . . with the process far more significantly than with its outcome." This is in line with the contention that Puritanism should have afforded a historical preparation for, and not a direct contribution to, the modern liberal outlook. It is scarcely astonishing that Walzer should write of the

---

did have some understanding of what we might today call the functions of rite and ceremony. (See the *History,* IV, 308–9 and the passage quoted below, pp. 189–190, from the *History,* V, 203–4; also *Essays,* II, 44.) Very rarely he will suggest "positive" functions of religion not necessarily having anything to do with rite or ceremony. (See, for example, *History,* I, 471.) His essay on the natural history of religion (*Essays,* II, 309–63) contains some points of value. He has no systematic, well-thought through position as a "social critic" of religion. The general level of his comprehension of religion as sociological and psychological phenomenon is certainly not very high. His more strictly philosophical performances, as in the remarkable *Dialogues concerning Natural Religion,* are quite a different matter.

111   Michael Walzer, *The Revolution of the Saints* (Cambridge, Mass.: Harvard University Press, 1965), p. 303.

lxii INTRODUCTION

Puritan saint: "The saint appeared at a certain moment . . . and is remembered afterward for the effects that he had rather than for his own motives and purposes."[112]

We are thus brought back once more to the effects of human action but not of human design. It is appropriate that Adam Smith, to whom unintended outcomes of action were so important and who had so acute a historical sense, should be allowed, in the section of the anthology dealing with history and sociology, to render again (as a third reading) the substance of his fine chapter in *The Wealth of Nations* (Bk. III, chap. 4), which deals with "how the commerce of the towns contributed to the improvement of the country." Smith remarks a variety of developments in the historical relations of city and country, contending among other things that commerce and manufacture gradually introduced order, government and individual liberty and security into the countryside. The changes Smith recounts amount to a "revolution"—and while it is not a novel thing that he should write that the revolution was brought about by "two different orders of people, who had not the least intention to serve the public" and who had neither "knowledge" nor "foresight" that the revolution was in fact being brought about by the "folly" of the one group and the "industry" of the other, nevertheless he has now presented this kind of thesis in connection with particular historical events that afford a significant exemplification of it and in such fashion that he reinforces the impression of the immense weight he places upon unintended social outcomes. Smith's writing of history is usually such that it is easy to believe he would have made a poor narrative historian. Narrative that is not an occasion for, or does not lead to, or does not in some way reinforce or illuminate a generalization or insight in sociology or economics or the like seems to have little interest for him. Accordingly Smith is very much what would once have been called the "philosophical" historian.

Adam Ferguson, in "Of the Political Arts," from his major work on moral and political science, also brings us back to unintended effects, about which he writes with his usual force. But he now goes a little beyond unintended effects, stating that human insti-

112 *Ibid.*, p. 18.

tutions previously developed without "concerted design" and from "instincts of nature" become a *"rude material on which the ingenuity of man is to be exercised."*[113] Ferguson is brilliantly clear on the point that "the first object of concert, or convention, on the part of man, is not to give society existence, but to perfect the society in which he finds himself already by nature placed; not to establish subordination, but to correct the abuse of a subordination already established." Ferguson might even have conceded that there are "subordinations" for which men may in the light of justifiable standards come to feel no tolerance at all. But he is seeking to achieve a delicate balance here. He knows that men often find themselves in social situations that both antedate them and cannot simply be disestablished by an arbitrary act or thought. The scope of "innovation" may accordingly be limited. Yet he is also well aware that "the exigencies of civil society" are not met out of "mere instinct"; that "nature" has ordained otherwise and so disposed of man's lot that, "being provided with intellectual faculties, he ever meets with a suitable occasion by which they are called into use."[114] What the past has precipitated is confronted by human intelligence or reason, which does not hesitate to criticize and revise.

Relevant elements in Ferguson's thought may be made somewhat more explicit than he made them. He struggles in his theory of society with three broad views or outlooks that have previously been referred to. One is that reason must operate against a background of the non-rational. The continuing results of the past in society provide reason with a kind of substance on which it may confer new form, new organization, but without which it would have nothing to organize. In this light, the past has produced a set of *givens* on which even a strenuous utopianism may in its own way draw and will frequently be constrained to draw. But this outlook, however useful within its limits, does not serve to solve problems about the value of various specific social arrangements. Here the view in which institutions incorporate wisdom (or perhaps foolishness) from the past becomes germane. In the first view,

113   *Principles of Moral and Political Science*, I, 261; italics supplied.
114   *Ibid.*, I, 262, 263, 265.

it is recognized that reason itself cannot function without "establishments," without antecedents in human experiences and sentiments taken up and consolidated into social arrangements. In the second view, questions arise of the extent to which various particular institutions that have come down from the past are streaked with rationality. Here one may ask about fitness of means for ends and seek to apply tests for assessment of non-instrumental values.

Finally, a third view or outlook may be called a "transcendence" view. Now again one sees particularly that social outcomes have gone beyond the intentions of individual actors. But a special twist may at this point be given to the notion of transcendence. Outcomes have indeed transcended intentions. And new intentions may now deliberately go beyond or transcend old outcomes. Ferguson can be said to have noted that there are occasions in the historical process when men become peculiarly aware of what has come down to them and seek seriously to reshape it. If what has come down is indeed, as Ferguson says in the present context, "a *rude* material," then *in* this present context he must see appreciable limitations in largely unintended institutional precipitations from the past; and he does write of the "rude material" that it is material "on which ingenuity is to be exercised." But at this interesting point that suggests the possibility of an active, deliberate transcendence, and where banalities will hardly do, Ferguson leaves us and provides nothing further. He might have done a number of things. Hypothetically, he might have written of a reconstruction of social structures even involving new ends emerging from old devices or forms.[115] He might have tried a searching examination of the op-

115   Troeltsch, referring to a very significant aspect of Spencer's views, remarks that "social structures created by older tendencies may be put into the service of new goals, of whose origins one knows nothing and of which one only discovers that they have been unconsciously constructed under cover of the older forms. . . . What cruelty, violence and superstition have wrought with a thousand horrors and terrors can be used by an individualized and moralized culture. Thereby the horrors of the militaristic period become tolerable, and the religious reverence of true piety can become connected even to imbecilic beliefs in ancestors and spirits since it transforms them into symbols for nobler and better metaphysical sentiments and actually feels that it was primitively and unconsciously latent in those phenomena." Ernst Troeltsch, *Der Historismus und Seine Probleme* (Tübingen: J. C. B. Mohr, 1922), p. 428.

timism about society to which he and the other Scots so strongly tended. He might more generally have ventured a mutual confrontation and systematic analysis of the several views noted. That one thinks of such posibilities is a witness to Ferguson's abilities, even if the possibilities point also to his inevitable limitations.

VII. *The Range of Sociological Concern*

Much of sociological relevance that was comprehended under moral philosophy has hardly, if at all, been touched upon as yet. It is the design of the following remarks (and of the seventh section of our anthology) to do further justice to the sheer range of sociological concern exhibited by the Scottish moralists. With this design, diversity of topic must be expected. Certain aspects of political sociology, contract, social norms, rank and stratification, demography, and what we would now call urban sociology are all treated in the work of the Scots and are important enough to require some attention.

The Scots were greatly interested in politics and in a number of issues bearing on politics that had a rather clearly sociological character. Hume's essay, "Of the Original Contract," which is not included herein, is a good example of the vigor with which they could attack political questions. The essay is plainly inspired by a desire on Hume's part to be realistic. He can be quite forthright in stating that "no compact or agreement . . . was expressly formed for general submission; an idea far beyond the comprehension of savages."[116] And much of his endeavor is directing toward showing how shallow, in the light of political and historical realities, certain kinds of social contract-oriented thought could be—particularly, one may say, such thought on this line as took the notion of a contract with great literalness and did not allow it enough of that "as if" or consciously fictional character that can lend it a certain significance and endow it with appreciable ethical and political force. Hume stresses the importance of conquest and usurpation in the origin of governments. He stresses the particular character of the sentiments and ideas of men with regard to their govern-

116 *Essays,* I, 445.

ments, obviously with the aim of showing that men very often do not think and "feel" in social contract terms: they tend to conceive that long possession gives a prince the title to rule, or they incline to the view that by their birth they owe allegiance to a particular ruler or form of government. Hume is further concerned with the circumstance that a certain willingness to acquiesce in authority is a requisite for minimum political and social stability. His view of various rules and conventions is affected by his sense of the over-riding importance of this willingness. The general obligation binding us to government, he asserts, is "the interest and necessities of society." This obligation is powerful; but the directing of the feeling of obligation "to this or that particular prince or form of government is frequently more uncertain and dubious." It is significant that Hume adds that in these cases present possession has "considerable authority," an authority greater than that which holds where we are concerned with private property, "because of the disorders which attend all revolutions and changes of government."[117]

Hume's concerns are undeniably those of a "philosopher," and his work need not be forced into frameworks that do not fit it. But one hardly forces it when one notes that one of the most urgent preoccupations of his essay on contract and of other writing of his by way of political analysis[118] is actually with questions of legitimacy, in the sense of what makes government seem legitimate in the eyes of a people, why long possession seems to confer legitimacy and so on. Questions such as these certainly touch on matters within the province of the sociologist today.

Adam Ferguson also had some concern with contract, as shown in "Of Contract, or the Principle of Conventional Obligation," reprinted below. Ferguson would of course have been among the last of men to be receptive to any doctrine of the actual beginning of society in a deliberate contract or agreement. It is hardly a matter for surprise that he should reject this. Society is a "natural" growth, and deliberate conventions, agreements, or contracts take place within a society already formed and possessed of a history

[117]   *Ibid.*, p. 459.
[118]   See his *Treatise*, II, 313–28.

or past. That history bequeaths norms or values to the members of any particular generation (and in Ferguson's view there are certain values that are likely to appear in any society). This legacy, together with men's value-dispositions in the present, may be said to constitute a kind of *moral environment of contract*, and contract does not and cannot stand alone. In contemplating moral obligation as apprehended by "the ordinary sense of mankind," Ferguson considers that "we find a clear apprehension of right and wrong prior to convention" or contract or agreement. Indeed, Ferguson goes on, "we find an acknowledgment that convention itself may be wrong; the completion of it worse; and the breach of it right." Further, "the obligation to abstain from harm and the right of every individual . . . to defend himself and his fellow creatures are prior to convention and are indeed the foundation upon which conventional obligation is binding." Contract, to be felt as binding, requires some source other than itself: "we must suppose some previous foundation upon which its obligation may rest";[119] and Ferguson is clearly disposed to look for such a foundation in the moral environment just referred to.

It happens that Ferguson's argument is connected with ideas relating to natural law, and natural law, important though it be for the Scottish moralists, is a topic that must substantially be left outside our range. But it may at least be noted that reference has previously been made to a justice that can be "found" and not merely "decreed by the will of a legislator." Ferguson's thought on contract is most relevant to this. The conception of a moral environment of contract, to which appeal may even be made against particular contracts for their violation of pre- or extra-contractual values, lends support to the notion of a justice that can be "found." Furthermore, modern sociological analysis has given some stress, if in slightly different terms, to the idea of a moral environment of contract. There is stress on "non-contractual" elements in contract, as when Parsons writes, for example, with regard to market transactions, that these are "actually entered into in accordance with a body of binding rules which are not part of the *ad hoc* agreement of the parties." The "binding rules" comprise

[119] *Principles of Moral and Political Science,* II, 217, 218, 219, 222.

an "institution" of contract within the already existing framework of which contractual relations occur.[120]

There is one other matter connected with natural law to which very brief attention may be given for its sociological relevance. Where there was concern to develop argument based on natural law, there was inevitably concern with the significance of such essential terms as "right" and "duty." Accordingly there may be found among the Scots a measure of preoccupation with what have been called law-norms, which attribute rights and duties.[121] The preoccupation led to the exercise of some care in the definition or specification of law-norms, with an indication of what they imply for the interrelation of human beings. A short passage from Thomas Reid is afforded in our anthology to give an example of this "logic of norms." There is certainly no intent here to suggest that all law must dissolve into sociology. But the logic of law-norms is of considerable sociological interest. To say no more, the analysis of social roles would be much the poorer without sustainment from this source. The mere elementary insight, which Reid possessed securely, that right and duty are so related that neither "makes sense" without the other is of some use, sociologically speaking. Reid's bit of analysis, taken from a brief chapter of his on "systems of natural jurisprudence," it will be noted, has an engagingly modern effect.

A different set of concerns is marked by the Scots' interest in rank and stratification and occupational orders. Adam Smith writes of "ambition" and of "the distinction of ranks" in a chapter, reproduced below, from *The Theory of Moral Sentiments*. His discussion is hardly a close analysis and it has at points a moralistic or homiletic effect, but he does concern himself with the topics his title announces, and his flair for the sociologically apt phrase is evident here as elsewhere, as when he observes that "place, that great object which divides the wives of aldermen, is the end of half the labors of human life."[122] Effectively, this chapter by Smith

---

[120]   Parsons, *The Structure of Social Action*, p. 311.
[121]   See the able analysis of law-norms given by Pitirim A. Sorokin in *Society, Culture and Personality* (New York: Harper & Brothers, 1947), pp. 71–88.
[122]   *The Theory of Moral Sentiments*, p. 80.

is a discussion within the realm of status, of differential assignment to different sets of persons of prestige or "honor." But Smith could of course also be concerned with stratification phenomena or phenomena pertaining to occupational orders that definitely carry more of a suggestion of class (by contrast with status), of the relationship of different groups to the market, and of their differing power on the market, as witness the passage, reproduced in our readings, from *The Wealth of Nations,* on the three great orders of society. It will be noted that in this passage Smith has some interesting if brief reflections on the character of the "consciousness," or knowledge of various interests (including their own) possessed by the members of the occupational orders. It may be salutary, too, to be reminded that Smith was hardly disposed to endorse unqualifiedly any and all manifestations on the market of the urge to profit.

From the matter of rank and stratification, we make another abrupt shift in our listing of sociological concerns to note that there was some concern on the part of the Scottish moralists with demographic problems. A very good example of this is afforded by Hume's lengthy essay, "Of the Populousness of Ancient Nations,"[123] a fragment of which will be found in this volume. Comparing societies in antiquity with those of the modern world, Hume wished to "consider whether it be probable, from what we know of the situation of society in both periods, that antiquity must have been more populous," as well as to ascertain whether ancient society was in fact "more populous."[124] The skeptical demographer is seen at work in Hume's critical remarks on relevant materials. This kind of skepticism was of course indispensable for the emergence of a rational modern demography.[125] The combination of demographic interest with an appreciable familiarity with classical sources, while it has certainly not been unique since Hume's

123   *Essays,* I, 381–443.
124   *Ibid.,* p. 383.
125   Mossner affords an interesting historical background for Hume's essay on population, reviewing some aspects of Hume's relationship to Robert Wallace, who was writing on the same subject about the same time. Mossner remarks that "the reasonings of Hume and Wallace were synthesized by . . . Malthus." *The Life of David Hume,* pp. 262–68.

day, is still provocative. It is as well to be reminded that the Scottish moralists could draw on materials in regard to which it would be truer to say that the skills required to utilize them have lapsed (among sociologists) than that they themselves have been unequivocally shown to be of little value.

A shift from demography to the circumstances of urban life will not seem particularly abrupt. Kames's sketch of "the character of a great city," also reproduced in our anthology, could easily pass as an essay in urban sociology, granted that it shows clear signs of its approximate date of composition. The number of subjects Kames manages to take up is impressive. But it must be confessed that he shows rather too much "facility" in handling them. At the same time, the main line of the argument is determinedly rational and, in the broad sense of the word, scientific. Kames is well aware of a number of things important in the sociological analysis of cities and to the urban planner. His essay accordingly retains point.

Some of the anthropological interests of the Scots remain to be considered, and with the consideration of these a reasonably extensive, if unavoidably incomplete, coverage of the Scottish outlook on human nature and society will have been achieved.

VIII. *The Anthropological Impulse*

Interest in matters anthropological is particularly pronounced in Kames and Monboddo. Kames held anthropological views that were followed for a long time after him, whether they were original with him or not. Monboddo, who had a downright gift for being wrong, nevertheless raised a number of intriguing anthropological questions. If there are still faint echoes of the laughter that greeted his responses, it is at any rate worth noting what the laughter was about.

Kames's *Sketches of the History of Man* reveals an eager ethnographic and comparative interest. Not only Greeks, Romans, and other Europeans appear in these volumes, but Caribbean Indians, Philippine Islanders, Tartars, and Chinese among others. Kames, however, is not generally an exceptionally incisive writer. It is not that he is incapable of shrewdness and insight, but he is likely enough to mix with these a measure of naïveté (and, incidentally, a piety so unremitting that it can become most annoying to a contemporary reader).[126] Kames also tends to exhibit a staggering optimism, going beyond the rather high level of optimism generally found in the Scots. It is utterly commonplace for him to comment that "the Deity has left none of his works imperfect."[127] This sort of bias is hardly of aid in his anthropology. But some of his anthropological presuppositions sustained their life long after he had passed from the scene. "I venture to suggest," he writes, "that as, with respect to individuals, there is a progress from infancy to maturity; so there is a similar progress in every nation, from its savage state to its maturity in arts and sciences."[128] Societies will generally go through the same stages in the development, say, of various institutions, although some allowance has to be made for individual peculiarities and differences of pace.[129] A proposition of this sort may perhaps be somewhat less antagonistically responded to today, in a time of some renewed thinking about social evolution, than a generation ago, but it is certain that Kames gives it no highly sophisticated application. It appears in him as a rather uncritical item of "method."[130] The passage presented in the anthology

---

126   The following may be allowed as an instance of both the naïveté and the piety. Wishing to attribute various "racial" differences to "nature" rather than to climate, Kames comes to grips with Montesquieu: "The most formidable antagonist remains still on hand, the celebrated Montesquieu, who is a great champion for the climate; observing, that in hot climates people are timid like old men, and in cold climates bold like young men. This in effect is to maintain that the torrid zone is an unfit habitation for men; that they degenerate in it, lose their natural vigor, and even in youth become like old men. That author certainly intended not any imputation on Providence; and yet, doth it not look like an imputation to maintain that so large a portion of the globe is fit for beasts only, not for men?" *Sketches*, I, 46.

127   *Ibid.*, I, 3.

128   *Ibid.*, III, 376.

129   See, for example, Kames's *Historical Law Tracts* (Edinburgh, 1758), I, 36–37.

130   Kames's biographer, Tytler, makes a good statement on the point: "On the supposition . . . of the universality of the savage state, Lord Kames thinks himself warranted to infer that the history of the progress of any one rude people from a state of barbarism to refinement is, in a great measure, the

following to illustrate his anthropological bent, given the title "The Development of Religious Belief" and excerpted from his lengthy sketch entitled "Principles and Progress of Theology," is a fair sample of his work. It will be clear to the reader familiar with anthropological literature that for a good many decades after Kames wrote the general level of discourse on topics such as he here deals with did not rise by very much.

Kames also has some concern with physical anthropology. In this connection it is well to recall his insistence on the truth of the story of the tower of Babel. The assumption of the truth of the confusion of Babel alone, he believes, can harmonize sacred and profane history. Originally, man was physically or biologically one and there was but one language. Yet now there is indubitably "natural" or "racial" diversity and there prevails a confusion of tongues. Had it not been for Babel all men would have progressed equally toward knowledge and civilization. But Babel scattered men over the earth and "deprived them of society and rendered them savages." They have since tended to emerge gradually from savagery, but some have actually remained in that state while others have shown unevenness in their advances from it.[131] What do the "racial" varieties of men signify, precisely? Whatever they may have meant to Kames, his conception of them does not seem to have affected seriously the notion that there is a generic human nature, a nature featuring very important traits in common, for many purposes overshadowing differences. Kames will write that all men have "a glimmering of the moral sense,"[132] or that "the sense of justice, and of other primary virtues, is universal. It belongs to man as such. Though it exists in very different degrees of strength, there perhaps never was a human creature absolutely void

---

history of the species; and that, in defect of the authentic records of any particular nation making distinctly this progress in a connected chain, it is allowable to draw from every quarter such facts as are illustrative of manners, habits of life, prevailing customs, ideas of morality, or the origin of arts and improvements, and adopt them without scruple as documents of the general history of man." *Memoirs of the Life and Writings of the Honorable Henry Home of Kames,* II, 149–50.

131   *Sketches,* I, 60–65.
132   *Ibid.,* III, 375.

of it.[133] In the form of a small volume on the art of thinking Kames wrote a manual of instruction in human nature and of moral edification, containing a variety of observations supplemented by illustrative historical and allegorical matter.[134] A few of his comments still have a certain cogency. "Barbarians," he writes, "are slaves to custom; polite people to fashions. The Hottentots are an instance of the former; the French of the latter."[135] One can still almost hear the "plus ça change plus c'est la même chose." And when Kames observes that "that reason which is favorable to our desires is always the best,"[136] he gives no occasion at all to think that he would have the observation apply in unequal degree to Hottentots and Frenchmen.

Monboddo makes a more colorful figure among the Scots than Kames. He was deeply enamored of "the ancient metaphysics" that has come down through the great classical Greek philosophers and that he believes is traceable back to Egypt through the intermediate figure of Pythagoras. On the foundation of this metaphysics he criticizes the philosophy and science of his own day, but, additionally, so great is his devotion to classical authors that he gathers from them the most dubious anthropological or ethnographic materials, to which he gives amazingly easy credence. Monboddo even writes that it is his observation that "those who are not scholars give no faith to the ancient authors, but judge from the opinions which they have formed from what they have themselves seen."[137] This was more particularly directed against Buffon, and it is impossible not to feel a strong note of disapproval in it. For his ethnographic purposes Monboddo adds to his classical authorities testimonies of travelers more or less of his own day, which, too, he simply cannot treat judiciously.

In his work *Of the Origin and Progress of Language*, Monboddo expounded the view that man was once in a state of nature and that some present-day men are still in it or close to it. This is to say that men, generally, once existed (as some men do even now)

133   *Essays on The Principles of Morality and Natural Religion*, p. 66.
134   *Introduction to the Art of Thinking* (New York: W. B. Gilley, 1818).
135   *Ibid.*, p. 110.
136   *Ibid.*, p. 30.
137   *Antient Metaphysics*, III, 152, note.

without culture and without language in particular, and even
without society, or at least without more than a quite rudimentary,
bare intercourse with others. All this certainly suggests the close-
ness of "natural man" to animals or "brutes," as Monboddo often
called them (although man always had the *potential* for culture
or civilization and language and differed in this regard, at least,
from the brutes). Given Monboddo's adherence to this view, some
of his peculiarities become more intelligible. Thus, the orangutan
is a great favorite of his.[138] It is most conspicuous in the first
volume of the book on language, haunts the third volume of
Antient Metaphysics, and is still to be traced in the terminal
(fourth, fifth, and sixth) volumes of the latter work. Monboddo
simply cannot let this beast be. He must "prove" its humanity, its
affiliation to the species man, time and again.[139] But he also holds
(with not very serious reservation) that the orangutan does not
speak, has not the art of language even if he has the potential to
acquire it. And, if the creature is unequivocally a man and yet does
not speak, there is reinforcement for Monboddo's much insisted
upon view that man in a natural state had no language and acquired it only painfully and over time.[140] Thus: "I have dwelt this
long upon the orangutan because, if I make him out to be a
man, I prove, by fact as well as argument, this fundamental
proposition upon which my whole theory hangs, that language is
not natural to man. And, *secondly,* I likewise prove that the natural

138   The beaver, curiously, is another: "It appears to me to have required
an extraordinary degree of sagacity to invent so artificial a thing as speech,
nor do I think that there is any animal other than man yet discovered, unless
perhaps it be the beaver, that has sagacity enough to have invented it." *Origin
and Progress of Language,* I, 459.
139   Incidentally, some orangutans are more definitely human than others.
See, for example, *Antient Metaphysics,* III, 44.
140   Monboddo repeatedly stresses how difficult it would be to "invent"
language. He even inclines to the view that the invention may have been beyond man's capacities alone. Thus, he writes that although he does not doubt
that men may "cultivate and improve" language once it has been invented,
he "can hardly believe but that in the first discovery of so artificial a method
of communication, men had supernatural assistance," and he is accordingly
"much inclined to listen to what the Egyptians tell us of a God, as they call
him, that is an intelligence superior to man, having first taught them the use
of language." *Origin and Progress of Language,* IV, 184.

state of man, such as I suppose it, is not a mere hypothesis, but a state which at present actually exists."[141]

The espousal of the humanity of the orangutan does hereby become more intelligible, if not a whit more correct. This espousal may also serve to stress again that there is a thrust in Monboddo's work toward the close association of humanity and non-human animality. Some of the stories he relates illustrate this. He is expansive on men with tails in the selection from his work in the anthology following, which exhibits some of his typical procedures and crotchets. He takes up stories about "sea men" and mermaids (whom he concedes to be "rare" in his day).[142] Nor does his credulity seem to be strained by relations of dogheaded men. But if man thus gets most closely (if most questionably) associated with the animal world, any conceivable anthropological gain Monboddo might have had from this is dissipated by his apparent inability to adduce or come to grips with genuine evidence in the whole matter.

Monboddo's tall tales are interesting in another light. The tales often suggest that men have been exceedingly various. And Monboddo avers, indeed, that "the scheme of Providence could not have been carried on, without a distinction of men, and of families of men."[143] He believes, then, that there are distinct "races" of men, but he is hardly clear on the point, and it is accordingly not easy to evaluate his position on the matter of uniformity of human nature. The very existence of men with tails and of dogheaded men and of similarly strange beings that Monboddo presumed, and even the presumption that the orangutan is human, could well be thought to argue in favor of "racial" differences, yet Monboddo does not argue the matter systematically.[144] There is another rather puzzling matter to be noted here. Man generally has achieved a cultural and social state and become possessed of a complex lin-

---

[141]   *Ibid.*, I, 359–60.

[142]   See *Antient Metaphysics*, III, 263.

[143]   *Ibid.*, III, 246.

[144]   It is interesting to note that he contends that the ancient Egyptians, for whose cultural achievements he has great regard, were Negroes, and takes David Hume to task for questioning the native abilities of Negroes. For Hume's speculation on the matter, see his *Essays*, I, 252, note.

guistic heritage, whereas men in the natural state were "mere
animals" who had not yet acquired intellect. In this sense there
has clearly been an ascent of man. Yet, curiously, man has also
degenerated "in later times"—in health, longevity, in stature, but
also in wisdom, for he has fallen away from the wisdom of the
ancients as well as from their physical standards.[145] This whole
matter is never clarified and Monboddo is not at pains to show
consistency with regard to it. Nor, in particular, is it evident just
what significance the degeneration that is presumed to have taken
place may have in regard to a "racial" differentiation of earlier and
later men.

Monboddo will aver that man's nature "may in some sense be
said to be the same, as he still has the same natural capabilities
that he had from the beginning," but he will add that "this nature
is by its original constitution susceptible of greater change than
the nature of any other animal known."[146] He does seem to hold to
the notion of a common human nature and of the importance of
the common elements, but there are ambiguities in his position and
he will always have his own twists. Thus, the idea that society
makes man human was generally congenial to the Scottish moralists. Monboddo in one way quite agrees with this, for he will
unhesitatingly aver that, in the absence of social intercourse, "it
is evident that the human mind would still have continued in a
state very little above that of the brutes."[147] Society makes men
human and was indispensable to the creation of language. Yet we
know that for Monboddo, somehow, "man," *potentially* capable
of cultural achievement, existed *before* such achievement. Needed
explication for this was never afforded.

There is a certain bizarre impressiveness about Monboddo. His
knowledge of many matters is very considerable and by no means
always inaccurate. His curiosity will sometimes lead him into
bypaths that are both rather fascinating and likely to have a
significance of their own.[148] It is true that his two books on lan-

[145]   See *Antient Metaphysics*, vol. III, Book II, chap. V; and William
Knight, *Lord Monboddo and Some of His Contemporaries*, pp. 29, 38.
[146]   *Origin and Progress of Language*, I, 44.
[147]   *Antient Metaphysics*, I, 147.
[148]   See, for example, the chapter on dreams in *Antient Metaphysics*, vol.
II, Book IV, at pp. 229–93.

guage and on metaphysics are intellectual museums, immense clutters now inspected only by an occasional scholar. But they preserve some elements that are still provocative. If it can hardly be claimed that he held defensible views on the more important matters he took up, he was yet wrong in interesting ways. The puzzles and ambiguities he created with his various statements about man in social and presocial conditions and man's presumed degeneration after an ascent to humanity may be regarded as constituting a double challenge in his time. There was a challenge to those who, notably like Adam Ferguson, wished to make the very presumption of humanity unqualifiedly contingent on the existence of a social state, to give their outlook (however justified it might be) a deeper foundation. There was a challenge to those who wanted a well-reasoned and consistent developmental representation of humanity to organize carefully and extend their relevant data and ideas. Monboddo had in his way a strong sense of movement or change, some feeling for problems in the evolution of the human species. His obsessive preoccupation with the orangutan may now appear quaint or even pathetic, but man's relation to the primates was an appreciably important matter long after his demise.[149] The chapter quoted from his work in this anthology no doubt also has its quaint features, but it would be erroneous to conclude from these that this avid anthropologist, metaphysician, classical scholar, and philologist was radically unworthy of the company he keeps with the other Scots here represented.

If the present state of sociological thought will unavoidably affect one's view of the work of the Scottish moralists, it may still be true that their work can in some measure operate independently to affect one's view of the present state of sociological thought. In the light of what the Scots have to say, it may not seem unreasonable to suggest they can intensify our awareness of a number of very important matters and sometimes hint at modes of analysis that we have tended to neglect and could profitably consider anew. These are not services to be despised. Hume once observed that the

---

149   While Monboddo contended that the orangutan was human, he did not consider as human the monkey or ape, "with or without a tail." *Origin and Progress of Language,* I, 311.

greater part of mankind might be divided into two classes, "that of *shallow* thinkers, who fall short of the truth, and that of *abstruse* thinkers, who go beyond it." He observed of the members of the latter class that they are "by far the most rare; and I may add, by far the most useful and valuable. They suggest hints, at least, and start difficulties, which they want, perhaps, skill to pursue, but which may produce fine discoveries when handled by men who have a more just way of thinking."[150] If by "more just" Hume meant more precise, some of the Scottish moralists, at least, met thoroughly respectable standards for precision and rigor and even technical quality of thought in the eighteenth century. But that the Scots were imaginative and vastly attracted by sweeping ideas (in sociological matters as in others), even if they could not always give them the development they or others might have wished, is beyond question. The qualified impartial spectator would have had to give them a high ranking as "abstruse thinkers" in the handling of sociological problems in their time. Their continuing vitality and suggestiveness should stand forth plain in the ensuing pages.

Louis Schneider

[150]   *Essays,* I, 287.

I. Aspects of
Human Psychology

1

David Hume

ON FEELING AND ASSOCIATION

It is EVIDENT that though all passions pass easily from one object to another related to it, yet this transition is made with greater facility where the more considerable object is first presented and the lesser follows it than where this order is reversed and the lesser takes the precedence. Thus it is more natural for us to love the son upon account of the father than the father upon account of the son; the servant for the master than the master for the servant; the subject for the prince than the prince for the subject. In like manner we more readily contract a hatred against a whole family where our first quarrel is with the head of it than where we are displeased with a son, or servant, or some inferior member. In short, our passions, like other objects, descend with greater facility than they ascend.

That we may comprehend wherein consists the difficulty of explaining this phenomenon, we must consider that the very same reason which determines the imagination to pass from remote to contiguous objects with more facility than from contiguous to remote causes it likewise to change with more ease the less for the greater than the greater for the less. Whatever has the greatest influence is most taken notice of; and whatever is most taken notice of presents itself most readily to the imagination. We are more

Reprinted from David Hume, *A Treatise of Human Nature*, T. H. Green and T. H. Grose, eds. (London, 1898), II, 132–33, 143–45. Title supplied.

apt to overlook in any subject what is trivial, than what appears of considerable moment; but especially if the latter takes the precedence and first engages our attention. Thus if any accident makes us consider the Satellites of Jupiter, our fancy is naturally determined to form the idea of that planet; but if we first reflect on the principal planet, it is more natural for us to overlook its attendants. The mention of the provinces of any empire conveys our thought to the seat of the empire; but the fancy returns not with the same facility to the consideration of the provinces. The idea of the servant makes us think of the master; that of the subject carries our view to the prince. But the same relation has not an equal influence in conveying us back again. And on this is founded that reproach of Cornelia to her sons, that they ought to be ashamed she should be more known by the title of the daughter of Scipio than by that of the mother of the Gracchi. This was, in other words, exhorting them to render themselves as illustrious and famous as their grandfather; otherwise the imagination of the people, passing from her who was intermediate and placed in an equal relation to both, would always leave them and denominate her by what was more considerable and of greater moment. On the same principle is founded that common custom of making wives bear the name of their husbands, rather than husbands that of their wives; as also the ceremony of giving the precedency to those whom we honor and respect. We might find many other instances to confirm this principle, were it not already sufficiently evident. . .

It may not be amiss, in treating of the affection we bear our acquaintance and relations, to observe some pretty curious phenomena which attend it. It is easy to remark in common life that children esteem their relation to their mother to be weakened in a great measure by her second marriage and no longer regard her with the same eye as if she had continued in her state of widowhood. Nor does this happen only when they have felt any inconveniences from her second marriage, or when her husband is much her inferior, but even without any of these considerations and merely because she has become part of another family. This also takes place with regard to the second marriage of a father but in a much less degree: and it is certain the ties of blood are not so much loosened in the latter case as by the marriage of a mother. These two phenomena are remarkable in themselves, but much more so when compared.

In order to produce a perfect relation between two objects, it is requisite not only that the imagination be conveyed from one to the other by resemblance, contiguity, or causation but also that it return back from the second to the first with the same ease and facility. At first sight this may seem a necessary and unavoidable consequence. If one object resemble another, the latter object must necessarily resemble the former. If one object be the cause of another, the second object is effect to its cause. It is the same case with contiguity: and therefore the relation being always reciprocal, it may be thought that the return of the imagination from the second to the first must also, in every case, be equally natural as its passage from the first to the second. But upon further examination we shall easily discover our mistake. For supposing the second object, beside its reciprocal relation to the first, to have also a strong relation to a third object; in that case the thought, passing from the first object to the second, returns not back with the same facility, though the relation continues the same; but is readily carried on to the third object by means of the new relation, which presents itself and gives a new impulse to the imagination. This new relation, therefore, weakens the tie between the first and second objects. The fancy is by its very nature wavering and inconstant and considers always two objects as more strongly related together where it finds the passage equally easy both in going and returning than where the transition is easy only in one of these motions. The double motion is a kind of a double tie and binds the objects together in the closest and most intimate manner.

The second marriage of a mother breaks not the relation of child and parent, and that relation suffices to convey my imagination from myself to her with the greatest ease and facility. But after the imagination is arrived at this point of view, it finds its object to be surrounded with so many other relations which challenge its regard that it knows not which to prefer and is at a loss what new object to pitch upon. The ties of interest and duty bind her to another family and prevent that return of the fancy from her to myself which is necessary to support the union. The thought has no longer the vibration requisite to set it perfectly at ease and indulge its inclination to change. It goes with facility but returns with difficulty, and by that interruption finds the relation much weakened from what it would be were the passage open and easy on both sides.

Now to give a reason why this effect follows not in the same degree upon the second marriage of a father, we may reflect on what has been proved already, that though the imagination goes easily from the view of a lesser object to that of a greater, yet it returns not with the same facility from the greater to the less. When my imagination goes from myself to my father, it passes not so readily from him to his second wife, nor considers him as entering into a different family, but as continuing the head of that family of which I am myself a part. His superiority prevents the easy transition of the thought from him to his spouse but keeps the passage still open for a return to myself along the same relation of child and parent. He is not sunk in the new relation he acquires, so that the double motion of vibration of thought is still easy and natural. By this indulgence of the fancy in its inconsistency, the tie of child and parent still preserves its full force and influence.

A mother thinks not her tie to a son weakened, because it is shared with her husband, nor a son his with a parent because it is shared with a brother. The third object is here related to the first as well as to the second, so that the imagination goes and comes along all of them with the greatest facility.

2

David Hume

SOME LIMITATIONS OF REASON

NOTHING IS MORE USUAL in philosophy and even in common life than to talk of the combat of passion and reason, to give the preference to reason and assert that men are only so far virtuous as they conform themselves to its dictates. Every rational creature, it is said, is obliged to regulate his actions by reason, and if any other motive or principle challenges the direction of his conduct, he ought to oppose it until it be entirely subdued, or at least brought to a conformity with that superior principle. On this method of thinking the greatest part of moral philosophy, ancient and modern, seems to be founded; nor is there an ampler field, as well for metaphysical arguments as popular declamations, than this, supposed preeminence of reason above passion. The eternity, invariableness, and divine origin of the former have been displayed to the best advantage: the blindness, unconstancy, and deceitfulness of the latter have been as strongly insisted on . . .

Since reason alone can never produce any action or give rise to volition, I infer that the same faculty is as incapable of preventing volition or of disputing the preference with any passion or emotion. This consequence is necessary. It is impossible reason could have the latter effect of preventing volition but by giving an impulse in a contrary direction to our passion, and that impulse,

Reprinted from David Hume, *A Treatise of Human Nature*, T. H. Green and T. H. Grose, eds. (London, 1898), II, 193, 194–95. Title supplied.

had it operated alone, would have been able to produce volition. Nothing can oppose or retard the impulse of passion but a contrary impulse; and if this contrary impulse ever arises from reason, that latter faculty must have an original influence on the will and must be able to cause, as well as hinder any act of volition. But if reason has no original influence, it is impossible it can withstand any principle which has such an efficacy or ever keep the mind in suspense a moment. Thus it appears that the principle which opposes our passion cannot be the same with reason and is only called so in an improper sense. We speak not strictly and philosophically when we talk of the combat of passion and of reason. Reason is and ought only to be the slave of the passions and can never pretend to any other office than to serve and obey them.

3

David Hume

OF THE IDEA OF NECESSARY
CONNECTION

THERE ARE NO IDEAS which occur in metaphysics more obscure and uncertain than those of *power, force, energy,* or *necessary connection,* of which it is every moment necessary for us to treat in all our disquisitions. We shall, therefore, endeavor, in this section, to fix, if possible, the precise meaning of these terms, and thereby remove some part of that obscurity which is so much complained of in this species of philosophy.

It seems a proposition which will not admit of much dispute that all our ideas are nothing but copies of our impressions, or in other words, that it is impossible for us to *think* of any thing which we have not antecedently *felt* either by our external or internal senses.... Complex ideas may perhaps be well known by definition, which is nothing but an enumeration of those parts or simple ideas that compose them. But when we have pushed up definitions to the most simple ideas and find still some ambiguity and obscurity, what resource are we then possessed of? By what invention can we throw light upon these ideas and render them altogether precise and determinate to our intellectual view? Produce the impressions or original sentiments from which the ideas are copied. These impressions are all strong and sensible. They admit not of

Reprinted from David Hume, *Enquiry concerning Human Understanding,* in *Essays,* T. H. Green and T. H. Grose, eds. (London: Longmans, Green, 1875), II, pp. 51–65.

ambiguity. They are not only placed in a full light themselves, but may throw light on their correspondent ideas, which lie in obscurity. And by this means, we may perhaps attain a new microscope or species of optics, by which, in the moral sciences, the most minute and most simple ideas may be so enlarged as to fall readily under our apprehension and be equally known with the grossest and most sensible ideas that can be the object of our enquiry.

To be fully acquainted, therefore, with the idea of power or necessary connection, let us examine its impression; and in order to find the impression with greater certainty, let us search for it in all the sources from which it may possibly be derived.

When we look about us toward external objects, and consider the operation of causes, we are never able, in a single instance, to discover any power or necessary connection, and quality which binds the effect to the cause and renders the one an infallible consequence of the other. We only find that the one does actually, in fact, follow the other. The impulse of one billiard-ball is attended with motion in the second. This is the whole that appears to the *outward* senses. The mind feels no sentiment or *inward* impression from this succession of objects: consequently, there is not, in any single, particular instance of cause and effect anything which can suggest the idea of power or necessary connection.

From the first appearance of an object, we never can conjecture what effect will result from it. But were the power or energy of any cause discoverable by the mind, we could foresee the effect even without experience, and might, at first, pronounce with certainty concerning it by the mere dint of thought and reasoning.

In reality, there is no part of matter that does ever, by its sensible qualities, discover any power or energy or give us ground to imagine that it could produce anything, or be followed by any other object, which we could denominate its effect. Solidity, extension, motion—these qualities are all complete in themselves and never point out any other event which may result from them. The scenes of the universe are continually shifting, and one object follows another in an uninterrupted succession; but the power or force which actuates the whole machine is entirely concealed from us and never discovers itself in any of the sensible qualities of body. We know that, in fact, heat is a constant attendant of flame, but what is the connection between them, we have no room so much as to conjecture or imagine. It is impossible, therefore, that the idea of power can be derived from the contemplation of bodies in single instances of their operation, because no bodies ever discover any power which can be the original of this idea.[1]

Since, therefore, external objects as they appear to the senses give us no idea of power or necessary connection, by their operation in particular instances, let us see whether this idea be derived from reflection on the operations of our own minds and be copied from any internal impression. It may be said that we are every moment conscious of internal power, while we feel that, by the simple command of our will, we can move the organs of our body or direct the faculties of our mind. An act of volition produces motion in our limbs or raises a new idea in our imagination. This influence of the will we know by consciousness. Hence we acquire the idea of power or energy; and are certain that we ourselves and all other intelligent beings are possessed of power. This idea then is an idea of reflection, since it arises from reflecting on the operations of our own mind and on the command which is exercised by will both over the organs of the body and faculties of the soul.

We shall proceed to examine this pretension and first with regard to the influence of volition over the organs of the body. This influence, we may observe, is a fact which, like all other natural events, can be known only by experience and can never be foreseen from any apparent energy or power in the cause which connects it with the effect and renders the one an infallible consequence of the other. The motion of our body follows upon the command of our will. Of this we are every moment conscious. But the means by which this is effected, the energy by which the will performs so extraordinary an operation, of this we are so far from being imme-

[1]   Mr. Locke, in his chapter of power says that finding from experience that there are several new productions in matter and concluding that there must somewhere be a power capable of producing them, we arrive at last by this reasoning at the idea of power. But no reasoning can ever give us a new, original, simple idea; as this philosopher himself confesses. This, therefore, can never be the origin of that idea.

diately conscious that it must forever escape our most diligent enquiry.

For first, is there any principle in all nature more mysterious than the union of soul with body by which a supposed spiritual substance acquires such an influence over a material one that the most refined thought is able to actuate the grossest matter? Were we empowered, by a secret wish, to remove mountains, or control the planets in their orbit; this extensive authority would not be more extraordinary nor more beyond our comprehension. But if by consciousness we perceived any power or energy in the will, we must know this power; we must know its connection with the effect; we must know the secret union of soul and body and the nature of both these substances by which the one is able to operate in so many instances upon the other.

Secondly, we are not able to move all the organs of the body with a like authority; though we cannot assign any reason besides experience for so remarkable a difference between one and the other. Why has the will an influence over the tongue and fingers, not over the heart or liver? This question would never embarrass us were we conscious of a power in the former case not in the latter. We should then perceive, independent of experience, why the authority of will over the organs of the body is circumscribed within such particular limits. Being in that case fully acquainted with the power or force by which it operates, we should also know why its influence reaches precisely to such boundaries and no farther.

A man suddenly struck with a palsy in the leg or arm or who had newly lost those members frequently endeavors, at first, to move them and employ them in their usual offices. Here he is as much conscious of power to command such limbs as a man in perfect health is conscious of power to actuate any member which remains in its natural state and condition. But consciousness never deceives. Consequently, neither in the one case nor in the other are we ever conscious of any power. We learn the influence of our will from experience alone. And experience only teaches us how one event constantly follows another without instructing us in the secret connection which binds them together and renders them inseparable.

Thirdly, we learn from anatomy that the immediate object of power in voluntary motion is not the member itself which is moved, but certain muscles and nerves and animal spirits and perhaps something still more minute and more unknown through which the motion is successively propagated ere it reach the member itself whose motion is the immediate object of volition. Can there be a more certain proof that the power, by which this whole operation is performed, so far from being directly and fully known by an inward sentiment or consciousness is to the last degree mysterious and unintelligible? Here the mind wills a certain event: immediately another event, unknown to ourselves, and totally different from the one intended, is produced: this event produces another, equally unknown: until at last, through a long succession, the desired event is produced. But if the original power were felt, it must be known; were it known, its effect must also be known since all power is relative to its effect. And vice versa, if the effect be not known the power cannot be known nor felt. How indeed can we be conscious of a power to move our limbs when we have no such power but only that to move certain animal spirits which, though they produce at last the motion of our limbs, yet operate in such a manner as is wholly beyond our comprehension?

We may, therefore, conclude from the whole, I hope, without any temerity, though with assurance that our idea of power is not copied from any sentiment or consciousness of power within ourselves when we give rise to animal motion or apply our limbs to their proper use and office. That their motion follows the command of the will is a matter of common experience, like other natural events, but the power or energy by which this is effected, like that in other natural events, is unknown and inconceivable.[2]

[2]   It may be pretended that the resistance which we meet with in bodies obliging us frequently to exert our force and call up all our power this gives us the idea of force and power. It is this *nisus* or strong endeavor, of which we are conscious, that is the original impression from which this idea is copied. But first we attribute power to a vast number of objects where we never can suppose this resistance or exertion of force to take place; to the Supreme

Shall we then assert that we are conscious of a power or energy in our own minds when, by an act or command of our will, we raise up a new idea, fix the mind to the contemplation of it, turn it on all sides, and at last dismiss it for some other idea when we think that we have surveyed it with sufficient accuracy? I believe the same arguments will prove that even this command of the will gives us no real idea of force or energy.

First, it must be allowed that when we know a power we know that very circumstance in the cause by which it is enabled to produce the effect: for these are supposed to be synonymous. We must, therefore, know both the cause and effect and the relation between them. But do we pretend to be acquainted with the nature of the human soul and the nature of an idea or the aptitude of the one to produce the other? This is a real creation; a production of something out of nothing which implies a power so great that it may seem at first sight beyond the reach of any being less than infinite. At least it must be owned that such a power is not felt, nor known, nor even conceivable by the mind. We only feel the event, namely, the existence of an idea, consequent to a command of the will; but the maner in which this operation is performed, the power by which it is produced, is entirely beyond our comprehension.

Secondly, the command of the mind over itself is limited as well as its command over the body, and these limits are not known by reason or any acquaintance with the nature of cause and effect, but only by experience and observation, as in all other natural events and in the operation of external objects. Our authority over our sentiments and passions is much weaker than that over our ideas, and even the latter authority is circumscribed within very

---

Being, who never meets with any resistance; to the mind in its command over its ideas and limbs in common thinking and motion where the effect follows immediately upon the will without any exertion or summoning up of force; to inanimate matter which is not capable of this sentiment. Secondly, this sentiment of an endeavor to overcome resistance has no known connection with any event: what follows it, we know by experience, but could not know it a priori. It must, however, be confessed that the animal *nisus* which we experience, though it can afford no accurate precise idea of power, enters very much into that vulgar, inaccurate idea, which is formed of it.

narrow boundaries. Will any one pretend to assign the ultimate reason of these boundaries or show why the power is deficient in one case and not in another?

Thirdly, this self-command is very different at different times. A man in health possesses more of it than one languishing with sickness. We are more master of our thoughts in the morning than in the evening, fasting, than after a full meal. Can we give any reason for these variations except experience? Where then is the power of which we pretend to be conscious? Is there not here, either in a spiritual or material substance, or both, some secret mechanism or structure of parts upon which the effect depends and which being entirely unknown to us renders the power or energy of the will equally unknown and incomprehensible?

Volition is surely an act of the mind with which we are sufficiently acquainted. Reflect upon it. Consider it on all sides. Do you find anything in it like this creative power, by which it raises from nothing a new idea, and with a kind of *fiat*, imitates the omnipotence of its Maker, if I may be allowed so to speak, who called forth into existence all the various scenes of nature? So far from being conscious of this energy in the will, it requires as certain experience as that of which we are possessed to convince us that such extraordinary effects do ever result from a simple act of volition.

The generality of mankind never find any difficulty in accounting for the more common and familiar operations of nature, such as the descent of heavy bodies, the growth of plants, the generation of animals, or the nourishment of bodies by food; but suppose that in all these cases, they perceive the very force or energy of the cause, by which it is connected with its effect, and is for ever infallible in its operation. They acquire by long habit such a turn of mind that upon the appearance of the cause they immediately expect with assurance its usual attendant and hardly conceive it possible that any other event could result from it. It is only on the discovery of extraordinary phenomena, such as earthquakes, pestilence, and prodigies of any kind, that they find themselves at a loss to assign a proper cause and to explain the manner in which the effect is produced by it. It is usual for men, in such difficulties, to have resource to some invisible intelligent principle, as the immediate cause of that event which surprises them and which they think, cannot be accounted for from the common powers of nature. But philosophers, who carry their scrutiny a little farther, immediately perceive that even in the most familiar events the energy of the cause is as unintelligible as in the most unusual, and that we only learn by experience the frequent Conjunction of objects, without being ever able to comprehend any thing like Connection between them. Here then, many philosophers think themselves obliged by reason to have recourse on all occasions to the same principle, which the vulgar never appeal to but in cases that appear miraculous and supernatural. They acknowledge mind and intelligence to be not only the ultimate and original cause of all things but the immediate and sole cause of every event which appears in nature. They pretend that those objects which are commonly denominated causes are in reality nothing but occasions, and that the true and direct principle of every effect is not any power or force in nature, but a volition of the Supreme Being, who wills that such particular objects should, forever, be conjoined with each other. Instead of saying that one billiard ball moves another by a force which it has derived from the author of nature, it is the Deity himself, they say, who by a particular volition moves the second ball, being determined to this operation by the impulse of the first ball: in consequence of those general laws, which he has laid down to himself in the government of the universe. But philosophers advancing still in their enquiries, discover that as we are totally ignorant of the power on which depends the mutual operation of bodies, we are no less ignorant of that power on which depends the operation of mind on body, or of body on mind; nor are we able either from our senses or consciousness to assign the ultimate principle in one case more than in the other. The same ignorance, therefore, reduces them to the same conclusion. They assert that the Deity is the immediate cause of the union between soul and body; and that they are not the organs of sense, which, being agitated by external objects, produce sensations in the mind; but that it is a particular volition of our omnipotent Maker, which excites such a sensation in consequence of such a motion in the organ. In like manner it is not any energy in the will that produces local motion in our members: it is God himself, who is pleased to second our will, in itself impotent, and to command that motion which we erroneously attribute to our own power and efficacy. Nor do philosophers stop at this conclusion. They sometimes extend the same inference to the mind itself in its internal operations. Our mental vision or conception of ideas is nothing but a revelation made to us by our Maker. When we voluntarily turn our thoughts to any object and raise up its image in the fancy; it is not the will which creates that idea: it is the universal Creator, who discovers it to the mind, and renders it present to us.

Thus, according to these philosophers, everything is full of God. Not content with the principle that nothing exists but by his will, that nothing possesses any power but by his concession, they rob nature and all created beings of every power in order to render their dependence on the Deity still more sensible and immediate. They consider not that by this theory they diminish, instead of magnifying, the grandeur of those attributes which they affect so much to celebrate. It argues surely more power in the Deity to delegate a certain degree of power to inferior creatures than to produce everything by his own immediate volition. It argues more wisdom to contrive at first the fabric of the world with such perfect foresight that, of itself, and by its proper operation it may serve all the purposes of providence than if the great Creator were obliged every moment to adjust its parts and animate by his breath all the wheels of that stupendous machine.

But if we would have a more philosophical confutation of this theory, perhaps the two following reflections may suffice.

First, it seems to me that this theory of the universal energy and operation of the Supreme Being is too bold ever to carry conviction with it to a man, sufficiently apprised of the weakness of human reason and the narrow limits to which it is confined in all its operations. Though the chain of arguments which conduct to it were ever so logical, there must arise a strong suspicion, if not an absolute assurance, that it has carried us quite beyond the reach of our faculties when it leads to conclusions so extraordinary and so remote from common life and experience. We are got into fairyland long ere we have reached the last steps of our theory and there we have no reason to trust our common method of argument or to think that our usual analogies and probabilities have any authority. Our line is too short to fathom such immense abysses. And however we may flatter ourselves that we are guided in every step which we take by a kind of verisimilitude and experience, we may be assured that this fancied experience has no authority when we thus apply it to subjects that lie entirely out of the sphere of experience. . .

Secondly, I cannot perceive any force in the arguments on which this theory is founded. We are ignorant, it is true, of the manner in which bodies operate on each other: their force or energy is entirely incomprehensible; but are we not equally ignorant of the manner or force by which a mind, even the supreme mind, operates either on itself or on body? Whence, I beseech you, do we acquire any idea of it? We have no sentiment or consciousness of this power in ourselves. We have no idea of the Supreme Being but what we learn from reflection on our own faculties. Were our ignorance, therefore, a good reason for rejecting anything, we should be led into that principle of denying all energy in the Supreme Being as much as in the grossest matter. We surely comprehend as little the operations of one as of the other. Is it more difficult to conceive that motion may arise from impulse than that it may arise from volition? All we know is our profound ignorance in both cases.[3]

3   I need not examine at length the *vis inertiae* which is so much talked of in the new philosophy, and which is ascribed to matter. We find by experience that a body at rest or in motion continues forever in its present state, until put from it by some new cause, and that a body impelled takes as much motion from the impelling body as it acquires itself. These are facts. When we call this a *vis inertiae*, we only mark these facts, without pretending to have any idea of the inert power; in the same manner as when we talk of gravity we mean certain effects without comprehending that active power. It was never the meaning of Sir Isaac Newton to rob second causes of all force or energy though some of his followers have endeavored to establish that theory upon his authority. On the contrary, that great philosopher had recourse to an etherial active fluid to explain his universal attraction though he was so cautious and modest as to allow that it was a mere hypothesis not to be insisted on without more experiments. I must confess that there is some-

But to hasten to a conclusion of this argument which is already drawn out to too great a length, we have sought in vain for an idea of power or necessary connection in all the sources from which we could suppose it to be derived. It appears that in single instances of the operation of bodies we never can by our utmost scrutiny discover anything but one event following another without being able to comprehend any force or power by which the cause operates or any connection between it and its supposed effect. The same difficulty occurs in contemplating the operations of mind on body where we observe the motion of the latter to follow upon the volition of the former but are not able to observe or conceive the tie which binds together the motion and volition, or the energy by which the mind produces this effect. The authority of the will over its own faculties and ideas is not a whit more comprehensible, so that upon the whole there appears not throughout all nature any one instance of connection which is conceivable by us. All events seem entirely loose and separate. One event follows another but we never can observe any tie between them. They seem conjoined but never connected. And as we can have no idea of any thing which never appeared to our outward sense or inward sentiment, the necessary conclusion seems to be that we have no idea of connection or power at all, and that these words are absolutely without any meaning when employed either in philosophical reasonings or common life.

But there still remains one method of avoiding this conclusion and one source which we have not yet examined. When any natural object or event is presented, it is impossible for us by any sagacity or penetration to discover or even conjecture without experience what event will result from it, or to carry our foresight beyond that object which is immediately present to the memory and senses. Even after one instance or experiment where we

---

thing in the fate of opinions a little extraordinary. Descartes insinuated that doctrine of the universal and sole efficacy of the Deity, without insisting on it. Malebranche and other Cartesians made it the foundation of all their philosophy. It had, however, no authority in England. Locke, Clarke, and Cudworth never so much as take notice of it, but supposed all along that matter has a real, though subordinate and derived power. By what means has it become so prevalent among our modern metaphysicians?

have observed a particular event to follow upon another, we are not entitled to form a general rule or foretell what will happen in like cases; it being justly esteemed an unpardonable temerity to judge of the whole course of nature from one single experiment, however accurate or certain. But when one particular species of event has always, in all instances, been conjoined with another, we make no longer any scruple of foretelling one upon the appearance of the other and of employing that reasoning which can alone assure us of any matter of fact or existence. We then call the one object, cause, the other, effect. We suppose that there is some connection between them, some power in the one, by which it infallibly produces the other, and operates with the greatest certainty and strongest necessity.

It appears then that this idea of a necessary connection among events arises from a number of similar instances which occur of the constant conjunction of these events, nor can that idea ever be suggested by any one of these instances surveyed in all possible lights and positions. But there is nothing in a number of instances different from every single instance which is supposed to be exactly similar except only that after a repetition of similar instances the mind is carried by habit upon the appearance of one event to expect its usual attendant and to believe that it will exist. This connection, therefore, which we feel in the mind, this customary transition of the imagination from one object to its usual attendant is the sentiment or impression from which we form the idea of power or necessary connection. Nothing farther is in the case. Contemplate the subject on all sides; you will never find any other origin of that idea. This is the sole difference between one instance, from which we can never receive the idea of connection and a number of similar instances by which it is suggested. The first time a man saw the communication of motion by impulse, as by the shock of two billiard balls, he could not pronounce that the one event was connected but only that it was conjoined with the other. After he had observed several instances of this nature, he then pronounces them to be connected. What alteration has happened to give rise to this new idea of connection? Nothing but that he now feels these events to be connected in his imagination, and can readily foretell the existence of one from the appearance of the other. When we say, therefore, that one object is connected with another we mean only that they have acquired a connection in our thought and give rise to this inference by which they become proofs of each other's existence: a conclusion which is somewhat extraordinary but which seems founded on sufficient evidence. Nor will its evidence be weakened by any general diffidence of the understanding or sceptical suspicion concerning every conclusion which is new and extraordinary. No conclusions can be more agreeable to scepticism than such as make discoveries concerning the weakness and narrow limits of human reason and capacity.

And what stronger instance can be produced of the surprising ignorance and weakness of the understanding than the present? For surely, if there be any relation among objects which it imports to us to know perfectly it is that of cause and effect. On this are founded all our reasonings concerning matter of fact or existence. By means of it alone we attain any assurance concerning objects which are removed from the present testimony of our memory and senses. The only immediate utility of all sciences is to teach us how to control and regulate future events by their causes. Our thoughts and enquires are, therefore, every moment employed about this relation; yet, so imperfect are the ideas which we form concerning it that it is impossible to give any just definition of cause except what is drawn from something extraneous and foreign to it. Similar objects are always conjoined with similar. Of this we have experience. Suitably to this experience, therefore, we may define a cause to be *an object followed by another and where all the objects similar to the first are followed by objects similar to the second.* Or, in other words, *where if the first object had not been the second never had existed.* The appearance of a cause always conveys the mind by a customary transition to the idea of the effect. Of this also we have experience. We may, therefore, suitably to this experience, form another definition of cause and call it *an object followed by another and whose appearance always conveys the thought to that other.* But though both these definitions be drawn from circumstances foreign to the cause, we cannot remedy this inconvenience or attain any more perfect definition which may point out that circumstance in the cause which gives it a connection with its effect. We have no idea of this connection nor even any distinct notion what it is we desire to know when we endeavor at a conception of it. We say, for instance, that the vibration of this string is the cause of this particular sound. But what do we mean by that affirmation? We either mean *that this vibration is followed by this sound and that all similar vibrations have been followed by similar sounds*, or *that this vibration is followed by this sound and that upon the appearance of one the mind anticipates the senses and forms immediately an idea of the other*. We may consider the relation of cause and effect in either of these two lights; but beyond these, we have no idea of it.[4]

To recapitulate, therefore, the reasonings of this section: every idea is copied from some preceding impression or sentiment, and

---

[4]   According to these explications and definitions, the idea of *power* is relative as much as that of *cause*; and both have a reference to an effect, or some other event constantly conjoined with the former. When we consider the *unknown* circumstance of an object by which the degree or quantity of its effect is fixed and determined we call that its power; and accordingly, it is allowed by all philosophers that the effect is the measure of the power. But if they had any idea of power as it is in itself, why could not they measure it in itself? The dispute whether the force of a body in motion be as its velocity, or the square of its velocity, this dispute, I say, needed not be decided by comparing its effects in equal or unequal times, but by a direct mensuration and comparison.

As to the frequent use of the words, force, power, energy, etc., which everywhere occur in common conversation, as well as in philosophy that is no proof that we are acquainted, in any instance, with the connecting principle between cause and effect, or can account ultimately for the production of one thing by another. These words, as commonly used, have very loose meanings annexed to them and their ideas are very uncertain and confused. No animal can put external bodies in motion without the sentiment of a *nisus* or endeavor, and every animal has a sentiment or feeling from the stroke or blow of an external object that is in motion. These sensations, which are merely animal and from which we can a priori draw no inference, we are apt to transfer to inanimate objects, and to suppose that they have some such feelings whenever they transfer or receive motion. With regard to energies, which are exerted without our annexing to them any idea of communicated motion, we consider only the constant experienced conjunction of the events; and as we *feel* a customary connection between the ideas, we transfer that feeling to the objects, as nothing is more usual than to apply to external bodies every internal sensation which they occasion.

where we cannot find any impression, we may be certain that there is no idea. In all single instances of the operation of bodies or minds, there is nothing that produces any impression nor consequently can suggest any idea of power or necessary connection. But when many uniform instances appear and the same object is always followed by the same event, we then begin to entertain the notion of cause and connection. We then *feel* a new sentiment or impression, to wit, a customary connection in the thought or imagination between one object and its usual attendant, and this sentiment is the original of that idea which we seek for. For as this idea arises from a number of similar instances and not from any single instance, it must arise from that circumstance in which the number of instances differ from every individual instance. But this customary connection or transition of the imagination is the only circumstance in which they differ. In every other particular they are alike. The first instance which we saw of motion communicated by the shock of two billiard balls (to return to this obvious illustration) is exactly similar to any instance that may, at present, occur to us, except only that we could not at first *infer* one event from the other, which we are enabled to do at present after so long a course of uniform experience. I know not whether the reader will readily apprehend this reasoning. I am afraid that should I multiply words about it or throw it into a greater variety of lights, it would only become more obscure and intricate. In all abstract reasonings, there is one point of view which, if we can happily hit, we shall go farther toward illustrating the subject than by all the eloquence and copious expression in the world. This point of view we should endeavor to reach and reserve the flowers of rhetoric for subjects which are more adapted to them.

4

Thomas Reid

INSTINCT AND THE INDUCTIVE PRINCIPLE

IT IS UNDENIABLE and indeed is acknowledged by all that when we have found two things to have been constantly conjoined in the course of nature, the appearance of one of them is immediately followed by the conception and belief of the other. The former becomes a natural sign of the latter, and the knowledge of their constant conjunction in time past, whether got by experience or otherwise, is sufficient to make us rely with assurance upon the continuance of that conjunction.

This process of the human mind is so familiar that we never think of inquiring into the principles upon which it is founded. We are apt to conceive it as a self-evident truth, that what is to come must be similar to what is past. Thus, if a certain degree of cold freezes water today and has been known to do so in all time past, we have no doubt but the same degree of cold will freeze water tomorrow, or a year hence. That this is a truth which all men believe as soon as they understand it, I readily admit; but the question is, Whence does its evidence arise? Not from comparing the ideas, surely. For when I compare the idea of cold with that of water hardened into a transparent solid body, I can perceive no connection between them: no man can show the one

Reprinted from Thomas Reid, *An Inquiry into the Human Mind*, in *Works*, W. Hamilton, ed. (6th ed.: Edinburgh, 1863), I, 197–99. Title supplied.

to be the necessary effect of the other; no man can give a shadow of reason why nature hath conjoined them. But do we not learn their conjunction from experience? True, experience informs us that they have been conjoined in time *past*; but no man ever had any experience of what is *future*: and this is the very question to be resolved, How we come to believe that the *future* will be like the *past*? Hath the Author of nature promised this? Or were we admitted to his council when he established the present laws of nature and determined the time of their continuance? No, surely. Indeed if we believe that there is a wise and good Author of nature, we may see a good reason why he should continue the same laws of nature and the same connections of things for a long time: because, if he did otherwise, we could learn nothing from what is past and all our experience would be of no use to us. But though this consideration, when we come to the use of reason, may confirm our belief of the continuance of the present course of nature, it is certain that it did not give rise to this belief; for children and idiots have this belief as soon as they know that fire will burn them. It must, therefore, be the effect of instinct, not of reason.

The wise Author of our nature intended that a great and necessary part of our knowledge should be derived from experience before we are capable of reasoning, and he hath provided means perfectly adequate to this intention. For first He governs nature by fixed laws, so that we find innumerable connections of things which continue from age to age. Without this stability of the course of nature there could be no experience; or it would be a false guide and lead us into error and mischief. If there were not a principle of veracity in the human mind, men's words would not be signs of their thoughts, and if there were no regularity in the course of nature, no one thing could be a natural sign of another. Secondly, He hath implanted in human minds an original principle by which we believe and expect the continuance of the course of nature and the continuance of those connections which we have observed in time past. It is by this general principle of our nature that when two things have been found connected in time past, the appearance of the one produces the belief of the other. . . . we agree with the author of the *Treatise of Human Nature* in this, that our belief of the continuance of nature's laws is not derived from reason. It is an instinctive prescience of the operations of nature, very like to that prescience of human actions which makes us rely upon the testimony of our fellow creatures, and as without the latter, we should be incapable of receiving information from men by language, so without the former, we should be incapable of receiving the information of nature by means of experience.

All our knowledge of nature beyond our original perceptions is got by experience and consists in the interpretation of natural signs. The constancy of nature's laws connects the sign with the thing signified; and by the natural principle just now explained, we rely upon the continuance of the connections which experience hath discovered and thus the appearance of the sign is followed by the belief of the thing signified.

Upon this principle of our constitution, not only acquired perception, but all inductive reasoning, and all our reasoning from analogy is grounded; and therefore, for want of another name, we shall beg leave to call it *the inductive principle*. It is from the force of this principle that we immediately assent to that axiom upon which all our knowledge of nature is built, that effects of the same kind must have the same cause; for *effects* and *causes* in the operations of nature mean nothing but signs and the things signified by them. We perceive no proper causality or efficiency in any natural cause, but only a connection established by the course of nature between it and what is called its effect. Antecendently to all reasoning, we have by our constitution an anticipation that there is a fixed and steady course of nature, and we have an eager desire to discover this course of nature. We attend to every conjunction of things which presents itself and expect the continuance of that conjunction. And when such a conjunction has been often observed, we conceive the things to be naturally connected and the appearance of one without any reasoning or reflection carries along with it the belief of the other.

5

Adam Smith

OF WONDER, OR OF THE
EFFECTS OF NOVELTY

IT IS EVIDENT that the mind takes pleasure in observing the resemblances that are discoverable between different objects. It is by means of such observations that it endeavors to arrange and methodise all its ideas and to reduce them into proper classes and assortments. Where it can observe but one single quality that is common to a great variety of otherwise widely different objects, that single circumstance will be sufficient for it to connect them all together to reduce them to one common class and to call them by one general name. It is thus that all things endowed with a power of self-motion, beasts, birds, fishes, insects, are classed under the general name of animal, and that these again, along with those which want that power are arranged under the still more general word substance: and this is the origin of those assortments of objects and ideas which in the schools are called genera and species, and of those abstract and general names, which in all languages are made use of to express them.

The further we advance in knowledge and experience the greater number of divisions and subdivisions of those genera and species we are both inclined and obliged to make. We observe a greater variety of particularities among those things which have a gross resemblance, and having made new divisions of them,

Reprinted from Adam Smith, *Essays on Philosophical Subjects* (London and Edinburgh, 1795), pp. 10–20.

according to those newly observed particularities, we are then no longer to be satisfied with being able to refer an object to a remote genus or very general class of things to many of which it has but a loose and imperfect resemblance. A person indeed unacquainted with botany may expect to satisfy your curiosity by telling you that such a vegetable is a weed, or perhaps in still more general terms that it is a plant. But a botanist will neither give nor accept of such an answer. He has broken and divided that great class of objects into a number of inferior assortments according to those varieties which his experience has discovered among them, and he wants to refer each individual plant to some tribe of vegetables with all of which it may have a more exact resemblance than with many things comprehended under the extensive genus of plants. A child imagines that it gives a satisfactory answer when it tells you that an object whose name it knows not is a thing and fancies that it informs you of something when it thus ascertains to which of the two most obvious and comprehensive classes of objects a particular impression ought to be referred; to the class of realities or solid substances which it calls *things*, or to that of appearances which it calls *nothings*.

Whatever, in short, occurs to us we are fond of referring to some species or class of things with all of which it has a nearly exact resemblance; and though we often know no more about them than about it, yet we are apt to fancy that by being able to do so we show ourselves to be better acquainted with it, and to have a more thorough insight into its nature. But when something quite new and singular is presented, we feel ourselves incapable of doing this. The memory cannot from all its stores cast up any image that nearly resembles this strange appearance. If by some of its qualities it seems to resemble and to be connected with a species which we have before been acquainted with, it is by others separated and detached from that, and from all the other assortments of things we have hitherto been able to make. It stands alone and by itself in the imagination and refuses to be grouped or confounded with any set of objects whatever. The imagination and memory exert themselves to no purpose and in vain look around all their classes of ideas in order to find one under which it may be arranged. They fluctuate to no purpose from thought to thought and we remain still uncertain and undetermined where to place it or what to think of it. It is this fluctuation and vain recollection together with the emotion or movement of the spirits that they excite which constitute the sentiment properly called *wonder*, and which occasion that staring, and sometimes that rolling of the eyes, that suspension of the breath, and that swelling of the heart which we may all observe both in ourselves and others when wondering at some new object, and which are the natural symptoms of uncertain and undetermined thought. What sort of a thing can that be? What is that like? are the questions which upon such an occasion we are all naturally disposed to ask. If we can recollect many such objects which exactly resemble this new appearance and which present themselves to the imagination naturally, and as it were of their own accord, our wonder is entirely at an end. If we can recollect but a few, and which it requires too some trouble to be able to call up, our wonder is indeed diminished but not quite destroyed. If we can recollect none, but are quite at a loss, it is the greatest possible.

With what curious attention does a naturalist examine a singular plant, or a singular fossil, that is presented to him? He is at no loss to refer it to the general genus of plants or fossils, but this does not satisfy him; and when he considers all the different tribes or species of either with which he has hitherto been acquainted, they all, he thinks, refuse to admit the new object among them. It stands alone in his imagination and as it were detached from all the other species of that genus to which it belongs. He labors, however, to connect it with some one or other of them. Sometimes he thinks it may be placed in this, and sometimes in that other assortment; nor is he ever satisfied till he has fallen upon one which in most of its qualities it resembles. When he cannot do this, rather than it should stand quite by itself, he will enlarge the precincts, if I may say so, of some species in order to make room for it, or he will create a new species on purpose to receive it and call it a "Play of Nature," or give it some other appellation, under which he arranges all the oddities that he knows not what else to do with. But to some class or other of known objects he must refer it, and betwixt it and them he must find out some resemblance or other, before he can get rid of that wonder, that uncertainty and anxious curiosity excited by its singular appearance and by its dissimilitude with all the objects he had hitherto observed.

As single and individual objects thus excite our wonder when, by their uncommon qualities and singular appearance, they make us uncertain to what species of things we ought to refer.them, so a succession of objects which follow one another in an uncommon train or order will produce the same effect though there be nothing particular in any one of them taken by itself.

When one accustomed object appears after another which it does not usually follow, it first excites, by its unexpectedness, the sentiment properly called surprise, and afterwards by the singularity of the succession, or order of its appearance, the sentiment properly called wonder. We start and are surprised at seeing it there and then wonder how it came there. The motion of a small piece of iron along a plain table is in itself no extraordinary object, yet the person who first saw it begin without any visible impulse in consequence of the motion of a loadstone at some little distance from it, could not behold it without the most extreme surprise; and when that momentary emotion was over, he would still wonder how it came to be conjoined to an event with which according to the ordinary train of things he could have so little suspected it to have any connection.

When two objects, however unlike, have often been observed to follow each other and have constantly presented themselves to the senses in that order, they come to be so connected together in the fancy that the idea of the one seems of its own accord to call up and introduce that of the other. If the objects are still observed to succeed each other as before, this connection, or as it has been called, this association of their ideas, becomes stricter and stricter and the habit of the imagination to pass from the conception of the one to that of the other grows more and more rivetted and confirmed. As its ideas move more rapidly than external objects, it is continually running before them, and therefore anticipates before it happens every event which falls out according to this ordinary course of things. When objects succeed each other in the same train in which the ideas of the imagination have thus been accustomed to move and in which, though not conducted by that chain of events presented to the senses, they have acquired a tendency to go on of their own accord, such objects appear all closely connected with one another and the thought glides easily along them without effort and without interruption. They fall in with the natural career of the imagination and as the ideas which represented such a train of things would seem all mutually to introduce each other, every last thought to be called up by the foregoing and to call up the succeeding; so when the objects themselves occur, every last event seems in the same manner to be introduced by the foregoing and to introduce the succeeding. There is no break, no stop, no gap, no interval. The ideas excited by so coherent a chain of things seem, as it were, to float through the mind of their own accord without obliging it to exert itself or to make any effort in order to pass from one of them to another.

But if this customary connection be interrupted, if one or more objects appear in an order quite different from that to which the imagination has been accustomed and for which it is prepared, the contrary of all this happens. We are at first surprised by the unexpectedness of the new appearance, and when that momentary emotion is over, we still wonder how it came to occur in that place. The imagination no longer feels the usual facility of passing from the event which goes before to that which comes after. It is an order or law of succession to which it has not been accustomed, and which it therefore finds some difficulty in following, or in attending to. The fancy is stopped and interrupted in that natural movement or career, according to which it was proceeding. Those two events seem to stand at a distance from each other; it endeavors to bring them together, but they refuse to unite; and it feels, or imagines it feels, something like a gap or interval between them. It naturally hesitates, and as it were, pauses upon the brink of this interval; it endeavors to find out something which may fill up the gap which, like a bridge, may so far at least unite those seemingly distant objects as to render the passage of the thought between them smooth and natural and easy. The supposition of a chain of intermediate though invisible events which succeed each other in a train similar to that in which the imagination has been accustomed to move, and which link together those two disjointed appearances, is the only means by which the imagination can fill up this interval, is the only bridge which, if one may say so, can smooth its passage from the one object to the other. Thus, when we observe the motion of the iron, in consequence of that of the loadstone, we gaze and hesitate, and feel a want of connection between two events which follow one another in so unusual a train. But when, with Descartes, we imagine certain invisible effluvia to circulate round one of them, and by their repeated impulses to impel the other, both to move toward it and to follow its motion, we fill up the interval between them, we join them together by a sort of bridge, and thus take off that hesitation and difficulty which the imagination felt in passing from the one to the other. That the iron should move after the loadstone seems upon this hypothesis in some measure according to the ordinary course of things. Motion after impulse is an order of succession with which of all things we are the most familiar. Two objects which are so connected seem no longer to be disjoined and the imagination flows smoothly and easily along them.

Such is the nature of this second species of wonder which arises from an unusual succession of things. The stop which is thereby given to the career of the imagination, the difficulty which it finds in passing along such disjointed objects, and the feeling of something like a gap or interval between them, constitute the whole essence of this emotion. Upon the clear discovery of a connecting chain of intermediate events, it vanishes altogether. What obstructed the movement of the imagination is then removed. Who wonders at the machinery of the opera house who has once been admitted behind the scenes? In the wonders of nature, however, it rarely happens that we can discover so clearly this connecting chain. With regard to a few even of them, indeed, we seem to have been really admitted behind the fences and our wonder accordingly is entirely at an end. Thus the eclipses of the sun and moon, which once, more than all the other appearances in the heavens, excited the terror and amazement of mankind, seem now no longer to be wonderful, since the connecting chain has been found out which joins them to the ordinary course of things. Nay, in those cases in which we have been less successful, even the vague hypotheses of Descartes and the yet more indetermined notions of Aristotle have with their followers contributed to give some coherence to the appearances of nature and might diminish though they could not destroy their wonder. If they did not completely fill up the interval between the two disjointed objects they bestowed upon them, however, some sort of loose connection which they wanted before.

That the imagination feels a real difficulty in passing along two events which follow one another in an uncommon order may be confirmed by many obvious observations. If it attempts to attend beyond a certain time to a long series of this kind, the continual efforts it is obliged to make in order to pass from one object to another and thus follow the progress of the succession, soon fatigue it, and if repeated too often, disorder and disjoint its whole frame. It is thus that too severe an application to study sometimes brings on lunacy and frenzy, in those especially who are somewhat advanced in life, but whose imaginations from being too late in applying have not got those habits which dispose them to follow easily the reasonings in the abstract sciences. Every step of a demonstration which to an old practitioner is quite natural and easy requires from them the most intense application of thought. Spurred on, however, either by ambition or by admiration for the subject, they still continue till they become, first confused, then giddy, and at last distracted. Could we conceive a person of the soundest judgment, who had grown up to maturity, and whose imagination had acquired those habits, and that mold which the constitution of things in this world necessarily impress upon it to be all at once transported alive to some other planet where nature was governed by laws quite different from those which take place here; as he would be continually obliged to attend to events which must to him appear in the highest degree jarring, irregular, and discordant, he would soon feel the same confusion and giddiness begin to come upon him which would at last end in the same manner, in lunacy and distraction. Neither to produce this effect is it necessary that the objects should be either great or interesting, or even uncommon, in themselves. It is sufficient that they follow one another in an uncommon order. Let any one attempt to look over even a game of cards and to attend particularly to every single stroke, and if he is unacquainted with the nature and rules of the game, that is, with the laws which regulate the succession of the cards, he will soon feel the same confusion and giddiness begin to come upon him which were it to be continued for days and months would end in the same manner, in lunacy and distraction. But if the mind be thus thrown into the most violent disorder when it attends to a long series of events which follow one another in an uncommon train, it must feel some degree of the same disorder when it observes even a single event fall out in this unusual manner: for the violent disorder can arise from nothing but the too frequent repetition of this smaller uneasiness.

That it is the unusualness alone of the succession which occasions this stop and interruption in the progress of the imagination, as well as the notion of an interval between the two immediately succeeding objects to be filled up by some chain of intermediate events is not less evident. The same orders of succession, which to one set of men seem quite according to the natural course of things, and such as require no intermediate events to join them, shall to another appear altogether incoherent and disjointed, unless some such events be supposed, and this for no other reason but because such orders of succession are familiar to the one and strange to the other. When we enter the workhouses of the most common artisans, such as dyers, brewers, distillers, we observe a number of appearances which present themselves in an order that seems to us very strange and wonderful. Our thought cannot easily follow it, we feel an interval between every two of them, and require some chain of intermediate events to fill it up and link them together. But the artisan himself, who has been for many years familiar with the consequences of all the operations of his art, feels no such interval. They fall in with what custom has made the natural movement of his imagination: they no longer excite his wonder, and if he is not a genius superior to his profession, so as to be capable of making the very easy reflection that those things, though familiar to him, may be strange to us, he will be disposed rather to laugh at than sympathize with our wonder. He cannot conceive what occasion there is for any connecting events to unite those appearances which seem to him to succeed each other very naturally. It is their nature, he tells us, to follow one another in this order and that accordingly they always do so. In the same manner bread has, since the world began, been the common nourishment of the human body and men have so long seen it, every day, converted into flesh and bones, substances in all respects so unlike it, that they have seldom had the curiosity to inquire by what process of intermediate events this change is brought about. Because the passage of the thought from the one object to the other is by custom become quite smooth and easy, almost without the supposition of any such process. Philosophers indeed who often look for a chain of invisible objects to join together two events that occur in an order familiar to all the world have endeavored to find out a chain of this kind between the two events I have just now mentioned, in the same manner as they have endeavored by a like intermediate chain to connect the gravity, the elasticity, and even the cohesion of natural bodies with some of their other qualities. These, however, are all of them such combinations of events as give no stop to the imaginations of the bulk of mankind, as excite no wonder, nor any apprehension that there is wanting the strictest connection between them. But as in those sounds, which to the greater part of men seem perfectly agreeable to measure and harmony, the nicer ear of a musician will discover a want, both of the most exact time, and of the most perfect coincidence: so the more practised thought of a philosopher, who has spent his whole life in the study of the connecting principles of nature will often feel an interval between two objects, which, to more careless observers, seem very strictly conjoined. By long attention to all the connections which have ever been presented to his observation, by having often compared them with one another, he has, like the musician, acquired, if one may say so, a nicer ear and a more delicate feeling with regard to things of this nature. And as to the one, that music seems dissonance which falls short of the most perfect harmony, so to the other, those events seem altogether separated and disjoined which fall short of the strictest and most perfect connection.

II. The Uniformity of
Human Nature

6

Francis Hutcheson

SENSATIONAL ANTHROPOLOGY

A LATE INGENIOUS AUTHOR (Lord Shaftsbury) has justly observed the absurdity of the monstrous taste which has possessed
both the readers and writers of travels. They are sparing enough
in accounts of the natural affections, the families, associations,
friendships, clans, of the Indians; and as transiently do they mention their abhorrence of treachery among themselves, their proneness to mutual aid and to the defence of their several states, their
contempt of death in defence of their country, or upon points of
honour. "These are but common stories.—No need to travel to the
Indies for what we see in Europe every day." The entertainment
therefore in these ingenious studies consists chiefly in exciting horror and making men stare. The ordinary employment of the bulk of
the Indians in support of their wives and offspring, or relations, has
nothing of the prodigious: but a human sacrifice, a feast upon enemies' carcasses, can raise an horror and admiration of the wondrous
barbarity of Indians, in nations no strangers to the massacre at
Paris, the Irish Rebellion, or the journals of the Inquisition. These
they behold with religious veneration, but the Indian sacrifices,
flowing from a like perversion of humanity by superstition, raise
the highest abhorrence and amazement. What is most surprising
in these studies is the wondrous credulity of some gentlemen of

Reprinted from Francis Hutcheson, *An Inquiry into the Original of
Our Ideas of Beauty and Virtue* (4th edition; London, 1738), pp. 206–7.
Title supplied.

great pretensions in other matters to caution of assent for these marvelous memoirs of monks, friars, sea captains, pirates; and for the histories, annals, chronologies, received by oral tradition, or hieroglyphics.

7

Francis Hutcheson

AGREEMENT AND DISAGREE-
MENT AMONG MEN

To PROVE that men have no *moral faculty*, or very dissimilar ones, we must show either that nations or great numbers of men hold all actions to be indifferent which don't appear to them to affect their own private interest, or that they are pleased with cruelty, treachery, ingratitude, unprovoked murders, and tortures, when not practiced toward themselves, just as much as with their contraries: they should in some nations be deemed as reputable and lovely as humanity, compassion, liberality, faith . . .

In some civilized states laws have obtained which we repute barbarous and impious. But look into the reasons for them, or the notions under which they were approved, and we generally find some alleged tendency to some public good. There may no doubt be found some few instances where immoderate zeal for their own grandeur, or that of their nation, has made legislators enact unjust laws without any moral species recommending them. This only proves that sometimes a different principle may overpower our sense of justice. But what foolish opinions have been received! What fantastic errors and dissimilitudes have been observed in the admired power of reasoning, allowed to be the characteristic of our species! Now almost all our diversities in moral sentiments and

Reprinted from Francis Hutcheson, *A System of Moral Philosophy* (Glasgow and London, 1755), I, pp. 91–92, 92–93, 300–302. Title supplied.

opposite approbations and condemnations arise from opposite conclusions of reason about the effects of actions upon the public, or the affections from which they flowed. The *moral sense* seems ever to approve and condemn uniformly the same immediate objects, the same affections and dispositions; though we reason very differently about the actions which evidence certain dispositions or their contraries. And yet reason, in which all these errors happen is allowed to be the natural principle; and the *moral faculty* is not, because of the diversities of approbation which yet arise chiefly from the diversity of reasonings . . .

Men differ much from each other in wisdom, virtue, beauty, and strength; but the lowest of them, who have the use of reason, differ in this from the brutes that by forethought and reflection they are capable of incomparably greater happiness or misery. Scarce any man can be happy who sees that all his enjoyments are precarious and depending on the will of others of whose kind intentions he can have no assurance. All men have strong desires of liberty and property, have notions of right, and strong natural impulses to marriage, families, and offspring, and earnest desires of their safety. It is true the generality may be convinced that some few are much superior to them in valuable abilities: this finer part of the species have imperfect rights to superior services from the rest: they are pointed out by nature as the fittest to be entrusted with the management of the common affairs of society in such plans of power as satisfy the community that its common interests shall be faithfully consulted. But without this satisfaction given, permanent power assumed by force over the fortunes of others must generally tend to the misery of the whole. Mere promises or professions give no security. The darkest and most dangerous tyrants may make the fairest shows till they are settled in power. We must therefore conclude that no endowments, natural or acquired, can give a perfect right to assume power over others without their consent.

This is intended against the doctrine of Aristotle and some others of the ancients "that some men are naturally slaves, of low genius but great bodily strength for labor: and others by nature masters of finer and wiser spirits, but weaker bodies: that the former are by nature destined to be subject to the latter, as the work beasts are subjected to men. That the inhabitants of certain countries, particularly Greece, are universally of finer spirits and destined to command and that the rest of the world are fitted for slavery. That by this subordination of the more stupid and imprudent to the wise and ingenious, the universal interest of the system is best promoted as that of the animal system is promoted by the power of the rational species over the irrational."

The power of education is surprising! This author in these justly admired books of politics is a zealous asserter of liberty and has seen the finest and most humane reasons for all the more equitable plans of civil power. He lived in that singular century in which Greece indeed produced more great and ingenious men than perhaps the world ever beheld at once; but had he lived to our times, he would have known that this beloved country for sixteen centuries hath seldom produced anything eminent in virtue, polity, arts, or arms; while great genii were often arising in the nations he had adjudged to slavery and barbarity.

Is it not abundantly known by experience that such as have a less fortunate capacity for the ingenious arts yet often surpass the ingenious in sagacity, prudence, justice, and firmness of mind, and all those abilities which fit a man for governing well? And then it is often found that men of less genius for arts or policy may have the loveliest turn of temper for all the sweet social virtues in private life and the most delicate sense of liberty . . .

Had providence intended that some men should have had a perfect right to govern the rest without their consent, we should have had as visible undisputed marks distinguishing these rulers from others as clearly as the human shape distinguishes men from beasts. Some nations would be found void of care, of forethought, of love of liberty, of notions of right of property, of storing up for futurity, without any wisdom or opinion of their own wisdom, or desires of knowledge; and perfectly easy in drudging for others and holding all things precariously while they had present supplies; never disputing about the wisdom of their rulers or having any suspicions or foreboding fears about their intentions. But where do we find any such tempers in the human shape?

8

David Hume

HUMAN UNIFORMITY AND
PREDICTABILITY

IT IS UNIVERSALLY ACKNOWLEDGED that there is a great uniformity among the actions of men in all nations and ages and that human nature remains still the same in its principles and operations. The same motives always produce the same actions: the same events follow from the same causes. Ambition, avarice, self-love, vanity, friendship, generosity, public spirit; these passions, mixed in various degrees, and distributed through society, have been from the beginning of the world and still are the source of all the actions and enterprises which have ever been observed among mankind. Would you know the sentiments, inclinations, and course of life of the Greeks and Romans? Study well the temper and actions of the French and English: you cannot be much mistaken in transferring to the former *most* of the observations which you have made with regard to the latter. Mankind are so much the same in all times and places that history informs us of nothing new or strange in this particular. Its chief use is only to discover the constant and universal principles of human nature, by showing men in all varieties of circumstances and situations and furnishing us with materials, from which we may form our observations and become acquainted with the regular springs of human

Reprinted from David Hume, *An Enquiry concerning Human Understanding,* in *Essays,* T. H. Green and T. H. Grose, eds. (London: Longmans Green, 1875), II, 68–75. Title supplied.

action and behavior. These records of wars, intrigues, factions, and revolutions are so many collections of experiments by which the politician or moral philosopher fixes the principles of his science; in the same manner as the physician or natural philosopher becomes acquainted with the nature of plants, minerals, and other external objects by the experiments which he forms concerning them. Nor are the earth, water, and other elements, examined by Aristotle, and Hippocrates more like to those, which at present lie under our observation than the men described by Polybius and Tacitus are to those who now govern the world.

Should a traveler returning from a far country bring us an account of men wholly different from any with whom we were ever acquainted, men who were entirely divested of avarice, ambition, or revenge, who knew no pleasure but friendship, generosity, and public spirit, we should immediately from these circumstances detect the falsehood and prove him a liar with the same certainty as if he had stuffed his narration with stories of centaurs and dragons, miracles, and prodigies. And if we would explode any forgery in history, we cannot make use of a more convincing argument than to prove that the actions ascribed to any person are directly contrary to the course of nature and that no human motives in such circumstances could ever induce him to such a conduct. The veracity of Quintus Curtius is as much to be suspected when he describes the supernatural courage of Alexander, by which he was hurried on singly to attack multitudes as when he describes his supernatural force and activity by which he was able to resist them. So readily and universally do we acknowledge a uniformity in human motives and actions as well as in the operations of body.

Hence likewise the benefit of that experience acquired by long life and a variety of business and company in order to instruct us in the principles of human nature and regulate our future conduct as well as speculation. By means of this guide we mount up to the knowledge of men's inclinations and motives from their actions, expressions, and even gestures; and again descend to the interpretation of their actions from our knowledge of their motives and inclinations. The general observations treasured up by a course of experience give us the clue of human nature and teach us to unravel all its intricacies. Pretexts and appearances no longer deceive us. Public declarations pass for the specious coloring of a cause. And though virtue and honor be allowed their proper weight and authority, that perfect disinterestedness, so often pretended to, is never expected in multitudes and parties, seldom in their leaders, and scarcely even in individuals of any rank or station. But were there no uniformity in human actions and were every experiment which we could form of this kind irregular and anomalous, it were impossible to collect any general observations concerning mankind, and no experience, however accurately digested by reflection, would ever serve to any purpose. Why is the aged husbandman more skillful in his calling than the young beginner, but because there is a certain uniformity in the operation of the sun, rain, and earth, toward the production of vegetables and experience teaches the old practitioner the rules by which this operation is governed and directed?

We must not, however, expect that this uniformity of human actions should be carried to such a length as that all men in the same circumstances will always act precisely in the same manner without making any allowance for the diversity of characters, prejudices, and opinions. Such a uniformity in every particular is found in no part of nature. On the contrary, from observing the variety of conduct in different men, we are enabled to form a greater variety of maxims which still suppose a degree of uniformity and regularity.

Are the manners of men different in different ages and countries? We learn thence the great force of custom and education which mold the human mind from its infancy and form it into a fixed and established character. Is the behavior and conduct of the one sex very unlike that of the other? It is thence we become acquainted with the different characters which nature has impressed upon the sexes and which she preserves with constancy and regularity. Are the actions of the same person much diversified in the different periods of his life from infancy to old age? This affords room for many general observations concerning the gradual change of our sentiments and inclinations and the different maxims which prevail in the different ages of human creatures. Even the characters, which are peculiar to each individual, have a uniformity in their influence; otherwise our acquaintance with the persons and our observation of their conduct could never teach us their dispositions or serve to direct our behavior with regard to them.

I grant it possible to find some actions which seem to have no regular connection with any known motives and are exceptions to all the measures of conduct, which have ever been established for the government of men. But if we would willingly know, what judgment should be formed of such irregular and extraordinary actions; we may consider the sentiments, commonly entertained with regard to those irregular events, which appear in the course of nature and the operations of external objects. All causes are not conjoined to their usual effects, with like uniformity. An artificer who handles only dead matter may be disappointed of his aim as well as the politician who directs the conduct of sensible and intelligent agents.

The vulgar who take things according to their first appearance attribute the uncertainty of events to such an uncertainty in the causes as makes the latter often fail of their usual influence though they meet with no impediment in their operation. But philosophers observing that almost in every part of nature there is contained a vast variety of springs and principles which are hid by reason of their minuteness or remoteness find that it is at least possible the contrariety of events may not proceed from any contingency in the cause but from the secret operation of contrary causes. This possibility is converted into certainty by farther observation when they remark that upon an exact scrutiny a contrariety of effects always betrays a contrariety of causes and proceeds from their mutual opposition. A peasant can give no better reason for the stopping of any clock or watch than to say that it does not commonly go right; but an artist easily perceives that the same force in the spring or pendulum has always the same influence on the wheels, but fails of its usual effect, perhaps by reason of a grain of dust, which puts a stop to the whole movement. From the observation of several parallel instances, philosophers form a maxim that the connection between all causes and effects is equally necessary and that its seeming uncertainty in some instances proceeds from the secret opposition of contrary causes.

Thus for instance, in the human body, when the usual symptoms of health or sickness disappoint our expectation, when medicines operate not with their wonted powers, when irregular events follow from any particular cause, the philosopher and physician are not surprised at the matter nor are ever tempted to deny, in general, the necessity and uniformity of those principles by which the animal economy is conducted. They know that a human body is a mighty complicated machine, that many secret powers lurk in it which are altogether beyond our comprehension, that to us it must often appear very uncertain in its operations, and that therefore the irregular events which outwardly discover themselves can be no proof that the laws of nature are not observed with the greatest regularity in its internal operations and government.

The philosopher, if he be consistent, must apply the same reasoning to the actions and volitions of intelligent agents. The most irregular and unexpected resolutions of men may frequently be accounted for by those who know every particular circumstance of their character and situation. A person of an obliging disposition gives a peevish answer, but he has the toothache, or has not dined. A stupid fellow discovers an uncommon alacrity in his carriage, but he has met with a sudden piece of good fortune. Or even when an action, as sometimes happens, cannot be particularly accounted for either by the person himself or by others, we know, in general, that the characters of men are to a certain degree inconstant and irregular. This is in a manner the constant character of human nature though it be applicable in a more particular manner to some persons who have no fixed rule for their conduct but proceed in a continued course of caprice and inconstancy. The internal principles and motives may operate in a uniform manner, notwithstanding these seeming irregularities; in the same manner as the winds, rain, clouds, and other variations of the weather are supposed to be governed by steady principles though not easily discoverable by human sagacity and inquiry.

Thus it appears not only that the conjunction between motives and voluntary actions is as regular and uniform as that between the cause and effect in any part of nature, but also that this regular conjunction has been universally acknowledged among mankind and has never been the subject of dispute either in philosophy or common life. Now, as it is from past experience that we draw all inferences concerning the future and as we conclude that objects will always be conjoined together, which we find to have always been conjoined, it may seem superfluous to prove that this experienced uniformity in human actions is a source whence we draw *inferences* concerning them. But in order to throw the argument into a greater variety of lights, we shall also insist, though briefly, on this latter topic.

The mutual dependence of men is so great in all societies that scarce any human action is entirely complete in itself, or is performed without some reference to the actions of others, which are requisite to make it answer fully the intention of the agent. The poorest artificer, who labors alone, expects at least the protection of the magistrate, to insure him the enjoyment of the fruits of his labor. He also expects that when he carries his goods to market and offers them at a reasonable price he shall find purchasers, and shall be able by the money he acquires to engage others to supply him with those commodities which are requisite for his subsistence. In proportion as men extend their dealings and render their intercourse with others more complicated, they always comprehend in their schemes of life a greater variety of voluntary actions which they expect from the proper motives to cooperate with their own. In all these conclusions, they take their measures from past experience in the same manner as in their reasonings concerning external objects; and firmly believe that men as well as all the elements are to continue in their operations the same that they have ever found them. A manufacturer reckons upon the labor of his servants for the execution of any work as much as upon the tools which he employs and would be equally surprised were his expectations disappointed. In short, this experimental inference and reasoning concerning the actions of others enters so much into human life that no man, while awake, is ever a moment without employing it. Have we not reason, therefore, to affirm that all mankind have always agreed in the doctrine of necessity according to the foregoing definition and explication of it?

Nor have philosophers ever entertained a different opinion from the people in this particular. For not to mention that almost every action of their life supposes that opinion, there are even few of the speculative parts of learning to which it is not essential. What would become of *history* had we not a dependence on the veracity of the historian according to the experience which we have had of mankind? How could *politics* be a science if laws and forms of government had not a uniform influence upon society? Where would be the foundation of *morals* if particular characters had no certain or determinate power to produce particular sentiments and if these sentiments had no constant operation on actions? And with what pretense could we employ our *criticism* upon any poet or polite author if we could not pronounce the conduct and sentiments of his actors, either natural or unnatural, to such characters and in such circumstances? It seems almost impossible, therefore, to engage either in science or action of any kind without acknowledging the doctrine of necessity and this *inference* from motives to voluntary actions, from characters to conduct.

And indeed, when we consider how aptly *natural* and *moral* evidence link together and form only one chain of argument we shall make no scruple to allow that they are of the same nature and derived from the same principles. A prisoner, who has neither money nor interest, discovers the impossibility of his escape as well when he considers the obstinacy of the gaoler as the walls and bars with which he is surrounded, and, in all attempts for his freedom, chooses rather to work upon the stone and iron of the one than upon the inflexible nature of the other. The same prisoner, when conducted to the scaffold, foresees his death as certainly from the constancy and fidelity of his guards as from the operation of the ax or wheel. His mind runs along a certain train of ideas: the refusal of the soldiers to consent to his escape; the action of the executioner; the separation of the head and body; bleeding, convulsive motions, and death. Here is a connected chain of natural causes and voluntary actions, but the mind feels no difference between them in passing from one link to another, nor is it less certain of the future event than if it were connected with the objects present to the memory or senses by a train of causes cemented together by what we are pleased to call a *physical* necessity. The same experienced union has the same effect on the mind, whether the united objects be motives, volition, and actions, or figure and motion. We may change the names of things, but their nature and their operation on the understanding never change.

Were a man, whom I know to be honest and opulent, and with whom I live in intimate friendship, to come into my house where I am surrounded with my servants, I rest assured that he is not to stab me before he leaves it in order to rob me of my silver standish; and I no more suspect this event than the falling of the house itself which is new and solidly built and founded.—*But he may have been seized with a sudden and unknown frenzy.*—So may a sudden earthquake arise and shake and tumble my house about my ears. I shall therefore change the suppositions. I shall say that I know with certainty that he is not to put his hand into the fire and hold it there until it be consumed: and this event I think I can foretell with the same assurance as that if he throw himself out at the window and meet with no obstruction, he will not remain a moment suspended in the air. No suspicion of an unknown frenzy can give the least possibility to the former event, which is so contrary to all the known principles of human nature. A man who at noon leaves his purse full of gold on the pavement at Charing Cross may as well expect that it will fly away like a feather as that he will find it untouched an hour after. Above one-half of human reasonings contain inferences of a similar nature, attended with more or less degrees of certainty, proportioned to our experience of the usual conduct of mankind in such particular situations.

9

Dugald Stewart

OF THE MORAL FACULTY

WITH RESPECT to the historical facts which have been quoted as proofs that the moral judgments of mankind are entirely factitious, we may venture to assert in general that none of them justify so very extravagant a conclusion, that a great part of them are the effects of misrepresentation, and that others lead to a conclusion directly the reverse of what has been drawn from them. It would hardly be necessary in the present times to examine them seriously were it not for the authority which, in the opinion of many, they still continue to derive from the sanction of Mr. Locke.

"Have there not been whole nations," says this eminent philosopher, "and those of the most civilized people, among whom the exposing their children, and leaving them in the fields to perish, by want or wild beasts, has been the practice, as little condemned or scrupled as the begetting them? Do they not still in some countries put them into the same graves with their mothers if they die in child-birth, or despatch them if a pretended astrologer declares them to have unhappy stars? And are there not places where, at a certain age, they kill or expose their *parents* without any remorse at all? . . . Where, then, are our innate ideas of justice, piety, grati-

Reprinted from Dugald Stewart, *Philosophy of the Active and Moral Powers,* vol. I, in *Collected Works,* W. Hamilton, ed. (Edinburgh, 1855), II, pp. 235–48.

tude; or where is that universal consent that assures us there are such inbred rules?"[1]

To this question of Locke's, so satisfactory an answer has been given by various writers that it would be superfluous to enlarge on the subject here. It is sufficient to refer *on the origin of infanticide* to Mr. Smith's *Theory of Moral Sentiments;*[2] and, *on the alleged impiety among some rude tribes of children toward their parents,* to Charron *Sur la Sagesse,*[3] and to an excellent note of Dr. Beattie's in his *Essay on Fable and Romance.*[4] The reasonings of the two last writers are strongly confirmed by Mr. Ellis in his *Voyage for the Discovery of a North-West Passage,* and by Mr. Curtis (afterwards Sir Roger Curtis), in a paper containing *some particulars with respect to the country of Labrador,* published in the *Philosophical Transactions* for the year 1773.

In order to form a competent judgment on facts of this nature, it is necessary to attend to a variety of considerations which have been too frequently overlooked by philosophers, and in particular, to make proper allowances for the three following:—1. For the different situations in which mankind are placed, partly by the diversity in their physical circumstances and partly by the unequal degrees of civilisation which they have attained. 2. For the diversity of their speculative opinions, arising from their unequal measures of knowledge or of capacity; and, 3. For the different moral import of the same action under different systems of external behavior.

---

[1]   *Essay,* Book I, ch. iii. § 9.—There are a series of curious dissertations by an anonymous author among the Pythagorean Fragments, collected by Gale, which carry out with great ingenuity and minuteness a doctrine correspondent to Locke's, in regard to the nature of *moral distinctions.* They are, of course, written in the Doric dialect. See the *Opuscula Mythologica Physica et Ethica.* Amstel. 1688, p. 704–31.—W.H.

[2]   Part V, chap. ii.

[3]   Liv. II, chap. viii. Charron's argument is evidently pointed at certain passages in Montaigne's *Essays,* in which that ingenious writer has fallen into a train of thought very similar to that which is the groundwork of Locke's reasonings against *innate practical principles.*

[4]   *Dissertations, Moral and Critical,* p. 524, 4to ed.—if there be any other.

1. (i.) In a part of the globe where the soil and climate are so favorable as to yield all the necessaries and many of the luxuries of life with little or no labor on the part of man, it may reasonably be expected that the ideas of men will be more loose concerning *the rights of property* than where nature has been less liberal in her gifts. As the right of property is founded *in the first instance* on the natural sentiment that *the laborer is entitled to the fruits of his own labor*, it is not surprising that where little or no labor is required for the gratification of our desires theft should be regarded as a very venial offence. There is here no contradiction in the moral judgments of mankind. Men feel *there* with respect to those articles which we appropriate with the most anxious care as we in this part of the world feel with respect to *air, light*, and *water*. If a country could be found in which no injustice was apprehended in depriving an individual of an enjoyment which he had provided for himself by a long course of persevering industry, the fact would be something to the purpose. But *this*, we may venture to say, has not yet been found to be the case in any quarter of the globe. That the circumstance I mentioned is the true explanation of the prevalence of theft in the South Sea Islands and of the venial light in which it is there regarded appears plainly from the accounts of our most intelligent navigators.

"There was another circumstance," says Captain Cook, speaking of the inhabitants of the Sandwich Islands, "in which the people perfectly resembled the other islanders we had visited. At first on their entering the ship, they endeavoured to steal everything they came near, or *rather to take it openly, as what we either should not resent, or not hinder*." (January, 1778.)

In another place, talking of the same people: "These islanders," says he, "merited our best commendations in their commercial intercourse, never once attempting to cheat us either ashore or alongside the ships. Some of them, indeed, as already mentioned, *at first* betrayed a thievish disposition; or rather, they thought that they had *a right* to everything they could lay their hands on; but they soon laid aside a conduct which, we convinced them, they could not persevere in with impunity."

In another part of the voyage (April, 1778), in which he gives an account of the American Indians near King George's Sound, he contrasts their notions on the subject of theft with those of the South Sea Islanders. "The inhabitants of the South Sea Islands, rather than be idle, would steal anything they could lay their hands on, without ever considering whether it could be of use to them or no. The novelty of the object was with them a sufficient motive for endeavouring, by any indirect means, to get possession of it; which marked, that in such cases they were rather actuated by a childish curiosity than by a dishonest disposition, *regardless of the modes of supplying real wants.* The inhabitants of Nootka, who invaded our property, have not such an apology. They were *thieves* in the strictest sense of the word; for they pilfered nothing from us but what they knew could be converted to the purposes of private utility, and had a *real value,* according to their estimation of things." He adds, that "he had abundant proof that stealing is much practiced among themselves"; but it is evident from the manner in which he expresses himself that *theft* was not *here* considered in the same venial or indifferent light as in those parts of the globe where the bounty of nature deprives exclusive property of almost all its value.[5]

In general it will be found that the ideas of rude nations on the subject of *property* are precise and decided, in proportion to *the degree of labor* to which they have been habituated in procuring the means of subsistence. Of one barbarous people (the Greenlanders), we are expressly told by a very authentic writer (Crantz) that their regard to property acquired by labor is not only strict but approaches to superstition. "Not one of them," says he, "will appropriate to himself a sea-dog in which he finds one or more harpoons with untorn thongs; nor even carry away drift-wood, or other things thrown up by the sea, *if they are covered with a stone,* because they consider this as an indication that they have already been appropriated by some other person."[6]

5   Cook's *Voyages, etc.,* of the dates specified. See also Anderson's *Remarks,* February, 1777, and December, 1777.
6   The following passage of Voltaire is perhaps liable to the charge of overrefinement; but it sufficiently shows that he saw clearly the general

1. (ii.) Another very remarkable instance of an apparent diversity in the moral judgments of mankind occurs in the contradictory opinions entertained by different ages and nations on the moral lawfulness of exacting *interest* for the use of money. Aristotle, in the first book of his *Politics* (6th chapter), speaking of the various ways of getting money, considers agriculture and the rearing of cattle as honorable and natural, because the earth itself and all animals are by nature fruitful; "but to make money from money, which is barren and unfruitful," he pronounces "to be the worst of all modes of accumulation, and the utmost corruption of artificial degeneracy. By commerce," he observes, "money is perverted from the purpose of exchange to that of gain. Still, however, this gain is obtained by the mutual transfer of different objects, but usury, by transferring merely the same object from one hand to another, generates money from money; and the interest thus generated is therefore called 'offspring,' as being precisely of the same nature, and of the same specific substance with that from which it proceeds."[7]—Similar sentiments with respect to *usury* (under which title was comprehended every *premium,* great or small, which was received by way of interest) occur in the Roman writers. "Concerning the arts," says Cicero, in his first book *De Officiis,*

---

principle on which the lax opinions of some nations on the subject of theft are to be explained.

"They may tell us that larceny was enjoined at Lacedaemon; that is simply an abuse of words. The same thing which we call *larceny* was not commanded at Lacedaemon; but in a city where everything was common, the permission that was given to carry off with dexterity what private individuals had appropriated to themselves contrary to law was a mode of punishing the spirit of property, which was prohibited among that people. *Thine* and *mine* was a crime, of which that we call *theft* was the punishment."—Voltaire's *Account of Newton's Discoveries.*

7   Gillies's translation. The argument of Aristotle is so extremely absurd and puerile that it could never have led this most acute and profound philosopher to the conclusion it is employed to support, but may be justly numbered among the instances in which speculative men have exerted their ingenuity to defend, by sophistical reasonings, the established prejudices of the times in which they lived, and in which the supposed evidence of the inference has served, in their estimation, to compensate for the weakness of the premises. It is, however, worthy of remark that the argument such as it is was manifestly suggested by the etymology of the word τόχos, (interest,) from the verb τίχτω, *pario;* an etymology which seems to imply that the principal gen-

"and the means of acquiring wealth, which are to be accounted liberal, and which mean, the following are the sentiments usually entertained. In the first place, those means of gain are in the *least* credit which incur the hatred of mankind, as those of tax-gatherers and usurers."[8] The same author (in the second book of the same work) mentions an anecdote of old Cato, who, being asked, "What he thought of lending money upon interest?" answered, "What do you think of the crime of murder?"[9]

In the code of the Jewish legislator, the regulations concerning loans imply manifestly that to exact a *premium* for the thing lent was an act of unkindness unsuitable to the fraternal relation in which the Israelites stood to one another. "Thou shalt not lend," it is said, "upon usury to thy brother: usury of money, usury of victuals, usury of anything that is lent."—"Unto the stranger thou mayest lend upon usury; but unto thy brother thou shalt not lend upon usury; that the Lord thy God may bless thee in all thou settest thy hand to, in the land whither thou goest to possess it."[10]

In consequence of this prohibition in the Mosaic law, the primitive Christians conceiving that they ought to look on all men, both Jews and Gentiles, as *brethren,* inferred (partly perhaps from the prohibition given by Moses, and partly from the general prejudices then prevalent against usury) that it was against the Christian law to take interest from any man. And accordingly there is no crime against which the fathers in their homilies declaim with more vehemence. The same abhorrence of usury of every kind appears in the canon law, insomuch that the penalty by that law is excommunication, nor is the usurer allowed burial until he has made

---

erates the interest. The same idea, too, occurs in the scene between Antonio and Shylock, in the *Merchant of Venice:*—

> "If thou wilt lend this money, lend it not
> As to thy friend, (for when did friendship take
> *A breed of barren metal from his friend?*)
> But lend it rather to thine enemy,
> Who, if he break, thou may'st with better face
> Exact the penalty."

8   Cap. xlii.
9   Cap. xxv.
10   *Deuteronomy* xxiii. 19, 20.

restitution of what he got by usury, or security is given that restitution shall be made after his death. About the middle of the
seventeenth century, we find the divines of the Church of England
very often preaching against all interest for the use of money, even
that which the law allowed, as a gross immorality. And not much
earlier it was the general opinion both of divines and lawyers that,
although law permitted a certain rate of interest to prevent greater
evils, and in compliance with the general corruption of men (as
the law of Moses permitted polygamy, and authorized divorce for
slight causes among the Jews), yet that the rules of morality did
not sanction the taking *any interest* for money, at least that it was
a very doubtful point whether they did. The same opinion was
maintained in the English House of Commons by some of the
members who were lawyers, in the debate upon a bill brought
in not much more than a hundred years ago.

I need not remark how completely the sentiments of mankind
are now changed upon the subject insomuch that a moralist or
divine would expose himself to ridicule if he should seriously think
it worth his while to use arguments to prove the lawfulness of a
practice which was formerly held in universal abhorrence. The
consistency of this practice (in cases where the debtor is able to
pay the interest) with the strictest morality appears to us so manifest and indisputable that it would be thought equally absurd to
argue for it as against it.[11]

The diversity of judgments, however, on this particular question, instead of proving a diversity in the *moral* judgments of mankind, affords an illustration of the uniformity of their opinions
concerning the fundamental rules of moral duty.

[11]   A learned gentleman, indeed, of the Middle Temple, Mr. Plowden
(a lawyer, I believe, of the Roman Catholic persuasion), who published
about thirty years ago a Treatise upon the *Law of Usury and Annuities* has
employed no less than fifty-nine pages of his work in considering the law of
usury in a *spiritual view,* in order to establish the following conclusion, "That
it is not sinful, but lawful for a British subject to receive legal interest for the
money he may lend, whether he receive it in annual dividends from the public,
or in interest from private individuals who may have borrowed it upon mort-
gage, bond, or otherwise."—Mr. Necker too in the notes annexed to his *Eloge
on Colbert* thought it necessary for him to offer an apology to the Church of
Rome for the freedom with which he ventured to write upon this critical
subject. "What I say regarding interest is from a political point of view and
has no reference to the respectable maxims of theology on that point."

In a state where there is little or no commerce, the great motive for borrowing being necessity, the value of a loan cannot be ascertained by calculation as it *may* be where money is borrowed for the purposes of trade. In such circumstances, therefore, every money lender who accepts of interest will be regarded in the same odious light in which pawnbrokers are considered among *us;* and "the man who putteth out his coin to usury," will naturally be classed (as he is in the words of Scripture) "with him who taketh a reward against the guiltless."[12]

These considerations, while they account for the origin of the opinions concerning the practice of taking interest for money among those nations of antiquity whose commercial transactions were few and insignificant, will be sufficient at the same time to establish its reasonableness and equity in countries where money is most commonly borrowed for the purposes of commercial profit, and where of consequence the use of it has a fixed and determinate value depending (like that of any commodity in general request) on the circumstances of the market at the time. In such countries *both* parties are benefited by the transaction, and even the state is a gainer in the end. The *lenders* of money are frequently widows and orphans who subsist on the interest of their slender funds, while the *borrowers* as frequently belong to the most opulent class of the community who wish to enlarge their capital and extend their trade and who by doing so are enabled to give farther encouragement to industry and to supply labor and bread to the indigent.

The prejudices, therefore, against usury among the ancient philosophers, were the natural result of the state of society which fell under their observation. The prohibition of usury among the Jews in their own mutual transactions, while they were permitted to take a *premium* for the money which they lent to strangers, was in perfect consistency with the other principles of their political code; commerce being interdicted as tending to an intercourse with idolaters and mortgages prevented by the indefeasible right which every man had to his lands.

1. (iii.) I shall only mention one instance more to illustrate the effects of different states of society in modifying the moral judg-

12   See *Psalm* 15:5.

ments of mankind. It relates to the crime of assassination, which we now justly consider as the most dreadful of any, but which must necessarily have been viewed in a very different light when laws and magistrates were unknown, and when the only check on injustice was *the principle of resentment.* As it is the nature of this principle not only to seek the punishment of the delinquent but to prompt the injured person to inflict the punishment with his own hand, so in every country the criminal jurisdiction of the magistrate has been the last branch of his authority that was established. Where the police, therefore, is weak, murders must not only be more frequent, but are really less criminal than in a society like ours where the private rights of individuals are completely protected by laws and where there hardly occurs an instance, excepting in a case of self-defense, in which one man can be justified for shedding the blood of another. And even when in a rude age a murder is committed from unjustifiable motives of self-interest or jealousy, yet the frequency of the occurrence prevents the minds of men from revolting so strongly at the sight of blood as we do at present. It is on this very principle that Mr. Mitford accounts for the manners and ideas that prevailed in the heroic ages of Greece.

But it is unnecessary on this head to appeal to the history of early times, or of distant nations. In our own country of Scotland about two centuries ago what shocking murders were perpetrated and seemingly without remorse by men who were by no means wholly destitute of a sense of religion and morality! Dr. Robertson[13] remarks, that "Buchanan relates the murder of Cardinal Beatoun and of Rizzio, without expressing those feelings which are natural to a man, or that indignation which became an historian. Knox, whose mind was fiercer and more unpolished, talks of the death of Beatoun and of the Duke of Guise, not only without censure, but with the utmost exultation. On the other hand, the Bishop of Ross mentions the assassination of the Earl of Murray with some degree of applause. Blackwood dwells on it with the most indecent triumph; and ascribes it directly to the hand of God. Lord Ruthven, the principal actor in the conspiracy against Rizzio,

13   *History of Scotland.*

wrote an account of it some time before his own death; and in all his long narrative there is not one expression of regret, or one symptom of compunction, for a crime no less dishonorable than barbarous. Morton, equally guilty of the same crime, entertained the same sentiments concerning it; and in his last moments, neither he himself, nor the ministers who attended him, seem to have considered it as an action which called for repentance. Even then he talks of *David's slaughter* as coolly as if it had been an innocent or commendable deed."[14]

The reflections of Dr. Robertson on these assassinations which were formerly so common in this country are candid and judicious. "In consequence of the limited power of our princes, the administration of justice was extremely feeble and dilatory. An attempt to punish the crimes of a chieftain, or even of his vassals, often excited rebellions and civil wars. To nobles haughty and independent, among whom the causes of discord were many and unavoidable, who were quick in discerning an injury, and impatient to revenge it; who esteemed it infamous to submit to an enemy, and cowardly to forgive him; who considered the right of punishing those who had injured them as a privilege of their order, and a mark of independency; such slow proceedings were extremely unsatisfactory. The blood of their adversary was, in their opinion, the only thing that could wash away an affront. Where that was not shed, their revenge was disappointed; their courage became suspected, and a stain was left on their honour. That vengeance which the impotent hand of the magistrate could not inflict, their own could easily execute. Under a government so feeble, men assumed, as in a state of nature, the right of judging and redressing their own wrongs.

[14]   The following lines, in which Sir David Lindsay reprobates the murder of his contemporary and enemy, Cardinal Beatoun, deserve to be added to the instances quoted by Dr. Robertson, as an illustration of the moral sentiments of our ancestors. They are expressed with a naïveté which places in a strong light both the moral and religious principles of that age.

> "As for this Cardinal, I grant,
> He was a man we well might want;
> *God will forgive it soon:*
> But of a sooth, the truth to say,
> Altho' the loun be well away,
> The fact was foully done."

And thus *assassination,* a crime of all others the most destructive to society, came not only to be allowed, but to be deemed honorable." In another passage he observes, "That mankind became thus habituated to blood, not only in times of war, but of peace; and from this, as well as other causes, contracted an amazing ferocity of temper and of manners."

2. The second cause I mentioned of the apparent diversity among mankind in their moral judgments is the diversity in their speculative opinions.

The manner in which this cause operates will appear obvious if it be considered that nature, by the suggestions of our moral principles, only recommends to us particular *ends,* but leaves it to our reason to ascertain the most effectual *means* by which these *ends* are to be attained. Thus nature points out to us our own happiness and also the happiness of our fellow-creatures as objects toward the attainment of which our best exertions ought to be directed, but she has left us to exercise our reason both in ascertaining what the constituents of happiness are and how they may be most completely secured. Hence, according to the different points of view in which these subjects of consideration may appear to different understandings, there must of necessity be a diversity of judgments with respect to the morality of the same actions. One man, for example, believes that the happiness of society is most effectually consulted by an implicit obedience *in all cases* to the will of the civil magistrate. Another, that the mischiefs to be apprehended from resistance and insurrection in cases of urgent necessity are trifling when compared with those which may result to ourselves and our posterity from an established despotism. The former will of course be an advocate for the duty of passive obedience; the latter for the *right* and in certain supposable cases for the *obligation* of resistance. Both of these men, however, agree in the general principle that it is our duty to promote to the utmost of our power the happiness of society, and they differ from each other only on a speculative question of expediency.

In like manner there is a wide diversity between the moral systems of ancient and modern times on the subject of suicide.

Both, however, agree in this, that it is the duty of man to obey the will of his Creator and to consult every intimation of it that his reason can discover as the supreme law of his conduct. They differed only in their *speculative opinions* concerning the interpretation of the will of God as manifested by the dispensations of his providence in the events of human life. The prejudices of the ancients on this subject were indeed founded in a very partial and erroneous view of circumstances (arising, however, not unnaturally from the unsettled state of society in the ancient republics), but they only afford an additional instance of the numerous mistakes to which human *reason* is liable, not of a fluctuation in the judgments of mankind concerning the fundamental rules of moral duty.

3. The different moral import too of the same material action under different systems of external behaviour deserves particular attention in forming an estimate of the moral sentiments of different ages and nations.

This difference is chiefly owing to two causes:—first, to the different conceptions of happiness and misery—of what is to be desired and shunned—which men are led to form in different states of society. Secondly, to the effect of accident which as it leads men to speak different languages in different countries so it leads them to express the same dispositions of the heart by different external observances.

3. (i.) Where the opinions of mankind vary concerning the external circumstances that constitute happiness, the external expressions of benevolence must vary of course. Thus, in the fact referred to by Locke concerning the Indians in the neighborhood of Hudson's Bay, the wishes of the agent parent being different from what we are accustomed to observe in this part of the world, the marks of filial affection on the part of the child must vary also. "In some countries honour is associated with suffering, and it is reckoned a favour to be killed with circumstances of torture. Instances of this occur in the manners of some American nations, and in the pride which an Indian matron feels when placed on the

funeral-pile of her deceased husband."[15] In such cases an action may have to us all the external marks of extreme cruelty, while it proceeded from a disposition generous and affectionate.

3. (ii.) A difference in the moral import of the same action often arises from the same accidental causes which lead men in different parts of the globe to express the same ideas by different arbitrary signs.

What happens in the trifling forms and ceremonies of behavior may serve to illustrate the operation of the same causes on more important occasions. "In the general principles of urbanity, politeness, or civility, we may venture to assert, that the opinions of all nations are agreed; but in the expression of this disposition we meet with endless varieties. In Europe, it is the form of respect to uncover the *head*; in Japan, the corresponding form is said to be to uncover *the foot* by dropping the slipper.[16] Persons unacquainted with any language but their own are apt to think the words they use natural and fixed expressions of things; while the words of a different language they consider as mere jargon, or the result of caprice. In the same manner, forms of behavior different from their own appear offensive and irrational, or a perverse substitution of absurd for reasonable manners.

"Among the varieties of this sort, we find actions, gestures, and forms of expression in their own nature indifferent, entered into the code of civil or religious duties, and enforced under the strongest sanctions of public censure or esteem; or under the strongest denunciations of the Divine indignation or favour.

"Numberless ceremonies and observances in the ritual of different sects are to be accounted for on the same principles which produce the diversity of names or signs for the same thing in the vocabulary of different languages. Thus, the generality of Chris-

15 See Dr. Ferguson's *Principles of Moral and Political Science*, Vol. II. p. 141. Part II. chap. ii. sect. 4.
16 "Even here," Sir Joshua Reynolds ingeniously remarks, "we may perhaps observe a general idea running through all the varieties; to wit, the general idea of making the body less in token of respect, whether by bowing the body, kneeling, prostration, pulling off the upper part of the dress, or throwing aside the lower."—*Discourses*.

tians when they pray take off their hats; the Jews when they pray put them on. Such acts, how strongly soever they may affect the imaginations of the multitude, may justly be considered as part of the arbitrary language of particular countries; implying no diversity whatever in the ideas or feelings of those among whom they are established."[17]

17   See Dr. Ferguson's *Principles of Moral and Political Philosophy,* Vol. II. pp. 142, 143. Part II. chap. ii. sect. 4.

III. Social Psychology and the Social Bond

10

Adam Smith

SELF-APPROBATION, SELF-DISAPPROBATION, AND THE MAN WITHIN THE BREAST

THE PRINCIPLE by which we naturally either approve or disapprove of our own conduct seems to be altogether the same with that by which we exercise the like judgments concerning the conduct of other people. We either approve or disapprove of the conduct of another man according as we feel that when we bring his case home to ourselves we either can or cannot entirely sympathize with the sentiments and motives which directed it. And in the same manner we either approve or disapprove of our own conduct according as we feel that when we place ourselves in the situation of another man and view it, as it were, with his eyes and from his station, we either can or cannot entirely enter into and sympathize with the sentiments and motives which influenced it. We can never survey our own sentiments and motives, we can never form any judgment concerning them unless we remove ourselves, as it were, from our own natural station and endeavor to view them as at a certain distance from us. But we can do this in no other way than by endeavoring to view them with the eyes of other people, or as other people are likely to view them. Whatever

Reprinted from Adam Smith, *The Theory of Moral Sentiments* (London and New York: G. Bell and Sons, 1892), pp. 161–65, 171–73, 192–94, 216. The title is from phrases of Smith's.

judgment we can form concerning them, accordingly, must always bear some secret reference either to what are or to what upon a certain condition would be, or to what, we imagine, ought to be the judgment of others. We endeavor to examine our own conduct as we imagine any other fair and impartial spectator would examine it. If, upon placing ourselves in his situation, we thoroughly enter into all the passions and motives which influenced it, we approve of it by sympathy with the approbation of this supposed equitable judge. If otherwise, we enter into his disapprobation and condemn it.

Were it possible that a human creature could grow up to manhood in some solitary place, without any communication with his own species, he could no more think of his own character, of the propriety or demerit of his own sentiments and conduct, of the beauty or deformity of his own mind, than of the beauty or deformity of his own face. All these are objects which he cannot easily see, which naturally he does not look at and with regard to which he is provided with no mirror which can present them to his view. Bring him into society, and he is immediately provided with the mirror which he wanted before. It is placed in the countenance and behavior of those he lives with which always mark when they enter into and when they disapprove of his sentiments; and it is here that he first views the propriety and impropriety of his own passions, the beauty and deformity of his own mind. To a man who from his birth was a stranger to society, the objects of his passions, the external bodies which either pleased or hurt him, would occupy his whole attention. The passions themselves, the desires or aversions, the joys or sorrows, which those objects excited, though of all things the most immediately present to him, could scarce ever be the objects of his thoughts. The idea of them could never interest him so much as to call upon his attentive consideration. The consideration of his joy could in him excite no new joy, nor that of his sorrow any new sorrow, though the consideration of the causes of those passions might often excite both. Bring him into society and all his own passions will immediately become the causes of new passions. He will observe that mankind approve of some of them and are disgusted by others. He will be elevated in the one case and cast down in the other; his desires and aversions, his joys and sorrows, will now often become the causes of new desires and new aversions, new joys, and new sorrows: they will now, therefore, interest him deeply and often call upon his most attentive consideration.

Our first ideas of personal beauty and deformity are drawn from the shape and appearance of others, not from our own. We soon become sensible, however, that others exercise the same criticism upon us. We are pleased when they approve of our figure and are disobliged when they seem to be disgusted. We become anxious to know how far our appearance deserves either their blame or approbation. We examine our persons limb by limb, and by placing ourselves before a looking-glass, or by some such expedient, endeavor, as much as possible, to view ourselves at the distance and with the eyes of other people. If after this examination we are satisfied with our own appearance, we can more easily support the most disadvantageous judgments of others. If, on the contrary, we are sensible that we are the natural objects of distaste, every appearance of their disapprobation mortifies us beyond all measure. A man who is tolerably handsome will allow you to laugh at any little irregularity in his person; but all such jokes are commonly unsupportable to one who is really deformed. It is evident, however, that we are anxious about our own beauty and deformity only upon account of its effect upon others. If we had no connection with society, we should be altogether indifferent about either.

In the same manner our first moral criticisms are exercised upon the characters and conduct of other people, and we are all very forward to observe how each of these affects us. But we soon learn that other people are equally frank with regard to our own. We become anxious to know how far we deserve their censure or applause, and whether to them we must necessarily appear those agreeable or disagreeable creatures which they represent us. We begin, upon this account, to examine our own passions and conduct and to consider how these must appear to them by considering how they would appear to us if in their situation. We suppose ourselves the spectators of our own behavior and endeavor to imagine what effect it would, in this light, produce upon us. This is the only looking-glass by which we can, in some measure, with the eyes of other people, scrutinize the propriety of our own conduct. If in this view it pleases us, we are tolerably satisfied. We can be more indifferent about the applause, and, in some measure, despise the censure of the world; secure that, however misunderstood or misrepresented, we are the natural and proper objects of approbation. On the contrary, if we are doubtful about it, we are often, upon that very account, more anxious to gain their approbation and provided we have not already, as they say, shaken hands with infamy, we are altogether distracted at the thought of their censure which then strikes us with double severity.

When I endeavor to examine my own conduct, when I endeavor to pass sentence upon it, and either to approve or condemn it, it is evident that in all such cases I divide myself, as it were, into two persons, and that I, the examiner and judge, represent a different character from that other I, the person whose conduct is examined into and judged of. The first is the spectator, whose sentiments with regard to my own conduct I endeavor to enter into, by placing myself in his situation, and by considering how it would appear to me, when seen from that particular point of view. The second is the agent, the person whom I properly call myself, and of whose conduct, under the character of a spectator, I was endeavoring to form some opinion. The first is the judge; the second the person judged of. But that the judge should, in every respect, be the same with the person judged of is as impossible as that the cause should, in every respect, be the same with the effect.

To be amiable and to be meritorious, that is, to deserve love and to deserve reward, are the great characters of virtue; and to be odious and punishable, of vice. But all these characters have an immediate reference to the sentiments of others. Virtue is not said to be amiable, or to be meritorius because it is the object of its own love, or of its own gratitude, but because it excites those sentiments in other men. The consciousness that it is the object of such favorable regards is the source of that inward tranquillity and self-satisfaction with which it is naturally attended, as the suspicion of the contrary gives occasion to the torments of vice. What so great happiness as to be beloved and to know that we deserve to be beloved? What so great misery as to be hated and to know that we deserve to be hated? . . .

II

As the love and admiration which we naturally conceive for some characters dispose us to wish to become ourselves the proper objects of such agreeable sentiments; so the hatred and contempt which we as naturally conceive for others dispose us, perhaps still more strongly, to dread the very thought of resembling them in any respect. Neither is it, in this case too, so much the thought of being hated and despised that we are afraid of as that of being hateful and despicable. We dread the thought of doing any thing which can render us the just and proper objects of the hatred and contempt of our fellow creatures; even though we had the most perfect security that those sentiments were never actually to be exerted against us. The man who has broken through all those measures of conduct which can alone render him agreeable to mankind, though he should have the most perfect assurance that what he had done was for ever to be concealed from every human eye, it is all to no purpose. When he looks back upon it and views it in the light in which the impartial spectator would view it, he finds that he can enter into none of the motives which influenced it. He is abashed and confounded at the thought of it and necessarily feels a very high degree of that shame which he would be exposed to, if his actions should ever come to be generally known. His imagination, in this case, too, anticipates the contempt and derision from which nothing saves him but the ignorance of those he lives with. He still feels that he is the natural object of these sentiments and still trembles at the thought of what he would suffer if they were ever actually exerted against him. But if what he had been guilty of was not merely one of those improprieties which are the objects of simple disapprobation, but one of those enormous crimes which excite detestation and resentment, he could never think of it as long as he had any sensibility left without feeling all the agony of horror and remorse; and though he could be assured that no man was ever to know it, and could even bring himself to believe that there was no God to revenge it, he would still feel enough of both these sentiments to embitter the whole of his life: he would still regard himself as the natural object of the hatred and indignation of all his fellow creatures; and if his heart was not grown callous by the habit of crimes, he could not think without terror and astonishment even of the manner in which mankind would look upon him, of what would be the expression of their countenance and of their eyes, if the dreadful truth should ever come to be known. These natural pangs of an affrighted conscience are the demons, the avenging furies, which, in this life, haunt the guilty, which allow them neither quiet nor repose, which often drive them to despair and distraction, from which no assurance of secrecy can protect them, from which no principle of irreligion can entirely deliver them, and from which nothing can free them but the vilest and most abject of all states, a complete insensibility to honor and infamy, to vice and virtue. Men of the most detestable characters, who in the execution of the most dreadful crimes had taken their measures so coolly as to avoid even the suspicion of guilt have sometimes been driven by the horror of their situation to discover of their own accord what no human sagacity could ever have investigated. By acknowledging their guilt, by submitting themselves to the resentment of their offended fellow citizens, and by thus satiating that vengeance of which they were sensible that they had become the proper objects they hoped by their death to reconcile themselves, at least in their own imagination, to the natural sentiments of mankind; to be able to consider themselves as less worthy of hatred and resentment; to atone in some measure for their crimes and by thus becoming the objects, rather of compassion than of horror, if possible to die in peace, and with the forgiveness of all their fellow creatures. Compared to what they felt before the discovery, even the thought of this, it seems, was happiness.

III

Let us suppose that the great empire of China, with all its myriads of inhabitants, was suddenly swallowed up by an earthquake, and let us consider how a man of humanity in Europe, who had no sort of connection with that part of the world, would be affected upon receiving intelligence of this dreadful calamity. He would, I imagine, first of all express very strongly his sorrow for the misfortune of that unhappy people, he would make many melancholy reflections upon the precariousness of human life and the vanity of all the labors of man, which could thus be annihilated in a moment. He would, too, perhaps, if he was a man of speculation, enter into many reasonings concerning the effects which this disaster might produce upon the commerce of Europe and the trade and business of the world in general. And when all this fine philosophy was over, when all these humane sentiments had been once fairly expressed, he would pursue his business or his pleasure, take his repose or his diversion with the same ease and tranquillity as if no such accident had happened. The most frivolous disaster which could befall himself would occasion a more real disturbance. If he were to lose his little finger tomorrow, he would not sleep tonight; but, provided he never saw them, he will snore with the most profound security over the ruin of a hundred millions of his brethren and the destruction of that immense multitude seems plainly an object less interesting to him than this paltry misfortune of his own. To prevent, therefore, this paltry misfortune to himself, would a man of humanity be willing to sacrifice the lives of a hundred millions of his brethren provided he had never seen them? Human nature startles with horror at the thought, and the world, in its greatest depravity and corruption, never produced such a villain as could be capable of entertaining it. But what makes this difference? When our passive feelings are almost always so sordid and so selfish, how comes it that our active principles should often be so generous and so noble? When we are always so much more deeply affected by whatever concerns ourselves than by whatever concerns other men, what is it which prompts the generous upon all occasions, and the mean upon many, to sacrifice their own interests to the greater interests of others? It is not the soft power of humanity, it is not that feeble spark of benevolence which nature has lighted up in the human heart that is thus capable of counteracting the strongest impulses of self-love. It is a stronger power, a more forcible motive, which exerts itself upon such occasions. It is reason, principle, conscience, the inhabitant of the breast, the man within, the great judge, and arbiter of our conduct. It is he who whenever we are about to act so as to affect the happiness of others calls to us with a voice capable of astonishing the most presumptuous of our passions that we are but one of the multitude in no respect better than any other in it; and that when we prefer ourselves so shamefully and so blindly to others, we become the proper objects of resentment, abhorrence, and execration. It is from him only that we learn the real littleness of ourselves, and of whatever relates to ourselves, and the natural misrepresentations of self-love can be corrected only by the eye of this impartial spectator. It is he who shows us the propriety of generosity and the deformity of injustice, the propriety of resigning the greatest interests of our own for the yet greater interests of others, and the deformity of doing the smallest injury to another in order to obtain the greatest benefit to ourselves. It is not the love of our neighbor, it is not the love of mankind, which upon many occasions prompts us to the practice of those divine virtues. It is a stronger love, a more powerful affection, which generally takes place upon such occasions; the love of what is honorable and noble, of the grandeur and dignity and superiority of our own characters.

IV

In solitude, we are apt to feel too strongly whatever relates to ourselves: we are apt to overrate the good offices we may have done and the injuries we may have suffered; we are apt to be too much elated by our own good and too much dejected by our own bad fortune. The conversation of a friend brings us to a better, that of a stranger to a still better temper. The man within the breast, the abstract and ideal spectator of our sentiments and conduct, requires often to be awakened and put in mind of his duty, by the presence of the real spectator; and it is always from that spectator, from whom we can expect the least sympathy and indulgence, that we are likely to learn the most complete lesson of self-command.

11

Adam Ferguson

OF THE PRINCIPLES OF UNION
AMONG MANKIND

MANKIND HAS ALWAYS wandered or settled, agreed or quarrelled, in troops and companies. The cause of their assembling, whatever it be, is the principle of their alliance or union.

In collecting the materials of history, we are seldom willing to put up with our subject merely as we find it. We are loth to be embarrassed with a multiplicity of particulars and apparent inconsistencies. In theory we profess the investigation of general principles and in order to bring the matter of our inquiries within the reach of our comprehension are disposed to adopt any system. Thus, in treating of human affairs, we would draw every consequence from a principle of union, or a principle of dissension. The state of nature is a state of war, or of amity, and men are made to unite from a principle of affection, or from a principle of fear, as is most suitable to the system of different writers. The history of our species indeed abundantly shows that they are to one another mutual objects both of fear and of love; and they who would prove them to have been originally either in a state of alliance, or of war, have arguments in store to maintain their assertions. Our attachment to one division, or to one sect, seems often to derive much of its force from an animosity conceived to an

Reprinted from Adam Ferguson, *An Essay on the History of Civil Society* (8th ed.; Philadelphia, 1819), pp. 28–34.

opposite one, and this animosity in its turn as often arises from a zeal in behalf of the side we espouse and from a desire to vindicate the rights of our party.

"Man is born in society," says Montesquieu, "and there he remains." The charms that detain him are known to be manifold. Together with the parental affection which instead of deserting the adult, as among the brutes, embraces more close as it becomes mixed with esteem and the memory of its early effects; we may reckon a propensity common to man and other animals, to mix with the herd, and, without reflection, to follow the crowd of his species. What this propensity was in the first moment of its operation, we know not, but with men accustomed to company, its enjoyments and disappointments are reckoned among the principal pleasures or pains of human life. Sadness and melancholy are connected with solitude; gladness and pleasure with the concourse of men. The track of a Laplander on the snowy shore gives joy to the lonely mariner, and the mute signs of cordiality and kindness which are made to him awaken the memory of pleasures which he felt in society. In fine, says the writer of a voyage to the North, after describing a mute scene of this sort, "We were extremely pleased to converse with men, since in thirteen months we had seen no human creature." (Collection of Dutch voyages.) But we need no remote observation to confirm this position: the wailings of the infant and the languors of the adult, when alone, the lively joys of the one and the cheerfulness of the other, upon return of company, are a sufficient proof of its solid foundations in the frame of our nature.

In accounting for actions we often forget that we ourselves have acted, and instead of the sentiments which stimulate the mind in the presence of its object, we assign as the motives of conduct with men those considerations which occur in the hours of retirement and cold reflection. In this mood frequently we can find nothing important besides the deliberate prospects of interest; and a great work, like that of forming society, must in our apprehension arise from deep reflections and be carried on with a view to the advantages which mankind derives from commerce and mutual support. But neither a propensity to mix with the herd nor the series of advantages enjoyed in that condition comprehend all the principles by which men are united together. Those bands are even of a feeble texture, when compared to the resolute ardor with which a man adheres to his friend, or to his tribe, after they have for some time run the career of fortune together. Mutual discoveries of generosity, joint trials of fortitude, redouble the ardor of friendship and kindle a flame in the human breast, which the considerations of personal interest or safety cannot suppress. The most lively transports of joy are seen and the loudest shrieks of despair are heard, when the objects of a tender affection are beheld in a state of triumph or of suffering. An Indian recovered his friend unexpectedly on the island of Juan Fernandes; he prostrated himself on the ground, at his feet. "We stood gazing in silence," says Dampier, "at this tender scene." If we would know what is the religion of a wild American, what it is in his heart that most resembles devotion, it is not his fear of the sorcerer, nor his hope of protection from the spirits of the air or the wood: it is the ardent affection with which he selects and embraces his friend; with which he clings to his side in every season of peril; and with which he invokes his spirit from a distance, when dangers surprise him alone. (Charlevoix, *History of Canada*.) Whatever proofs we may have of the social disposition of man in familiar and contiguous scenes, it is possibly of importance to draw our observations from the examples of men who live in the simplest condition and who have not learned to affect what they do not actually feel.

Mere acquaintance and habitude nourish affection, and the experience of society brings every passion of the human mind upon its side. Its triumphs and prosperities, its calamities and distresses, bring a variety and a force of emotion which can only have place in the company of our fellow creatures. It is here that a man is made to forget his weakness, his cares of safety, and his subsistence, and to act from those passions which make him discover his force. It is here he finds that his arrows fly swifter than the eagle and his weapons wound deeper than the paw of the lion or the tooth of the boar. It is not alone his sense of a support which is near nor the love of distinction in the opinion of his tribe that inspire his courage, or swell his heart with a confidence that exceeds what his natural forces should bestow. Vehement passions of animosity or attachment are the first exertions of vigor in his breast; under their influence every consideration, but that of his object, is forgotten; dangers and difficulties only excite him the more.

That condition is surely favorable to the nature of any being in which his force is increased; and if courage be the gift of society to man, we have reason to consider his union with his species as the noblest part of his fortune. From this source are derived not only the force but the very existence of his happiest emotions; not only the better part but almost the whole of his rational character. Send him to the desert alone, he is a plant torn from his roots: the form indeed may remain, but every faculty droops and withers; the human personage and the human character cease to exist.

Men are so far from valuing society on account of its mere external conveniences that they are commonly most attached where those conveniences are least frequent; and are there most faithful where the tribute of their allegiance is paid in blood. Affection operates with the greatest force where it meets with the greatest difficulties: in the breast of the parent, it is most solicitous amidst the dangers and distresses of the child; in the breast of a man, its flame redoubles where the wrongs or sufferings of his friend, or his country, require his aid. It is in short from this principle alone that we can account for the obstinate attachment of a savage to his unsettled and defenseless tribe, when temptations on the side of ease and of safety might induce him to fly from famine and danger to a station more affluent and more secure. Hence the sanguine affection which every Greek bore to his country, and hence the devoted patriotism of an early Roman. Let those examples be compared with the spirit which reigns in a commercial state where men may be supposed to have experienced, in its full extent, the interest which individuals have in the preservation of their country. It is here indeed, if ever, that man is sometimes found a detached and a solitary being: he has found an object which sets him in competition with his fellow creatures, and he deals with them as he does with his cattle and his soil, for the sake of the profits they bring. The mighty engine which we suppose to have formed society only tends to set its members at variance or to continue their intercourse after the bands of affection are broken.

12

Adam Ferguson

OF THE PRINCIPLES OF
SOCIETY IN HUMAN
NATURE

THE GENERAL COMBINATION of parts in the system of nature, the mutual subserviency of different orders of being on
this globe, the natural attachment of individuals in every species
of living creature to some others of their kind, and the frequency
of gregarious and political assemblage in the description of different animals must greatly facilitate the admission of society as a
part in the destination of man, or indeed, joined to the fact that
men are actually found in society, render argument on the subject of his qualification for such a state entirely superfluous.

The purpose of what follows on this subject, therefore, is rather
to specify the character of human society than to evince its reality
as the state or condition in which man is destined to act.

In a mixed scene of benevolence and malice, it is indeed of
importance to determine how far man is by his nature limited to
one or to the other, or how far he is equally susceptible of either
and deeply concerned in the one, as a good which he ought to
choose, and in the other, as an evil which he ought to avoid.

Authors, admitting the reality of man's actual place in society,
have endeavored to collect the appearances which mark his fitness or unfitness for this condition, in order to determine, each in

Reprinted from Adam Ferguson, *Principles of Moral and Political Science* (London and Edinburgh, 1792), I, 26–36.

his own way, the much agitated question relating to the state of nature.

These appearances highly merit our attention; they serve to characterize the species to which we belong, and the scenes in which we ourselves are destined to act. They may be collected from any of the transactions of men, whether in cooperation or opposition; the first, in the case of families, tribes, companies, nations, and empires; the second, in the rivalship or competition of parties, whether single men, or communities.

Families may be considered as the elementary forms of society, or establishments the most indispensably necessary to the existence and preservation of the kind. As families may exist apart, and without any necessary communication of one group with another, so they still continue to be formed in whatever numbers mankind may be leagued into larger communities: they are the nurseries of men; the basis of empires, as well as of nations and tribes; and the compartments of which the greatest fabrics of political establishment are composed, so that, however little we may need information on the subject of family connections, it is material to have in our view the principles on which they are formed, as the constituents of a social character, indelible in every age and in every state of society, whether voluntary or forced.

In families, no doubt, the first occasion or motive to union is the mutual inclination of the sexes, a disposition which is known to suspend, or to exceed in force, every other affection or passion of the human mind. Its effect, in particular instances, is an exclusive attachment of the parties, not like the corresponding disposition in the other animals, merely periodical and temporary, but a foundation of continual society, extending to all times and seasons; the result of it, in the general history of mankind, is such as to have rendered some institution of marriage universal or common. In this institution, the relation of husband and wife is accompanied with that of parent and child, and the increase of numbers is procured without consulting the mind, or the intention of the parties. This effect is to the race what the vital motion of the heart is to the individual; too necessary to the preservation of nature's works to be entrusted to the precarious will or intention of those most nearly concerned.

That the birth of a man is more painful and hazardous, that the state of his infancy is more helpless, and of longer duration, than is exemplified in the case of any other species, may be ranked with the apparent comparative defects of his animal nature; but this circumstance, we may venture to affirm, like many others of his seeming defects, is of a piece with that superior destination which remains to be fulfilled in the subsequent history of mankind.

His birth is marked with circumstances that make a deep impression in the parent's breast: it is at once a delivery from anxiety, danger, and pain; it is an acquisition, of which the value is indefinite and fondly enhanced; it is the opening of a new blossom of hope in a breast still trembling with fear, and awake to every sentiment of tender concern, solicitude, and love.

The only effort of the child, or all he can do for himself, is to raise the feeble cry of distress, in which he announces at once the glad tidings of life and his need of assistance; and his cry is more powerful to obtain this assistance than the most vigorous exertions of which the young of other animals, at their entry into life, are capable; it reaches the ear and the heart of those who have means, understanding, and power fitted to supply the relief which is wanted, and who continue through life to seek the advantage of their child in preference to any interest of their own.

Were the infant capable of observing the state to which he is born, he would find himself confederate in a league to which, besides the pleasure of serving him, he contributes nothing. His inability to make any return, however, but interests the more a tender affection of which he is the object, and the solicitude he brings serves but to rivet that affection by the continued repetition of its cares.

His first smile of complacency and his first attempts to cling, with an appearance of predilection, to the breast that supports him are an ample reward for all the pains which his birth, or his preservation, has occasioned. No one has yet been so bold as to maintain that in this instance the human heart is incapable of love and formed alone for interested connections: that a mother, in presenting the breast to her child, has a view only to some future returns of advantage to herself.

If, in this relation, the period of anxiety, on the part of the parent, and of dependence or weakness on the part of the young be prolonged beyond the time that is usual in the case of other animals, these seeming disadvantages are more than compensated in the pleasure which a parent enjoys from the continuation of his cares and in the effect of a dependence which is the germ of that social connection which man is destined to have with his kind in a much higher form than is known in any other species of animals.

The infant's ground of connection with his parents in the earlier period of life is that of being placed in their hands and in a relation with them from which he cannot recede. He is born in society, and while unconscious of benefit or wrong, is anxiously preserved in his state. When he begins to perceive his condition and is in any measure left to choose for himself; he is ever at the heel of his parent and dreads being left behind as the most fatal misfortune. At every interval of separation, he longs to recover the company in which he was born, and feels, through life, whatever may affect the honor or welfare of his family as the most serious concern of his own.

Before the force of the first family affection is spent, relations multiply and instinctive attachments grow into habit. Brothers and sisters come to cooperate in the same cause together; and a third generation sometimes appears, before the second or the third are separated from the original stock; collaterals grow up together, still apprised of their relation, and even when separated are taught to regard consanguinity as a bond of connection which extends beyond the limits of acquaintance or personal intercourse of any sort.

It is thus that the supposed descendants of a race are multiplied into a tribe, in which many families are included, adopting some common point of honor, or some common cause, in which the kindred partake.

Under this denomination of a tribe or clan, numbers of men are leagued together and often endeared by the experience of affection, fidelity, and courage, while they mutually support and are supported, or run the career of fortune together.

The tenderness of parents had a specific name in the language of the Greeks. In ours, it is termed natural affection, as being peculiarly inspired by nature and precluding even the choice of its object.

Natural affection springs up in the soul as the milk springs in the mother's breast to furnish a nourishment to her child. Whether piety in the child be natural, in the same sense, may be questioned. He clings indeed to the parent's breast, or shrinks from a stranger; but these are perhaps no more than the first efforts of self-preservation, in which he abides by that which he has experienced to be friendly or safe, and declines, as doubtful, what is strange or unknown; and habit may confirm the predilection he has formed while he continues to apprehend, in the person of his parent, the source of every comfort of which he has any experience, or which he is any way qualified to receive.

That the relation of consanguinity beyond that of brother and sister, at least, operates as a mere occasion of acquaintance, intimacy, and cooperation in the same cause together is still less susceptible of doubt. Relations are attached, or are at variance, according as their humors agree; but the spirit of clanship, which is so frequent in human nature, abundantly proves a disposition in man to avail himself of every pretence upon which he can league with those among whom his lot and his acquaintance has fallen.

Company is the solace of human life, and it will not be disputed that in the absence of every interested design companions meet from a common dislike of solitude, or a common inclination to the same pursuits and occupations; nor will it be doubted that from mere acquaintance persons tried in fidelity, affection, and good understanding actually become friends on the most permanent foundations of attachment and confidence.

The love of company is a principle common to man with all the gregarious animals. So far, it is merely instinctive and gratified indiscriminately in the presence of a fellow creature of the same species. Animals, endowed with this instinct, will force their way through every impediment to join the herd they affect, but beyond the mere concourse of numbers rarely appear to have any selection or choice.

With man, the fact is different; he is ever disposed to select his company, and to shun, as well as to embrace, an acquaintance. The characters of men are unequal, and the choice of one frequently implies the rejection of another. But to select a companion, or a friend, is not to be unsociable: it is to affect society, but to know the distinction of good and evil in this important connection.

As men have a greater extent and variety of concerns, whether mistaken or real, in which their pursuits may interfere, so they have more frequent occasions of strife than are incident to individuals of any other species of gregarious animals. What we term reason in man, or intelligence so imperfect as his, is more liable than instinct to err and mistake its objects. Hence offenses are taken and given, and the minds of men alienated from one another upon imaginary as well as upon real grounds of dislike.

Mere estrangement approaches to jealousy; and men do not desire to associate with persons entirely unknown. Hence the species is never observed to act in one, but in manifold troops and companies, and although without any physical bar to prevent their union, are still observed under the notion of independence and freedom to affect separation.

Hence the multiplicity of hordes in barbarous ages; but, in human nature, separation itself has an effect in straitening the bands of society, for the members of each separate nation feel their connection the more that the name of fellow countryman stands in contradistinction to that of an alien.

In this divided state of the world incompatible interests are formed, or at least apprehended; and the members of different societies are engaged on opposite sides; affection to one society becomes animosity to another; and they are not always to be reckoned of the most sociable disposition who equally fawn upon all. Indifference, more than candor, is likely to produce the appearance of impartiality when the cause of our friend or our country is at stake.

Even here, however, what seems to divide the species tends

also to unite them in leagues more extensive than they would otherwise form. Hence the coalition of families, tribes and extensive tracts of country into nations under political establishments that combine the strength and the resources of many for common protection and safety.

The love of company is gratified in the resorts of a few; and predilection ever implies acquaintance and esteem; but national establishments far exceed these bounds and comprehend, in the same state or community, persons far removed from one another and mutually unknown.

Nations are formed upon a principle of expediency, and to obtain security against foreign enemies, or domestic disorders; but, notwithstanding this origin, the name of a country ever carries an object of the warmest affection, hence the ardent enthusiasm, with which the good citizen sacrifices to a public cause every personal consideration of ease, profit, and safety.

The progress of national enlargement by increase of people, or successive annexations of territory, is not restricted within any special limits. Ambition often leads the growing state to extend its dimensions far beyond any real advantage, and in the result of war, communities, once proud of their separate establishments and the lustre of their history, are made to discontinue their own institutions and to receive the laws by which they are governed from abroad.

When provinces remote from one another, without any national intercourse, participation of language, manners, or interest, are reduced to acknowledge a common head, or to join in their contributions to enrich a common master, the associating principle in such examples, if we must call it by that name, is force, or rather the ambition of sovereigns, than the will of the people, or even the interests of state. Upon this principle, the inhabitants of cities and territories, unknown to one another, become fellow subjects, and owe their connection to the force by which they were subdued, and by which they are kept in subjection. But this force itself was the combination of numbers employed in conquest.

The conquered become an accession to empire in which nations are absorbed, or changed into provinces that have no feeling of attachment, nor even community of interest. But, if empires thus extend beyond the limits to which the social affections of man have reached, these affections nevertheless continue to subsist in different divisions of the largest dominion. They subsist in the family, in the neighborhood, in the select company of acquaintance, and in the attachment of friends. There even arises, in the largest empires, a national spirit, with which the subject cordially serves his sovereign and contends for the honor and safety of his country.

The mind of man has a fellow feeling with what befalls a fellow creature, which is so much conceived as an appurtenance of human nature as in common language to be called humanity and considered as a characteristic of the species. Under the effects of this disposition, even to be a stranger is a recommendation and a ground of regard.

Much remains to be observed on this subject that cannot be classed with the appurtenances of mere animal nature. Where man rises above this predicament, his destination to range with a system and make a part in a comprehensive order of things becomes still more conspicuous. His understanding is a power of comprehension, qualifying him to perceive and to estimate the bearings of a whole through all its parts to some common end, or beneficial effect, and his moral judgments give sanction to the propriety of his own character or action in the society of his fellow creatures. The great distinction of right and wrong, of virtue and vice, on which men experience such extremes of complacence or indignation, of esteem or contempt, is formed on the dictates of a social disposition, which receives with favor and love what constitutes the good of mankind, or rejects, with disapprobation and abhorrence, what is of a contrary nature.

Man's specific talent for expression and communication, also notwithstanding the diversity of tongues which with other circumstances contributes to keep separate hordes in a state of estrangement from one another, serves upon the whole to reunite the efforts of mankind to one common purpose of advancement in the progress of intelligence. The lights of science are communicated from the parts in which they sprang up, to the remotest corners of the habitable world. The works of singular genius are a common benefit to mankind, and the whole species, on every quarter, in every nation, and in every age, cooperates together for one common end of information, invention, science, and art. No one member of this great body is detached from the whole, or can enjoy his good, or suffer his evil, without some participation with others.

13

Dugald Stewart

THE DESIRE OF SOCIETY

ABSTRACTING FROM THOSE AFFECTIONS which interest us in the happiness of others and from all the advantages which we ourselves derive from the social union, we are led by a natural and instinctive desire to associate with our species. This principle is easily discernible in the minds of children long before the dawn of reason. "Attend only," says an intelligent and accurate observer, "to the eyes, the features, and the gestures of a child on the breast when another child is presented to it; both instantly, previous to the possibility of instruction or habit, exhibit the most evident expressions of joy. Their eyes sparkle, and their features and gestures demonstrate, in the most unequivocal manner, a mutual attachment. When farther advanced, children, who are strangers to each other, though their social appetite be equally strong, discover a mutual shyness of approach, which, however, is soon conquered by the more powerful instinct of association."[1]

In the lower animals, too, very evident traces of the same instinct appear. In some of these we observe a species of union strikingly analogous to political associations among men; in others we observe occasional unions among individuals to accomplish a particular purpose—to repel, for example, a hostile assault—but

---

Reprinted from Dugald Stewart, *Philosophy of the Active and Moral Powers of Man,* in *Collected Works,* W. Hamilton, ed. (Edinburgh, 1855), VII, 135–42.

[1]   Smellie's *Philosophy of Natural History,* p. 416.

there are also various tribes which discover a desire of society and a pleasure in the company of their own species without an apparent reference to any farther end. Thus we frequently see horses, when confined alone in an enclosure, neglect their food and break the fences to join their companions in the contiguous field. Every person must have remarked the spirit and alacrity with which this animal exerts himself on the road when accompanied by another animal of his own species in comparison of what he discovers when traveling alone; and with respect to oxen and cows, it has been asserted that even in the finest pasture they do not fatten so rapidly in a solitary state as when they feed together in a herd.

What is the final cause of the associating instinct in such animals as have now been mentioned, it is not easy to conjecture, unless we suppose that it was intended merely to augment the sum of their enjoyments. But whatever opinion we may form on this point, it is indisputable that the instinctive determination is a strong one and that it produces striking effects on the habits of the animal, even when external circumstances are the most unfavorable to its operation. Horses and oxen, for example, when deprived of companions of their own species, associate and become attached to each other. The same thing sometimes happens between individuals that belong to tribes naturally hostile, as between dogs and cats, or between a cat and a bird.

If these facts be candidly considered, there will appear but little reason to doubt the existence of the social instinct in our own species when it is so agreeable to the general analogy of nature as displayed through the rest of the animal creation. As this point, however, has been controverted warmly by authors of eminence, it will be necessary to consider it with some attention.

The question with respect to the social or the solitary nature of man seems to me to amount to this, whether man has any disinterested principles which lead him to unite with his fellow creatures, or whether the social union be the result of prudential views of self-interest, suggested by the experience of his own insufficiency to procure the objects of his natural desires. Of these two opinions Hobbes has maintained the latter and has endeavored to establish it by proving that in what he calls the state of nature every man is an enemy to his brother, and that it was the experience of the evils arising from these hostile dispositions that induced men to unite in a political society. In proof of this he insists on the terror which children feel at the sight of a stranger; on the apprehension which, he says, a person naturally feels when he hears the tread of a foot in the dark; on the universal invention of locks and keys; and on various other circumstances of a similar nature.

That this theory of Hobbes is contrary to the universal history of mankind cannot be disputed. Man has always been found in a social state; and there is reason even for thinking, that the principles of union which nature has implanted in his heart operate with the greatest force in those situations in which the advantages of the social union are the smallest. As society advances, the relations among individuals are continually multiplied and man is rendered the more necessary to man; but it may be doubted if in a period of great refinement the social affections be as warm and powerful as when the species were wandering in the forest.

Besides, it does not seem to be easy to conceive in what manner Hobbes's supposition could be realized. Surely, if there be a foundation for anything laid in the constitution of man's nature it is for family union. The infant of our species continues longer in a helpless state and requires longer the protecting care of both parents than the young of any other animal. Before the first child is able to provide for itself a second and a third are produced and thus the union of the sexes, supposing it at first to have been merely casual, is insensibly confirmed by habit and cemented by the common interest which both parents take in their offspring. So just is the simple and beautiful statement of the fact given by Montesquieu, "that man is born in society, and there he remains."

From these considerations, it appears that the social union does not take its rise from views of self-interest, but that it forms a necessary part of the condition of man from the constitution of his nature. It is true indeed that before he begins to reflect he finds himself connected with society by a thousand ties, so that, independently of any social instinct, prudence would undoubtedly prevent him from abandoning his fellow creatures. But still it is evident that the social instinct forms a part of human nature and has a tendency to unite men even when they stand in no need of each other's assistance. Were the case otherwise, prudence and the social disposition would be only different names for the same principle, whereas it is matter of common remark that although the two principles be by no means inconsistent when kept within reasonable bounds, yet that the former, when it rises to any excess, is in a great measure exclusive of the latter. I hinted, too, already, that it is in societies where individuals are most independent of each other as to their animal wants that the social principles operate with the greatest force.

According to the view of the subject now given, the multiplied wants and necessities of man in his infant state, by laying the foundation of the family union, impose upon our species as a necessary part of their condition those social connections which are so essential to our improvement and happiness. . . . The considerations now stated afford a beautiful illustration of the beneficent design with which the physical condition of man is adapted to the principles of his moral constitution, an adaptation so striking that it is not surprising those philosophers, who are fond of simplifying the theory of human nature, should have attempted to account for the origin of these principles from the habits which our external circumstances impose. In this, as in many other instances, their attention has been misled by the spirit of system from those wonderful combinations of means to particular ends which are everywhere conspicuous in the universe. It is not by the physical condition of man that the essential principles of his mind are formed, but the one is fitted to the other by the same superintending wisdom which adapts the fin of the fish to the water and the wing of the bird to the air and which scatters the seeds of the vegetable tribes in those soils and exposures where they are fitted to vegetate. It is not the wants and necessities of his animal being which *create* his social principles and which produce an artificial and interested league among individuals who are naturally solitary and hostile; but, determined by instinct to society, endowed with innumerable principles which have a reference to his fellow creatures, he is placed by the condition of his birth in that element where alone the perfection and happiness of his nature are to be found.

In speaking of the lower animals, I before observed that such of them as are instinctively social discover the secret workings of nature even when removed from the society of their kind. This fact amounts, in *their* case, to a demonstration of that mutual adaptation of the different parts of nature to each other which I have just remarked. It demonstrates that the structure of their *internal* frame is purposely adjusted to that *external* scene in which they are destined to be placed. As the lamb, when it strikes with its forehead while yet unarmed, proves that it is not its weapons which determine its instincts, but that it has preexistent instincts suited to its weapons, so when we see an animal, deprived of the sight of his fellows, cling to a stranger, or disarm, by his caresses, the rage of an enemy, we perceive the workings of a social instinct not only not superinduced by external circumstances, but manifesting itself in spite of circumstances which are adverse to its operation. The same remark may be extended to man. When in solitude he languishes, and by making companions of the lower animals, or by attaching himself to inanimate objects, strives to fill up the void of which he is conscious. "Were I in a desert" (says an author who, amid all his extravagances and absurdities, sometimes writes like a *wise* man, and where the moral feelings are at all concerned, never fails to write like a *good* man)—"Were I in a desert, I would find out wherewith in it to call forth my affections. If I could not do better, I would fasten them upon some sweet myrtle, or seek some melancholy cypress to connect myself to; I would court their shade and greet them kindly for their protection. I would cut my name upon them and swear they were the loveliest trees throughout the desert. If their leaves withered, I would teach myself to mourn, and when they rejoiced, I would rejoice along with them."

The Count de Lauzun was confined by Louis XIV for nine years in the Castle of Pignerol, in a small room where no light could enter but from a chink in the roof. In this solitude he attached himself to a spider and contrived for some time to amuse himself with attempting to tame it, with catching flies for its support, and with superintending the progress of its web. The jailer discovered his amusement and killed the spider, and the Count used afterwards to declare that the pang he felt on the occasion could be compared only to that of a mother for the loss of a child.[2]

This anecdote is quoted by Lord Kames in his *Sketches* and by the late Lord Auckland in his *Principles of Penal Law*. It is remarkable that both these learned and respectable writers should have introduced it into their works on account of the shocking incident of the jailer and as a proof of the pure and unprovoked malice of which some minds are capable, without taking any notice of it as a beautiful picture of the feelings of a man of sensibility in a state of solitude and of his disposition to create to himself some object upon which he may rest those affections which have a reference to society.

It will be said that *these* are the feelings of one who has experienced the pleasures of social life and that no inference can be drawn from such facts in opposition to Hobbes. But if they do not prove in man an instinctive impulse toward society prior to experience, they at least prove that he feels a delight in the society of his fellow creatures, which no view of self-interest is sufficient to explain.

It does not belong to our present speculation to illustrate the importance of the social union to our improvement and our happiness. Its subserviency to both (abstracting entirely from its necessity for the complete gratification of our physical wants) is much greater than we should be disposed at first to apprehend. In proof of this, it is sufficient to mention here its connection with the culture of our intellectual faculties and with the development of our moral principles. Illustrations of this may be drawn from the low state in which both these parts of our nature are generally found in the deaf and dumb and from the effects which a few months'

2   In Delille's poem on *the Imagination*, the same anecdote, which is here told of the Count de Lauzun, is attributed to Pelisson, a celebrated literary and political character in the reign of Louis XIV, who was confined four years in the Bastile, on account of his connection with the disgraced minister *Foucquet*. See end of Chant vi.

education sometimes has in unfolding their mental powers. The pleasing change which in the meantime takes place in their once vacant countenances, when animated and lighted up by an active and inquisitive mind, cannot escape the notice of the most careless observer.

IV. Individual Actions and Unintended Social Outcomes

14

Thomas Reid

BEES AND MEN: INSTINCT
AND THE LIMITATIONS
OF REASON

By INSTINCT, I mean a natural blind impulse to certain actions, without having any end in view, without deliberation, and
very often without any conception of what we do.

Thus, a man breathes while he is alive by the alternate contrac-
tion and relaxation of certain muscles by which the chest, and of
consequence the lungs, are contracted and dilated. There is no
reason to think that an infant newborn knows that breathing is
necessary to life in its new state, that he knows how it may be performed, or even that he has any thought or conception of that
operation. Yet he breathes as soon as he is born, with perfect
regularity, as if he had been taught and got the habit by long
practice.

By the same kind of principle, a newborn child, when its
stomach is emptied and nature has brought milk into the mother's
breast, sucks and swallows its food as perfectly as if it knew the
principles of that operation and had got the habit of working
according to them.

Sucking and swallowing are very complex operations. Anatomists describe about thirty pairs of muscles that must be em-

Reprinted from Thomas Reid, *Essays on the Active Powers of Man,* in
Works, W. Hamilton, ed. (Edinburg, 1863), II, 545–47, 558, 560.
Title supplied.

ployed in every draught. Of those muscles, every one must be
served by its proper nerve and can make no exertion but by some
influence communicated by the nerve. The exertion of all those
muscles and nerves is not simultaneous. They must succeed each
other in a certain order, and their order is no less necessary than
the exertion itself.

This regular train of operations is carried on according to the
nicest rules of art by the infant who has neither art, nor science,
nor experience, nor habit.

That the infant feels the uneasy sensation of hunger, I admit,
and that it sucks no longer than till this sensation be removed.
But who informed it that this uneasy sensation might be removed,
or by what means? That it knows nothing of this is evident, for it
will as readily suck a finger, or a bit of stick, as the nipple.

By a like principle it is that infants cry when they are pained
or hurt; that they are afraid when left alone, especially in the dark;
that they start when in danger of falling; that they are terrified
by an angry countenance, or an angry tone of voice, and are
soothed and comforted by a placid countenance, and by soft and
gentle tones of voice.

In the animals we are best acquainted with, and which we look
upon as the more perfect of the brute creation, we see much the
same instincts as in the human kind, or very similar ones, suited
to the particular state and manner of life of the animal.

Besides these, there are in brute animals instincts peculiar to
each tribe by which they are fitted for defense, for offense, or for
providing for themselves and for their offspring.

It is not more certain that nature hath furnished various animals
with various weapons of offense and defense than that the same
nature hath taught them how to use them: the bull and the ram to
butt, the horse to kick, the dog to bite, the lion to use his paws, the
boar his tusks, the serpent his fangs, and the bee and wasp their
sting.

The manufactures of animals, if we may call them by that name,
present us with a wonderful variety of instincts belonging to particular species, whether of the social or of the solitary kind; the
nests of birds, so similar in their situation and architecture in the

same kind, so various in different kinds; the webs of spiders, and of other spinning animals; the ball of the silkworm; the nests of ants and other mining animals; the combs of wasps, hornets, and bees; the dams and houses of beavers.

The instinct of animals is one of the most delightful and instructive parts of a most pleasant study, that of natural history, and deserves to be more cultivated than it has yet been.

Every manufacturing art among men was invented by some man, improved by others, and brought to perfection by time and experience. Men learn to work in it by long practice which produces a habit. The arts of men vary in every age and in every nation and are found only in those who have been taught them.

The manufactures of animals differ from those of men in many striking particulars.

No animal of the species can claim the invention. No animal ever introduced any new improvement or any variation from the former practice. Every one of the species has equal skill from the beginning, without teaching, without experience or habit. Every one has its art by a kind of inspiration. I do not mean that it is inspired with the principles or rules of the art, but with the ability and inclination of working in it to perfection, without any knowledge of its principles, rules, or end.

The more sagacious animals may be taught to do many things which they do not by instinct. What they are taught to do, they do with more or less skill, according to their sagacity and their training. But in their own arts, they need no teaching nor training, nor is the art ever improved or lost. Bees gather their honey and their wax, they fabricate their combs, and rear their young at this day, neither better nor worse than they did when Virgil so sweetly sung their works.

The work of every animal is indeed like the works of nature, perfect in its kind, and can bear the most critical examination of the mechanic or the mathematician. One example from the animal last mentioned may serve to illustrate this.

Bees, it is well known, construct their combs with small cells on both sides, fit both for holding their store of honey and for rearing their young. There are only three possible figures of the cells, which can make them all equal and similar, without any useless interstices. These are the equilateral triangle, the square, and the regular hexagon.

It is well known to mathematicians that there is not a fourth way possible in which a plane may be cut into little spaces that shall be equal, similar, and regular, without leaving any interstices. Of the three, the hexagon is the most proper, both for conveniency and strength. Bees, as if they knew this, make their cells regular hexagons.

As the combs have cells on both sides, the cells may either be exactly opposite, having partition against partition, or the bottom of a cell may rest upon the partitions between the cells on the other side which will serve as a buttress to strengthen it. The last way is best for strength; accordingly, the bottom of each cell rests against the point where three partitions meet on the other side, which gives it all the strength possible.

The bottom of a cell may either be one plane perpendicular to the side-partition or it may be composed of several planes meeting in a solid angle in the middle point. It is only in one of these two ways that all the cells can be similar without losing room. And for the same intention, the planes of which the bottom is composed, if there be more than one, must be three in number and neither more nor fewer.

It has been demonstrated that by making the bottoms of the cells to consist of three planes meeting in a point, there is a saving of material and labor no way inconsiderable. The bees, as if acquainted with these principles of solid geometry, follow them most accurately; the bottom of each cell being composed of three planes which make obtuse angles with the side-partitions and with one another and meet in a point in the middle of the bottom; the three angles of this bottom being supported by three partitions on the other side of the comb and the point of it by the common intersection of those three partitions.

One instance more of the mathematical skill displayed in the structure of a honecomb deserves to be mentioned.

It is a curious mathematical problem at what precise angle the three planes which compose the bottom of a cell ought to meet in order to make the greatest possible saving, or the least expense, of material and labor.

This is one of those problems belonging to the higher parts of mathematics which are called problems of *maxima* and *minima*. It has been resolved by some mathematicians, particularly by the ingenious Mr. Maclaurin, by a fluxionary calculation, which is to be found in the "Transactions of the Royal Society of London." He has determined precisely the angle required, and he found, by the most exact mensuration the subject could admit, that it is the very angle in which the three planes in the bottom of the cell of a honey-comb do actually meet.

Shall we ask here, who taught the bee the properties of solids, and to resolve problems of *maxima* and *minima*? If a honey-comb were a work of human art, every man of common sense would conclude without hesitation that he who invented the construction must have understood the principles on which it is constructed.

We need not say that bees know none of these things. They work most geometrically, without any knowledge of geometry; somewhat like a child, who, by turning the handle of an organ, makes good music, without any knowledge of music.

The art is not in the child but in him who made the organ. In like manner, when a bee makes its comb so geometrically, the geometry is not in the bee but in that great Geometrician who made the bee and made all things in number, weight, and measure. . .

We have seen how by instinct and habit—a kind of mechanical principles—man, without any expense of thought, without deliberation or will, is led to many actions necessary for his preservation and well-being, which, without those principles, all his skill and wisdom would not have been able to accomplish.

It may perhaps be thought that his deliberate and voluntary actions are to be guided by his reason.

But it ought to be observed that he is a voluntary agent long before he has the use of reason. Reason and virtue, the prerogatives of man, are the latest growth. They come to maturity by slow degrees and are too weak in the greater part of the species to secure the preservation of individuals and of communities and to produce that varied scene of human life in which they are to be exercised and improved.

Therefore, the wise Author of our being hath implanted in human nature many inferior principles of action, which, with little or no aid of reason or virtue, preserve the species and produce the various exertions and the various changes and revolutions which we observe upon the theater of life.

In this busy scene, reason and virtue have access to act their parts and do often produce great and good effects; but whether they interpose or not, there are actors of an inferior order that will carry on the play and produce a variety of events, good or bad.

Reason, if it were perfect, would lead men to use the proper means of preserving their own lives and continuing their kind. But the Author of our being hath not thought fit to leave this task to reason alone, otherwise the race would long ago have been extinct. He hath given us, in common with other animals, appetites by which those important purposes are secured whether men be wise or foolish, virtuous, or vicious.

Reason, if it were perfect, would lead men neither to lose the benefit of their active powers by inactivity nor to overstrain them by excessive labor. But nature hath given a powerful assistant to reason, by making inactivity a grievous punishment to itself; and by annexing the pain of lassitude to excessive labor.

Reason, if it were perfect, would lead us to desire power, knowledge, and the esteem and affection of our fellowmen, as means of promoting our own happiness and of being useful to others. Here again, nature, to supply the defects of reason, hath given us a strong natural desire of those objects which leads us to pursue them without regard to their utility. . .

We are placed in this world by the Author of our being, surrounded with many objects that are necessary or useful to us, and with many that may hurt us. We are led not by reason and self-love only, but by many instincts and appetites and natural desires to seek the former and to avoid the latter.

But of all the things of this world, man may be the most useful or the most hurtful to man. Every man is in the power of every man with whom he lives. Every man has power to do much good to his fellowmen and to do more hurt.

We cannot live without the society of men, and it would be impossible to live in society, if men were not disposed to do much of that good to men, and but little of that hurt which it is in their power to do.

But how shall this end, so necessary to the existence of human society, and consequently to the existence of the human species be accomplished?

If we judge from analogy, we must conclude that in this, as in other parts of our conduct, our rational principles are aided by principles of an inferior order similar to those by which many brute animals live in society with their species, and that by means of such principles, that degree of regularity is observed which we find in all societies of men, whether wise or foolish, virtuous or vicious.

The benevolent affections planted in human nature appear therefore no less necessary for the preservation of the human species than the appetites of hunger and thirst.

15

Adam Smith

THE INVISIBLE HAND

They [the rich] consume little more than the poor; and in spite of their natural selfishness and rapacity, though they mean only their own conveniency, though the sole end which they propose from the labors of all the thousands whom they employ be the gratification of their own vain and insatiable desires, they divide with the poor the produce of all their improvements. They are led by an invisible hand to make nearly the same distribution of the necessaries of life which would have been made had the earth been divided into equal portions among all its inhabitants; and thus, without intending, without knowing it, advance the interest of the society and afford means to the multiplication of the species.

II

As every individual . . . endeavors as much as he can both to employ his capital in the support of domestic industry, and so to direct that industry that its produce may be of the greatest value, every individual necessarily labors to render the annual revenue of the society as great as he can. He generally indeed neither in-

---

The first quotation is reprinted from *The Theory of Moral Sentiments* (London and New York: G. Bell and Sons, 1892), pp. 264–65, the second from *The Wealth of Nations* (Edinburgh: Adam and Charles Black, 1863), p. 199. Title supplied.

tends to promote the public interest nor knows how much he is promoting it. By preferring the support of domestic to that of foreign industry, he intends only his own security; and by directing that industry in such a manner as its produce may be of the greatest value, he intends only his own gain, and he is in this, as in many other cases, led by an invisible hand to promote an end which was no part of his intention. Nor is it always the worse for the society that it was no part of it. By pursuing his own interest he frequently promotes that of the society more effectually than when he really intends to promote it. I have never known much good done by those who affected to trade for the public good. It is an affectation indeed not very common among merchants and very few words need be employed in dissuading them from it.

16

Adam Ferguson

UNINTENDED
ESTABLISHMENTS

MANKIND, in following the present sense of their minds, in striving to remove inconveniences, or to gain apparent and contiguous advantages, arrive at ends which even their imagination could not anticipate, and pass on, like other animals, in the track of their nature, without perceiving its end. He who first said, "I will appropriate this field; I will leave it to my heirs," did not perceive that he was laying the foundation of civil laws and political establishments. He who first ranged himself under a leader did not perceive that he was setting the example of a permanent subordination, under the pretense of which the rapacious were to seize his possessions and the arrogant to lay claim to his service.

Men in general are sufficiently disposed to occupy themselves in forming projects and schemes, but he who would scheme and project for others will find an opponent in every person who is disposed to scheme for himself. Like the winds that come we know not whence and blow whithersoever they list, the forces of society are derived from an obscure and distant origin. They arise, long before the date of philosophy, from the instincts, not from the speculations of men. The crowd of mankind are directed,

Reprinted from Adam Ferguson, *An Essay on the History of Civil Society* (8th ed.; Philadelphia, 1819), pp. 221–26. Title supplied.

in their establishments and measures, by the circumstances in which they are placed; and seldom are turned from their way to follow the plan of any single projector.

Every step and every movement of the multitude, even in what are termed enlightened ages, are made with equal blindness to the future, and nations stumble upon establishments, which are indeed the result of human action, but not the execution of any human design. (De Retz's *Memoirs*). If Cromwell said that man never mounts higher than when he knows not whither he is going, it may with more reason be affirmed of communities that they admit the greatest revolutions where no change is intended and that the most refined politicians do not always know whither they are leading the state by their projects.

If we listen to the testimony of modern history and to that of the most authentic parts of the ancient; if we attend to the practice of nations in every quarter of the world, and in every condition, whether that of the barbarian or the polished, we shall find very little reason to retract this assertion. No constitution is formed by concert, no government is copied from a plan. The members of a small state contend for equality; the members of a greater find themselves classed in a certain manner that lays a foundation for monarchy. They proceed from one form of government to another by easy transitions and frequently under old names adopt a new constitution. The seeds of every form are lodged in human nature; they spring up and ripen with the season. The prevalence of a particular species is often derived from an imperceptible ingredient mingled in the soil.

We are therefore to receive with caution the traditionary histories of ancient legislators and founders of states. Their names have long been celebrated; their supposed plans have been admired; and what were probably the consequences of an early situation is in every instance considered as an effect of design. An author and a work, like cause and effect, are perpetually coupled together. This is the simplest form under which we can consider the establishment of nations; and we ascribe to a previous design what came to be known only by experience, what no human wisdom could foresee, and what, without the concurring humor and disposition of his age, no authority could enable an individual to execute.

If men, during ages of extensive reflection, and employed in the search of improvement, are wedded to their institutions, and, laboring under heavy acknowledged inconveniences, cannot break loose from the trammels of custom, what shall we suppose their humor to have been in the times of Romulus and Lycurgus? They were not surely more disposed to embrace the schemes of innovators, or to shake off the impressions of habit; they were not more pliant and ductile, when their minds were more circumscribed.

We imagine perhaps that rude nations must have so strong a sense of the defects under which they labor and be so conscious that reformations are requisite in their manners, that they must be ready to adopt, with joy, every plan of improvement, and to receive every plausible proposal with implicit compliance. And we are thus inclined to believe that the harp of Orpheus could effect in one age what the eloquence of Plato could not produce in another. We mistake, however, the characteristic of simple ages: mankind then appear to feel the fewest defects and are then least desirous to enter on reformations.

The reality, in the meantime, of certain establishments at Rome and at Sparta, cannot be disputed; but it is probable that the government of both these states took its rise from the situation and genius of the people, not from the projects of single men; that the celebrated warrior and statesman, who are considered as the founders of those nations, only acted a superior part among numbers who were disposed to the same institution; and that they left to posterity a renown, pointing them out as the inventors of many practices which had been already in use and which helped to form their own manners and genius, as well as those of their countrymen.

It has been formerly observed, that, in many particulars, the customs of simple nations coincide with what is ascribed to the invention of early statesmen; that the model of republican government, the senate, and the assembly of the people; that even the equality of property, or the community of goods, were not reserved to the invention or contrivance of singular men.

If we consider Romulus as the founder of the Roman state, certainly he who killed his brother, that he might reign alone, did not desire to come under restraints from the controlling power of the senate, nor to refer the councils of his sovereignty to the decision of a collective body. Love of dominion is, by its nature, averse to restraint; and this chieftain, like every leader in a rude age, probably found a class of men ready to intrude on his councils, and without whom he could not proceed. He met with occasions on which, as at the sound of a trumpet, the body of the people assembled and took resolutions, which any individual might in vain dispute, or attempt to control; and Rome, which commenced on the general plan of every artless society, found lasting improvements in the pursuit of temporary expedients, and digested her political frame in adjusting the pretensions of parties which arose in the state.

17

Dugald Stewart

GOVERNMENT, UNINTENDED DEVELOPMENTS, EXPEDIENCY, INNOVATION

IN EVERY SOCIETY . . . which, in consequence of the general spirit of its government, enjoys the blessings of tranquillity and liberty, a great part of the political order which we are apt to ascribe to legislative sagacity is the natural result of the selfish pursuits of individuals. . .

In every state of society which has yet existed, the multitude has in general acted from the immediate impulse of passion, or from the pressure of their wants and necessities; and therefore, what we commonly call the political order is, at least in a great measure, the result of the passions and wants of man combined with the circumstances of his situation; or in other words, it is chiefly the result of the wisdom of nature. So beautifully indeed do these passions and circumstances act in subserviency to her designs, and so invariably have they been found in the history of past ages to conduct him in time to certain beneficial arrangements, that we can hardly bring ourselves to believe that the end was not foreseen by those who were engaged in the pursuit. Even in those rude periods of society, when, like the lower animals, he

Reprinted from Dugald Stewart, *Collected Works*, W. Hamilton, ed., (Edinburgh, 1854), II, 227 and *Collected Works,* W. Hamilton, ed. (Edinburgh, 1856), IX, 417–24. Title supplied.

follows blindly his instinctive principles of action, he is led by an invisible hand and contributes his share to the execution of a plan of the nature and advantages of which he has no conception. The operations of the bee when it begins, for the first time, to form its cell convey to us a striking image of the efforts of unenlightened man, in conducting the operations of an infant government. . .

I before took notice . . . of that natural aristocracy which we find in every community arising from the original differences among men in respect of intellectual and moral qualities. That these were intended to lay a foundation for civil government, no man can doubt who does not reject altogether the inferences which are drawn from the appearances of design in the human constitution.

As the possession of power, however, is to the best of men a source of corruption, the general utility requires that some checks should be imposed on the pretensions of the aristocracy; and the only effectual checks may be easily perceived to be a *popular assembly* on the one hand to secure the enactment of equal laws, and a *single magistrate* on the other possessing the sole executive power to prevent the competitions and rivalships among the order of nobility.

The fact which I have now stated with respect to the existence of a natural aristocracy in every community, as well as the advantages to be derived from it, if properly restrained and regulated, and the mischiefs to be apprehended from it, on a contrary supposition, are eloquently described in the following passage from Lord Bolingbroke:—"It seems to me that in order to sustain the moral system of the universe, at a certain point far below that of ideal perfection (for we are made capable of conceiving what we are not capable of attaining), it has pleased the author of Nature to mingle, from time to time, among the societies of men, a few, and but a few, of those on whom He has been graciously pleased to confer a larger portion of the ethereal spirit than in the ordinary course of His providence He bestows on the sons of men. These are they who engross almost the whole reason of the species, who are born to direct, to guide, and to preserve. . . . If they retire from the world, their splendor accompanies them and enlightens even the darkness of their retreat. If they take a part in public life, the effect is never indifferent. They either appear the instruments of Divine vengeance, and their course through the world is marked by desolation and oppression, by poverty and servitude; or they are the guardian angels of the country they inhabit, studious to avert the most distant evil, and to procure peace and plenty, and the greatest of human blessings—Liberty."[1]

Since then there is in every society a natural aristocracy arising partly from original inequalities among men, and partly from the influence of birth and fortune, in what manner shall the legislator avail himself of the assistance of those who compose it and at the same time guard against the dangers to be apprehended from their uncontrolled authority? The answer seems obvious. Form that order of men who, from their situation in life, are most likely to comprehend the greatest number of individuals of this description into a *senate* possessing no share of the executive power and control their legislative proceedings by the executive magistrate, *on the one hand*, and by an assembly of popular representatives *on the other*.

"The people without the senate," says Harrington, "would want wisdom; the senate without the people would want honesty."[2]

In stating these general principles, I would not be understood to insinuate that it is possible to devise a plan of government universally applicable to all the situations of mankind. On the contrary, nothing can be more certain or more evident than this— that as the form of a government has an influence on the character of the people, so there is a certain national character necessary to support the government, and which, while it continues the same, will render all violent innovations impracticable. Even where a despotism is established, the situation of the people can be improved only by very slow degrees; and any violent attempt to alter it has in general produced only a change of masters, after a short paroxysm of bloodshed and anarchy.

Neither would I wish it to be understood that governments have in general taken their rise from political wisdom. On the contrary,

1   *Letter on the Spirit of Patriotism, Works,* Vol. IV, pp. 187, 190.
2   *Oceana.*

almost every one of which we have any account has been the gradual result of time and experience, of circumstances and emergencies. This we may affirm to have been universally the case with those which have taken their rise in the rude periods of society; for surely no person without extreme credulity can listen to the accounts in ancient historians of those fabulous legislators, who by the force of eloquence or the reputation of wisdom assembled together a set of savages, who formerly wandered in the woods, convinced them of the utility of government and persuaded them to submit to any regulations they should think proper to prescribe. The case is considerably different in a more enlightened age. A statesman may avail himself of the power he possesses in introducing new institutions which in process of time may produce important effects on the character of a nation; or a people who have been trained to political order under one form of government may, after a violent revolution, choose (like the American States) to introduce among themselves a new set of usages and institutions. But even in such instances, there are certain limits within which innovations are practicable. They must have a certain degree of reference to the character and manners of the people, otherwise it is impossible that they should permanently maintain the good order or secure the happiness of the community. . .

We may observe, farther, as a proof of the impossibility of establishing general political rules, which are to apply universally to mankind, that the institutions which it is expedient for a state to adopt are often determined by circumstances external to itself; by the relation, for example, in which it stands to the states in its neighborhood.

Thus when Charles the Seventh of France, under the pretense of keeping always on foot a force sufficient to defend the kingdom against the sudden invasions of the English, established the first standing army known in Europe,[3] self-preservation made it necessary for the other nations of the Continent to follow his example; and in this manner a change which essentially affected their in-

3   A.D. 1445. See Robertson, Vol. I, p. 94 [Dublin edit. 1770. *Charles V., Preliminary View of the State of Europe*, Sect. ii].

ternal policy was recommended to them, or rather forced upon them, by the measures of a foreign prince.

The extent of territory too, and the amount of population which a state may possess with advantage (in either of which a change will require a correspondent change in the political institutions), may frequently depend on circumstances external to itself. In the case of states placed in the neighborhood of each other, a certain equality is necessary to procure to each that degree of consideration which may secure its independence. In the opinions of many politicians, the happiest situation and the most favorable to the human character, in which mankind have ever been placed, is where they have been formed into small and independent republics; but in modern Europe, the republics of the same extent, with those of ancient Greece, appear so insignificant when compared with the extensive monarchies with which they are surrounded, that they resemble (to borrow an allusion of Dr. Ferguson's) the shrubs in a wood which are choked by the trees under whose shadow they grow.[4] The disproportion is so great as to frustrate the advantages with which they would otherwise be attended. The same author remarks, that "when the kingdoms of Spain were united; when the great fiefs in France were annexed to the Crown, it was no longer expedient for the nations of Great Britain to continue disjoined."[5] Abstracting entirely from their relative interests, or the comparative advantages which they derived from the union of the crowns, the alternations in the state of the great continental powers rendered that event equally necessary to the safety of both.

These miscellaneous remarks may, I hope, be of some use as a supplement to the theoretical views of government given by Montesquieu and his commentators.

I now proceed to make a few observations on the peculiar advantages of that combination of political powers which takes place in our own constitution.

Before, however, I enter on this subject, it may be proper for me

[4]   *Essay on Civil Society*, Part I. Sect. ix. p. 100, edit. 1793.
[5]   Ibid., p. 99.

to explain the idea I annex to the word *constitution*, a word often used in a very vague and inaccurate manner and which has sometimes been defined in such a way as to convey a false notion of the *origin* of our government. Such an explanation is the more necessary as in consequence of an erroneous conception of the true import of this expression, some foreign politicians have been led to assert that in England there is no constitution at all; inasmuch as there are no fundamental laws of superior authority to the acts of the existing legislature. The English government (it is said) has been the gradual offspring of circumstances and events, and its different parts arose at different times—some of them from acts of the legislature prompted by emergencies and some of them from long-established customs or usages, of which it is not always possible to trace the origin, so that no part of it is sanctioned by an authority paramount to that which gives force to every other law by which we are governed. It is pretended therefore that there are no fundamental or essential principles in our government which fix a limit to the possibility of legislative enroachment and to which an appeal could be made if a particular law should appear to be hostile to the rights and liberties of the people. But surely the conclusion in this argument does not follow from the premises. For do we not every day speak of laws being *constitutional* or *unconstitutional*; and do not these words convey to men of plain understanding a very distinct and intelligible meaning, a meaning which no person can pretend to misapprehend, who is not disposed to cavil about expressions?

It appears to me that what we call the *constitution* differs from our other laws, not in its *origin*, but in the *importance of the subject to which it refers and in the systematical connection of its different principles*. It may, I think, be defined to be that form of government and that mode of administering it which is agreeable to the *general* spirit and tendency of our established laws and usages.

According to this view of the subject, I apprehend that the constitution *taken as a whole* ought to modify every new institution which is introduced, so that it may accord with its general *spirit*;

although every part of this constitution *taken separately*, arose itself from no higher authority than the common acts of our present legislature.

To illustrate this proposition it may be proper to remark that although the constitution was the gradual result of circumstances which may be regarded as accidental and irregular, yet that the very mode of its formation necessarily produced a certain consistence and analogy in its different parts, so as to give to the whole a sort of systematical appearance. For unless every new institution which was successively introduced had possessed a certain reference or affinity to the laws and usages existing before, it could not possibly have been permanent in its operation. Wherever a constitution has existed for ages and men have enjoyed tranquillity under it, it is a proof that its great and fundamental principles are all animated by the same congenial spirit. In such a constitution, when any law contrary to the spirit of the rest is occasionally introduced, it soon falls into desuetude and oblivion, while those which accord in their general character and tendency acquire additional stability from the influence of time and from the mutual support which they lend to each other. Of such a law we may say with propriety that it is *unconstitutional*, not because we dispute the authority from which it proceeds, but because it is contrary to the spirit and analogy of the laws which we have been accustomed to obey.

Something similar to this obtains with respect to languages. *These*, as well as governments, are the gradual result of time and experience, and not of philosophical speculation; yet every language, in process of time, acquires a great degree of systematical beauty. When a new word, or a new combination of words, is introduced, it takes its rise from the same origin with every other expression which the language contains—the desire of an individual to communicate his own thoughts or feelings to others. But this consideration alone is not sufficient to justify the use of it. Before it is allowed by good writers or speakers to incorporate itself with those words which have the sanction of time in their favor, it must be shown that it is not disagreeable to the general analogy of the language, otherwise it is soon laid aside as an innovation, revolting, anomalous, and *ungrammatical*. It is much in the same manner that we come to apply the epithet *unconstitutional* to a law.

The zeal therefore which genuine patriots have always shown for the maintenance of the constitution, so far from being unreasonable, will be most strongly felt by the prudent and intelligent, because such men know that political wisdom is much more the result of experience than of speculation and that when a Constitution has been matured by such slow steps as ours has been, in consequence of the struggles of able and enlightened individuals, jealous of their liberties and anxious to preserve them, it may be considered as the result of the accumulated experience and wisdom of ages; possessing *on that very account* the strongest of all possible recommendations and sanctions, as experimental proof of its excellence, of its fitness to perpetuate itself, and to promote the happiness of those who live under it.

V. Anticipations of Functionalism

18

Adam Smith

OF THE INFLUENCE OF FORTUNE UPON THE SENTIMENTS OF MANKIND, WITH REGARD TO THE MERIT OR DEMERIT OF ACTIONS

Introduction

WHATEVER PRAISE or blame can be due to any action must belong either, first, to the intention or affection of the heart from which it proceeds, or secondly, to the external action or movement of the body which this affection gives occasion to, or lastly, to the good or bad consequences which actually and in fact proceed from it. These three different things constitute the whole nature and circumstances of the action and must be the foundation of whatever quality can belong to it.

That the two last of these three circumstances cannot be the foundation of any praise or blame, is abundantly evident; nor has the contrary ever been asserted by anybody. The external action or

Reprinted from Adam Smith, *The Theory of Moral Sentiments* (London and New York: G. Bell & Sons, 1892), pp. 133–57.

movement of the body is often the same in the most innocent and in the most blamable actions. He who shoots a bird and he who shoots a man both of them perform the same external movement: each of them draws the trigger of a gun. The consequences which actually, and in fact, happen to proceed from any action are, if possible, still more indifferent either to praise or blame than even the external movement of the body. As they depend, not upon the agent, but upon fortune, they cannot be the proper foundation for any sentiment, of which his character and conduct are the objects.

The only consequences for which he can be answerable, or by which he can deserve either approbation or disapprobation of any kind, are those which were some way or other intended, or those which, at least, show some agreeable or disagreeable quality in the intention of the heart, from which he acted. To the intention or affection of the heart, therefore, to the propriety or impropriety, to the beneficence or hurtfulness of the design, all praise or blame, all approbation or disapprobation of any kind, which can justly be bestowed upon any action, must ultimately belong.

When this maxim is thus proposed in abstract and general terms there is nobody who does not agree to it. Its self-evident justice is acknowledged by all the world and there is not a dissenting voice among all mankind. Every body allows that how different soever the accidental, the unintended, and unforeseen consequences of different actions, yet, if the intentions or affections from which they arose were, on the one hand, equally proper and equally beneficent, or on the other, equally improper and equally malevolent, the merit or demerit of the actions is still the same, and the agent is equally the suitable object either of gratitude or of resentment.

But how well soever we may seem to be persuaded of the truth of this equitable maxim when we consider it after this manner, in abstract, yet when we come to particular cases, the actual consequences which happen to proceed from any action have a very great effect upon our sentiments concerning its merit or demerit and almost always either enhance or diminish our sense of both. Scarce, in any one instance, perhaps, will our sentiments be found, after examination, to be entirely regulated by this rule, which we all acknowledge ought entirely to regulate them.

This irregularity of sentiment, which every body feels, which scarce any body is sufficiently aware of, and which nobody is willing to acknowledge, I proceed now to explain; and I shall consider first the cause which gives occasion to it, or the mechanism by which nature produces it; secondly, the extent of its influence; and, last of all, the end which it answers, or the purpose which the Author of nature seems to have intended by it.

Of the Causes of This Influence of Fortune

The causes of pain and pleasure, whatever they are, or however they operate, seem to be the objects which, in all animals, immediately excite those two passions of gratitude and resentment. They are excited by inanimated as well as by animated objects. We are angry, for a moment, even at the stone that hurts us. A child beats it, a dog barks at it, a choleric man is apt to curse it. The least reflection indeed corrects this sentiment and we soon become sensible that what has no feeling is a very improper object of revenge. When the mischief, however, is very great, the object which caused it becomes disagreeable to us ever after, and we take pleasure to burn or destroy it. We should treat in this manner the instrument which had accidentally been the cause of the death of a friend, and we should often think ourselves guilty of a sort of inhumanity if we neglected to vent this absurd sort of vengeance upon it.

We conceive in the same manner a sort of gratitude for those inanimated objects which have been the causes of great or frequent pleasure to us. The sailor, who, as soon as he got ashore, should mend his fire with the plank upon which he had just escaped from a shipwreck would seem to be guilty of an unnatural action. We should expect that he would rather preserve it with care and affection, as a monument that was, in some measure, dear to him. A man grows fond of a snuffbox, of a penknife, of a staff which he has long made use of, and conceives something like a real love and affection for them. If he breaks or loses them, he is vexed out of all proportion to the value of the damage. The house which we have long lived in, the tree whose verdure and shade we have long enjoyed, are both looked upon with a sort of respect that seems due to such benefactors. The decay of the one, or the ruin of the other, affects us with a kind of melancholy, though we should sustain no loss by it. The dryads and the lares of the ancients, a sort of genii of trees and houses, were probably first suggested by this sort of affection which the authors of those superstitions felt for such objects and which seemed unreasonable if there was nothing animated about them.

But before any thing can be the *proper* object of gratitude or resentment, it must not only be the cause of pleasure or pain; it must likewise be capable of feeling them. Without this other quality, those passions cannot vent themselves with any sort of satisfaction upon it. As they are excited by the causes of pleasure and pain, so their gratification consists in retaliating those sensations upon what gave occasion to them, which it is to no purpose to attempt upon what has no sensibility. Animals, therefore, are less improper objects of gratitude and resentment than inanimated objects. The dog that bites, the ox that gores, are both of them punished. If they have been the causes of the death of any person, neither the public nor the relations of the slain can be satisfied unless they are put to death in their turn, nor is this merely for the security of the living, but, in some measure, to revenge the injury of the dead. Those animals, on the contrary, that have been remarkably serviceable to their masters become the objects of a very lively gratitude. We are shocked at the brutality of that officer mentioned in the Turkish Spy who stabbed the horse that had carried him across an arm of the sea, lest that animal should afterward distinguish some other person by a similar adventure.

But, though animals are not only the causes of pleasure and pain, but are also capable of feeling those sensations, they are still far from being complete and perfect objects either of gratitude or resentment, and those passions still feel that there is something wanting to their entire gratification. What gratitude chiefly desires is not only to make the benefactor feel pleasure in his turn, but to make him conscious that he meets with this reward on account of his past conduct, to make him pleased with that conduct, and to satisfy him that the person upon whom he bestowed his good offices was not unworthy of them. What most of all charms us in our benefactor is the concord between his sentiments and our own, with regard to what interests us so nearly as the worth of our own character and the esteem that is due to us. We are delighted to find a person who values us as we value ourselves and distinguishes us from the rest of mankind, with an attention not unlike that with which we distinguish ourselves. To maintain in him these agreeable and flattering sentiments is one of the chief ends proposed by the returns we are disposed to make to him. A generous mind often disdains the interested thought of exorting new favors from its benefactor by what may be called the importunities of its gratitude. But to preserve and to increase his esteem is an interest which the greatest mind does not think unworthy of its attention. And this is the foundation of what I formerly observed that when we cannot enter into the motives of our benefactor, when his conduct and character appear unworthy of our approbation, let his services have been ever so great, our gratitude is always sensibly diminished. We are less flattered by the distinction, and to preserve the esteem of so weak, or so worthless a patron, seems to be an object which does not deserve to be pursued for its own sake.

The object, on the contrary, which resentment is chiefly intent upon is not so much to make our enemy feel pain in his turn as to make him conscious that he feels it upon account of his past conduct, to make him repent of that conduct, and to make him sensible that the person whom he injured did not deserve to be treated in that manner. What chiefly enrages us against the man who injures or insults us is the little account which he seems to make of us, the unreasonable preference which he gives to himself above us, and that absurd self-love by which he seems to imagine that other people may be sacrificed at any time to his convenience or his humor. The glaring impropriety of this conduct, the gross insolence and injustice which it seems to involve in it, often shock and exasperate us more than all the mischief which we have suffered. To bring him back to a more just sense of what is due to other people, to make him sensible of what he owes us, and of the wrong that he has done to us, is frequently the principal end proposed in our revenge, which is always imperfect when it cannot accomplish this. When our enemy appears to have done us no injury, when we are sensible that he acted quite properly, that in his situation we should have done the same thing and that we deserved from him all the mischief we met with, in that case, if we have the least spark either of candor or justice, we can entertain no sort of resentment.

Before any thing therefore can be the complete and proper object, either of gratitude or resentment, it must possess three different qualifications. First, it must be the cause of pleasure in the one case and of pain in the other. Secondly, it must be capable of feeling those sensations. And thirdly, it must not only have produced those sensations, but it must have produced them from design, and from a design that is approved of in the one case and disapproved of in the other. It is by the first qualification that any object is capable of exciting those passions; it is by the second, that it is in any respect capable of gratifying them; the third qualification is not only necessary for their complete satisfaction, but, as it gives a pleasure or pain that is both exquisite and peculiar, it is likewise an additional exciting cause of those passions.

As what gives pleasure or pain therefore, either in one way or another, is the sole exciting cause of gratitude and resentment; though the intentions of any person should be ever so proper and beneficent, on the one hand, or ever so improper and malevolent on the other; yet, if he has failed in producing either the good or the evil which he intended, as one of the exciting causes is wanting in both cases, less gratitude seems due to him in the one, and less resentment in the other. And, on the contrary, though in the intentions of any person, there was either no laudable degree of benevolence on the one hand, or no blamable degree of malice on the other; yet, if his actions should produce either great good or great evil, as one of the exciting causes takes place upon both these occasions, some gratitude is apt to arise toward him in the one and some resentment in the other. A shadow of merit seems to fall upon him in the first, a shadow of demerit in the second. And as the consequences of actions are altogether under the empire of fortune, hence arises her influence upon the sentiments of mankind with regard to merit and demerit.

Of the Extent of This Influence of Fortune

The effect of this influence of fortune is first to diminish our sense of the merit or demerit of those actions which arose from the most laudable or blamable intentions when they fail of producing their proposed effects; and, secondly, to increase our sense of the merit or demerit of actions beyond what is due to the motives or affections from which they proceed when they accidentally give occasion either to extraordinary pleasure or pain.

1. First, I say, though the intentions of any person should be ever so proper and beneficent on the one hand, or ever so improper or malevolent on the other, yet, if they fail in producing their effects, his merit seems imperfect in the one case and his demerit incomplete in the other. Nor is this irregularity of sentiment felt only by those who are immediately affected by the consequences of any action. It is felt in some measure even by the impartial spectator. The man who solicits an office for another without obtaining it is regarded as his friend and seems to deserve his love and affection. But the man who not only solicits but procures it is more peculiarly considered as his patron and benefactor and is entitled to his respect and gratitude. The person obliged, we are apt to think, may with some justice imagine himself on a level with the first; but we cannot enter into his sentiments if he does not feel himself inferior to the second. It is common indeed to say that we are equally obliged to the man who has endeavored to serve us as to him who actually did so. It is the speech which we constantly make upon every unsuccessful attempt of this kind, but which, like all other fine speeches, must be understood with a grain of allowance. The sentiments which a man of generosity entertains for the friend who fails may often indeed be nearly the same with those he conceives for him who succeeds, and the more generous he is,

the more nearly will those sentiments approach to an exact level. With the truly generous, to be beloved, to be esteemed by those whom they themselves think worthy of esteem, gives more pleasure and thereby excites more gratitude than all the advantages which they can ever expect from those sentiments. When they lose those advantages therefore they seem to lose but a trifle, which is scarce worth regarding. They still, however, lose something. Their pleasure therefore and consequently their gratitude is not perfectly complete, and accordingly, if between the friend who fails and the friend who succeeds all other circumstances are equal, there will even in the noblest and best mind be some little difference of affection in favor of him who succeeds. Nay, so unjust are mankind in this respect that though the intended benefit should be procured, yet if it is not procured by the means of a particular benefactor, they are apt to think that less gratitude is due to the man who with the best intentions in the world could do no more than help it a little forward. As their gratitude is in this case divided among the different persons who contributed to their pleasure, a smaller share of it seems due to any one. Such a person, we hear men commonly say, intended no doubt to serve us, and we really believe exerted himself to the utmost of his abilities for that purpose. We are not, however, obliged to him for this benefit, since, had it not been for the concurrence of others, all that he could have done would never have brought it about. This consideration, they imagine, should even in the eyes of the impartial spectator diminish the debt which they owe to him. The person himself who has unsuccessfully endeavored to confer a benefit has by no means the same dependency upon the gratitude of the man whom he meant to oblige, nor the same sense of his own merit toward him, which he would have had in the case of success.

Even the merit of talents and abilities which some accident has hindered from producing their effects seems in some measure imperfect even to those who are fully convinced of their capacity to produce them. The general who has been hindered by the envy of ministers from gaining some great advantage over the enemies of his country regrets the loss of the opportunity for ever after. Nor is it only upon account of the public that he regrets it. He laments that he was hindered from performing an action which would have added a new lustre to his character in his own eyes, as well as in those of every other person. It satisfies neither himself nor others to reflect that the plan or design was all that depended on him, that no greater capacity was required to execute it than what was necessary to concert it, that he was allowed to be every way capable of executing it, and that had he been permitted to go on, success was infallible. He still did not execute it, and though he might deserve all the approbation which is due to a magnanimous and great design, he still wanted the actual merit of having performed a great action. To take the management of any affair of public concern from the man who has almost brought it to a conclusion is regarded as the most invidious injustice. As he had done so much, he should, we think, have been allowed to acquire the complete merit of putting an end to it. It was objected to Pompey that he came in upon the victories of Lucullus and gathered those laurels which were due to the fortune and valor of another. The glory of Lucullus, it seems, was less complete even in the opinion of his own friends when he was not permitted to finish that conquest which his conduct and courage had put in the power of almost any man to finish. It mortifies an architect when his plans are either not executed at all or when they are so far altered as to spoil the effect of the building. The plan, however, is all that depends upon the architect. The whole of his genius is to good judges as completely discovered in that as in the actual execution. But a plan does not even to the most intelligent give the same pleasure as a noble and magnificent building. They may discover as much both of taste and genius in the one as in the other. But their effects are still vastly different and the amusement derived from the first never approaches to the wonder and admiration which are sometimes excited by the second. We may believe of many men that their talents are superior to those of Caesar and Alexander and that in the same situations they would perform still greater actions. In the meantime, however, we do not behold them with that astonishment and admiration with which those two heroes have been regarded in all ages and nations. The calm judgments of the mind may approve of them more, but they want the splendor of great actions to dazzle and transport it. The superiority of virtues and talents has not, even upon those who acknowledge that superiority, the same effect with the superiority of achievements.

As the merit of an unsuccessful attempt to do good seems thus in the eyes of ungrateful mankind to be diminished by the miscarriage, so does likewise the demerit of an unsuccessful attempt to do evil. The design to commit a crime, how clearly soever it may be proved, is scarce ever punished with the same severity as the actual commission of it. The case of treason is perhaps the only exception. That crime immediately affecting the being of the government itself, the government is naturally more jealous of it than of any other. In the punishment of treason, the sovereign resents the injuries which are immediately done to himself; in the punishment of other crimes, he resents those which are done to other men. It is his own resentment which he indulges in the one case; it is that of his subjects which by sympathy he enters into in the other. In the first case therefore, as he judges in his own cause, he is very apt to be more violent and sanguinary in his punishments than the impartial spectator can approve of. His resentment too rises here upon smaller occasions and does not always, as in other cases, wait for the perpetration of the crime, or even for the attempt to commit it. A treasonable concert, though nothing has been done, or even attempted in consequence of it, nay, a treasonable conversation, is in many countries punished in the same manner as the actual commission of treason. With regard to all other crimes, the mere design upon which no attempt has followed is seldom punished at all and is never punished severely. A criminal design and a criminal action, it may be said, indeed, do not necessarily suppose the same degree of depravity and ought not therefore to be subjected to the same punishment. We are capable, it may be said, of resolving and even of taking measures to execute many things which when it comes to the point, we feel ourselves altogether incapable of executing. But this reason can have no place when the design has been carried the length of the last attempt. The man, however, who fires a pistol at his enemy but misses him is punished with death by the laws of scarce any country. By the old law of Scotland, though he should wound him, yet, unless death ensues within a certain time, the assassin is not liable to the last punishment. The resentment of mankind, however, runs so high against this crime, their terror for the man who shows himself capable of committing it is so great that the mere attempt to commit it ought in all countries to be capital. The attempt to commit smaller crimes is almost always punished very lightly and sometimes is not punished at all. The thief, whose hand has been caught in his neighbor's pocket before he had taken any thing out of it, is punished with ignominy only. If he had got time to take away a handkerchief, he would have been put to death. The house-breaker, who has been found setting a ladder to his neighbor's window, but had not got into it, is not exposed to the capital punishment. The attempt to ravish is not punished as a rape. The attempt to seduce a married woman is not punished at all, though seduction is punished severely. Our resentment against the person who only attempted to do a mischief is seldom so strong as to bear us out in inflicting the same punishment upon him which we should have thought due if he had actually done it. In the one case, the joy of our deliverance alleviates our sense of the atrocity of his conduct; in the other, the grief of our misfortune increases it. His real demerit, however, is undoubtedly the same in both cases, since his intentions were equally criminal; and there is in this respect, therefore, an irregularity in the sentiments of all men, and a consequent relaxation of discipline, in the laws of, I believe, all nations, of the most civilized as well as of the most barbarous. The humanity of a civilized people disposes them either to dispense with or to mitigate punishments wherever their natural indignation is not goaded on by the consequences of the crime. Barbarians, on the other hand, when no actual consequence has happened from any action, are not apt to be very delicate or inquisitive about the motives.

The person himself who, either from passion or from the influence of bad company, has resolved and perhaps taken measures to perpetrate some crime, but who has fortunately been prevented by an accident which put it out of his power, is sure, if he has any remains of conscience to regard this event all his life after as a

great and signal deliverance. He can never think of it without
returning thanks to Heaven for having been thus graciously
pleased to save him from the guilt in which he was just ready to
plunge himself and to hinder him from rendering all the rest of his
life a scene of horror, remorse, and repentance. But though his
hands are innocent, he is conscious that his heart is equally guilty
as if he had actually executed what he was so fully resolved upon.
It gives great ease to his conscience, however, to consider that the
crime was not executed, though he knows that the failure arose
from no virtue in him. He still considers himself as less deserving
of punishment and resentment, and this good fortune either dimin-
ishes, or takes away altogether, all sense of guilt. To remember how
much he was resolved upon it has no other effect than to make him
regard his escape as the greater and more miraculous, for he still
fancies that he has escaped, and he looks back upon the danger to
which his peace of mind was exposed, with that terror, with which
one who is in safety may sometimes remember the hazard he was
in of falling over a precipice and shudder with horror at the
thought.

2. The second effect of this influence of fortune is to increase
our sense of the merit or demerit of actions beyond what is due to
the motives or affection from which they proceed when they happen to give occasion to extraordinary pleasure or pain. The agreeable or disagreeable effects of the action often throw a shadow of
merit or demerit upon the agent, though in his intention there was
nothing that deserved either praise or blame, or at least that deserved them in the degree in which we are apt to bestow them.
Thus, even the messenger of bad news is disagreeable to us and, on
the contrary, we feel a sort of gratitude for the man who brings us
good tidings. For a moment we look upon them both as the authors,
the one of our good, the other of our bad fortune, and regard them
in some measure as if they had really brought about the events
which they only give an account of. The first author of our joy is
naturally the object of a transitory gratitude: we embrace him
with warmth and affection and should be glad, during the instant
of our prosperity, to reward him as for some signal service. By the
custom of all courts, the officer who brings the news of a victory

is entitled to considerable preferments, and the general always chooses one of his principal favorites to go upon so agreeable an errand. The first author of our sorrow is, on the contrary, just as naturally the object of a transitory resentment. We can scarce avoid looking upon him with chagrin and uneasiness, and the rude and brutal are apt to vent upon him that spleen which his intelligence gives occasion to. Tigranes, King of Armenia, struck off the head of the man who brought him the first account of the approach of a formidable enemy. To punish in this manner the author of bad tidings seems barbarous and inhuman; yet, to reward the messenger of good news is not disagreeable to us; we think it suitable to the bounty of kings. But why do we make this difference, since, if there is no fault in the one, neither is there any merit in the other? It is because any sort of reason seems sufficient to authorize the exertion of the social and benevolent affections, but it requires the most solid and substantial to make us enter into that of the unsocial and malevolent.

But though in general we are averse to enter into the unsocial and malevolent affections, though we lay it down for a rule that we ought never to approve of their gratification, unless so far as the malicious and unjust intention of the person against whom they are directed renders him their proper object; yet, upon some occasions, we relax of this severity. When the negligence of one man has occasioned some unintended damage to another, we generally enter so far into the resentment of the sufferer as to approve of his inflicting a punishment upon the offender much beyond what the offence would have appeared to deserve had no such unlucky consequence followed from it.

There is a degree of negligence which would appear to deserve some chastisement though it should occasion no damage to anybody. Thus, if a person should throw a large stone over a wall into a public street without giving warning to those who might be passing by and without regarding where it was likely to fall, he would undoubtedly deserve some chastisement. A very accurate police would punish so absurd an action, even though it had done no mischief. The person who has been guilty of it shows an insolent contempt of the happiness and safety of others. There is real injustice in his conduct. He wantonly exposes his neighbor to what no man in his senses would choose to expose himself to and evidently wants that sense of what is due to his fellow creatures which is the basis of justice and of society. Gross negligence, therefore, is, in the law, said to be almost equal to malicious design.[1] When any unlucky consequences happen from such carelessness, the person who has been guilty of it is often punished as if he had really intended those consequences; and his conduct, which was only thoughtless and insolent and what deserved some chastisement, is considered as atrocious and as liable to the severest punishment. Thus if by the imprudent action above mentioned he should accidentally kill a man, he is by the laws of many countries, particularly by the old law of Scotland, liable to the last punishment. And though this is no doubt excessively severe, it is not altogether inconsistent with our natural sentiments. Our just indignation against the folly and inhumanity of his conduct is exasperated by our sympathy with the unfortunate sufferer. Nothing, however, would appear more shocking to our natural sense of equity than to bring a man to the scaffold merely for having thrown a stone carelessly into the street without hurting anybody. The folly and inhumanity of his conduct, however, would in this case be the same; but still our sentiments would be very different. The consideration of this difference may satisfy us how much the indignation even of the spectator is apt to be animated by the actual consequences of the action. In cases of this kind there will, if I am not mistaken, be found a great degree of severity in the laws of almost all nations; as I have already observed that in those of an opposite kind there was a very general relaxation of discipline.

There is another degree of negligence which does not involve in it any sort of injustice. The person who is guilty of it treats his neighbor as he treats himself, means no harm to anybody, and is far from entertaining any insolent contempt for the safety and happiness of others. He is not, however, so careful and circumspect in his conduct as he ought to be, and deserves upon this account some degree of blame and censure, but no sort of punish-

1   Lata culpa prope dolum est.

ment. Yet, if by a negligence[2] of this kind he should occasion some damage to another person, he is by the laws of, I believe, all countries obliged to compensate it. And though this is no doubt a real punishment, and what no mortal would have thought of inflicting upon him, had it not been for the unlucky accident which his conduct gave occasion to, yet this decision of the law is approved of by the natural sentiments of all mankind. Nothing, we think, can be more just than that one man should not suffer by the carelessness of another and that the damage occasioned by blamable negligence should be made up by the person who was guilty of it.

There is another species of negligence[3] which consists merely in a want of the most anxious timidity and circumspection with regard to all the possible consequences of our actions. The want of this painful attention, when no bad consequences follow from it, is so far from being regarded as blamable that the contrary quality is rather considered as such. That timid circumspection which is afraid of everything is never regarded as a virtue, but as a quality which more than any other incapacitates for action and business. Yet, when from a want of this excessive care, a person happens to occasion some damage to another, he is often by the law obliged to compensate it. Thus, by the Aquilian law, the man, who not being able to manage a horse that had accidentally taken fright, should happen to ride down his neighbor's slave is obliged to compensate the damage. When an accident of this kind happens, we are apt to think that he ought not to have ridden such a horse and to regard his attempting it as an unpardonable levity; though without this accident we should not only have made no such reflection, but should have regarded his refusing it as the effect of timid weakness and of an anxiety about merely possible events which it is to no purpose to be aware of. The person himself, who by an accident even of this kind has involuntarily hurt another, seems to have some sense of his own ill desert with regard to him. He naturally runs up to the sufferer to express his concern for what has happened and to make every acknowledg-

2   Culpa levis.
3   Culpa levissima.

ment in his power. If he has any sensibility, he necessarily desires to compensate the damage and to do every thing he can to appease that animal resentment which he is sensible will be apt to arise in the breast of the sufferer. To make no apology, to offer no atonement, is regarded as the highest brutality. Yet, why should he make an apology more than any other person? Why should he, since he was equally innocent with any other bystander, he thus singled out from among all mankind to make up for the bad fortune of another? This task would surely never be imposed upon him, did not even the impartial spectator feel some indulgence for what may be regarded as the unjust resentment of that other.

Of the Final Cause of This Irregularity of Sentiments

Such is the effect of the good or bad consequence of actions upon the sentiments both of the person who performs them and of others; and thus, fortune, which governs the world, has some influence where we should be least willing to allow her any and directs in some measure the sentiments of mankind with regard to the character and conduct both of themselves and others. That the world judges by the event, and not by the design, has been in all ages the complaint and is the great discouragement of virtue. Everybody agrees to the general maxim that as the event does not depend on the agent it ought to have no influence upon our sentiments with regard to the merit or propriety of his conduct. But when we come to particulars, we find that our sentiments are scarce in any one instance exactly conformable to what this equitable maxim would direct. The happy or unprosperous event of any action is not only apt to give us a good or bad opinion of the prudence with which it was conducted, but almost always too animates our gratitude or resentment, our sense of the merit or demerit of the design.

Nature, however, when she implanted the seeds of this irregularity in the human breast, seems, as upon all other occasions, to have intended the happiness and perfection of the species. If the hurtfulness of the design, if the malevolence of the affection,

were alone the causes which excited our resentment, we should
feel all the furies of that passion against any person in whose breast
we suspected or believed such designs or affections were harbored,
though they had never broken out into any actions. Sentiments,
thoughts, intentions, would become the objects of punishment,
and if the indignation of mankind run as high against them as
against actions, if the baseness of the thought which had given
birth to no action seemed in the eyes of the world as much to call
aloud for vengeance as the baseness of the action, every court of
judicature would become a real inquisition. There would be no
safety for the most innocent and circumspect conduct. Bad wishes,
bad views, bad designs, might still be suspected; and while these
excited the same indignation with bad conduct, while bad intentions were as much resented as bad actions, they would equally
expose the person to punishment and resentment. Actions, therefore, which either produce actual evil, or attempt to produce it,
and thereby put us in the immediate fear of it, are by the Author
of nature rendered the only proper and approved objects of human
punishment and resentment. Sentiments, designs, affections,
though it is from these that according to cool reason human
actions derive their whole merit or demerit, are placed by the
great Judge of hearts beyond the limits of every human jurisdiction
and are reserved for the cognizance of his own unerring tribunal.
That necessary rule of justice, therefore, that men in this life are
liable to punishment for their actions only, not for their designs
and intentions, is founded upon this salutary and useful irregularity in human sentiments concerning merit or demerit, which at
first sight appears so absurd and unaccountable. But every part
of nature, when attentively surveyed, equally demonstrates the
providential care of its Author, and we may admire the wisdom
and goodness of God even in the weakness and folly of men.

Nor is that irregularity of sentiments altogether without its
utility, by which the merit of an unsuccessful attempt to serve, and
much more that of mere good inclinations and kind wishes, appears
to be imperfect. Man was made for action and to promote by the
exertion of his faculties such changes in the external circumstances
both of himself and others as may seem most favorable to the

happiness of all. He must not be satisfied with indolent benevolence, nor fancy himself the friend of mankind, because in his
heart he wishes well to the prosperity of the world. That he may
call forth the whole vigor of his soul and strain every nerve in
order to produce those ends which it is the purpose of his being
to advance, nature has taught him that neither himself nor mankind can be fully satisfied with his conduct, nor bestow upon it the
full measure of applause, unless he has actually produced them.
He is made to know that the praise of good intentions without the
merit of good offices will be but of little avail to excite either the
loudest acclamations of the world or even the highest degree of
self-applause. The man who has performed no single action of
importance, but whose whole conversation and deportment express the justest, the noblest, and most generous sentiments, can
be entitled to demand no very high reward, even though his in-
utility should be owing to nothing but the want of an opportunity
to serve. We can still refuse it him without blame. We can still
ask him, What have you done? What actual service can you produce to entitle you to so great recompence? We esteem you and
love you, but we owe you nothing. To reward indeed that latent
virtue which has been useless only for want of an opportunity to
serve, to bestow upon it those honors and preferments which,
though in some measure it may be said to deserve them, it could
not with propriety have insisted upon is the effect of the most
divine benevolence. To punish, on the contrary, for the affections
of the heart only, where no crime has been committed, is the most
insolent and barbarous tyranny. The benevolent affections seem
to deserve most praise when they do not wait until it becomes
almost a crime for them not to exert themselves. The malevolent,
on the contrary, can scarce be too tardy, too slow, or deliberate.

   It is even of considerable importance that the evil which is
done without design should be regarded as a misfortune to the
doer as well as to the sufferer. Man is thereby taught to reverence
the happiness of his brethren, to tremble lest he should, even
unknowingly, do anything that can hurt them, and to dread that
animal resentment which, he feels, is ready to burst out against
him if he should, without design, be the unhappy instrument of

their calamity. As, in the ancient heathen religion, that holy ground which had been consecrated to some god was not to be trod upon but upon solemn and necessary occasions and the man who had even ignorantly violated it became piacular from that moment, and, until proper atonement should be made, incurred the vengeance of that powerful and invisible being to whom it had been set apart; so, by the wisdom of nature, the happiness of every innocent man is, in the same manner, rendered holy, consecrated, and hedged round against the approach of every other man, not to be wantonly trod upon, not even to be, in any respect, ignorantly and involuntarily violated, without requiring some expiation, some atonement in proportion to the greatness of such undesigned violation. A man of humanity, who accidentally and without the smallest degree of blamable negligence has been the cause of the death of another man feels himself piacular, though not guilty. During his whole life he considers this accident as one of the greatest misfortunes that could have befallen him. If the family of the slain is poor and he himself in tolerable circumstances, he immediately takes them under his protection, and without any other merit, thinks them entitled to every degree of favor and kindness. If they are in better circumstances, he endeavors by every submission, by every expression of sorrow, by rendering them every good office which he can devise, or they accept of, to atone for what has happened, and to propitiate, as much as possible, their, perhaps natural, though no doubt most unjust resentment for the great, though involuntary, offense which he has given them.

The distress which an innocent person feels, who, by some accident, has been led to do something which, if it had been done with knowledge and design, would have justly exposed him to the deepest reproach, has given occasion to some of the finest and most interesting scenes both of the ancient and of the modern drama. It is this fallacious sense of guilt, if I may call it so, which constitutes the whole distress of Oedipus and Jocasta upon the Greek, of Monimia and Isabella upon the English, theater. They are all of them in the highest degree piacular, though not one of them is in the smallest degree guilty.

Notwithstanding, however, all these seeming irregularities of sentiment, if man should unfortunately either give occasion to those evils which he did not intend, or fail in producing that good which he intended, nature has not left his innocence altogether without consolation, nor his virtue altogether without reward. He then calls to his assistance that just and equitable maxim, that those events which did not depend upon our conduct ought not to diminish the esteem that is due to us. He summons up his whole magnanimity and firmness of soul and strives to regard himself, not in the light in which he at present appears, but in that in which he ought to appear, in which he would have appeared had his generous designs been crowned with success, and in which he would still appear, notwithstanding their miscarriage, if the sentiments of mankind were either altogether candid and equitable or even perfectly consistent with themselves. The more candid and humane part of mankind entirely go along with the efforts which he thus makes to support himself in his own opinion. They exert their whole generosity and greatness of mind to correct in themselves this irregularity of human nature and endeavor to regard his unfortunate magnanimity in the same light in which, had it been successful, they would without any such generous exertion have naturally been disposed to consider it.

19

Dugald Stewart

OF THE SPECULATION
CONCERNING FINAL CAUSES

*Opinion of Lord Bacon on the Subject—Final Causes
Rejected by Descartes, and by the Majority of French Philosophers—Recognized as Legitimate Objects of Research
by Newton—Tacitly Acknowledged by All as a Useful Logical Guide, even in Sciences Which Have no Immediate
Relation to Theology*

THE STUDY OF FINAL CAUSES may be considered in two different points of view: first, as subservient to the evidences of natural
religion, and secondly, as a guide and auxiliary in the investigation of physical laws. Of these views it is the latter alone which
is immediately connected with the principles of the inductive
logic; and it is to this, accordingly, that I shall chiefly direct my
attention in the following observations. I shall not, however, ad-
here so scrupulously to a strict arrangement as to avoid all reference to the former where the train of my reflections may naturally
lead to it. The truth is that the two speculations will, on examination, be found much more nearly allied than might at first sight
be apprehended.

Reprinted from Dugald Stewart, *Elements of the Philosophy of the
Human Mind*, Vol. II, in *Collected Works*, W. Hamilton, ed. (Edinburgh, 1854), III, 335–57.

I before observed that the phrase final cause was first introduced by Aristotle and that the extension thus given to the notion of *causation* contributed powerfully to divert the inquiries of his followers from the proper objects of physical science. In reading the strictures of Bacon on this mode of philosophizing, it is necessary always to bear in mind that they have a particular reference to the theories of the schoolmen; and if they should sometimes appear to be expressed in terms too unqualified, due allowances ought to be made for the undistinguishing zeal of a reformer, in attacking prejudices consecrated by long and undisturbed prescription. *"The search after final causes is barren, and, like a virgin consecrated to God, produces nothing."*—Bacon. Had a similar remark occurred in any philosophical work of the eighteenth century, it might perhaps have been fairly suspected to savor of the school of Epicurus, although, even in such a case, the quaintness and levity of the conceit would probably have inclined a cautious and candid reader to interpret the author's meaning with an indulgent latitude. On the present occasion, however, Bacon is his own best commentator; and I shall therefore quote, in a faithful though abridged translation, the preparatory passage by which this allusion is introduced.

"The second part of *metaphysics* is the investigation of *final causes,* which I object to, not as a speculation which ought to be neglected, but as one which has, in general, been very improperly regarded as a branch of *physics.* If this were merely a fault of arrangement, I should not be disposed to lay great stress upon it, for arrangement is useful chiefly as a help to perspicuity, and does not affect the substantial matter of science: but in this instance a disregard of *method* has occasioned the most fatal consequences to philosophy; inasmuch as the consideration of *final* causes in physics has supplanted and banished the study of *physical* causes; the fancy amusing itself with illusory explanations derived from the former, and misleading the curiosity from a steady prosecution of the latter." After illustrating this remark by various examples, Bacon adds: "I would not, however, be understood by these observations to insinuate that the *final causes* just mentioned may not be founded in truth and in a *metaphysical* view extremely worthy of attention, but only that when such disquisitions invade and over-run the appropriate province of *physics,* they are likely to lay waste and ruin that department of knowledge." The passage concludes with these words: "And so much concerning *metaphysics,* the part of which relating to *final causes,* I do not deny, has been often enlarged upon in physical, as well as in metaphysical treatises. But while, in the latter of these, it is treated of with propriety, in the former it is altogether misplaced; and *that,* not merely because it violates the rules of a logical order, but because it operates as a powerful obstacle to the progress of inductive science."[1]

The epigrammatic maxim which gave occasion to these ex-tracts has, I believe, been oftener quoted (particularly by French writers) than any other sentence in Bacon's works; and as it has in general been stated without any reference to the context in the form of a detached aphorism, it has been commonly supposed to convey a meaning widely different from what appears to have been annexed to it by the author. The remarks with which he has prefaced it and which I have here submitted to the consideration of my readers sufficiently show, not only that he meant his propo-sition to be restricted to the abuse of final causes in the physics of Aristotle, but that he was anxious to guard against the possibility of any misapprehension or misrepresentation of his opinion. A fur-ther proof of this is afforded by the censure which in the same paragraph he bestows on Aristotle for "substituting nature instead of God, as the fountain of final causes, and for treating of them rather as subservient to logic than to theology."

A similar observation may be made on another sentence in Bacon, in the interpretation of which a very learned writer, Dr. Cudworth, seems to have altogether lost sight of his usual candor. "It is incredible what a host of fictions has been introduced into philosophy, by the reduction of natural operations to the parallel of human actions."—Bacon. "If," says Cudworth, "the Advancer of Learning here speaks of those who unskilfully attribute their own properties to inanimate bodies (as when they say that matter *desires* forms as the female does the male, and that heavy bodies descend down *by appetite* toward the center, that they may rest

[1]   *De Aug. Scient.* lib. iii. cap. iv. v.

therein), there is nothing to be reprehended in the passage. But if his meaning be extended further to take away all final causes from the things of nature, then is it the very spirit of atheism and infidelity. It is no *idol of the cave or den* (to use that affected language), that is, no prejudice or fallacy imposed on ourselves, from the attributing our own animalish properties to things without us, to think that the frame and system of this whole world was contrived by a perfect understanding and mind."

It is difficult to conceive that any person who had read Bacon's works and who, at the same time, was acquainted with the theories which it was their great object to explode could for a moment have hesitated about rejecting the latter interpretation as altogether absurd; and, yet, the splenetic tone which marks the conclusion of Cudworth's strictures plainly shows that he had a decided leaning to it, in preference to the former.[2] The comment does no honor to his liberality, and on the most favorable supposition, must be imputed to a superstitious reverence for the remains of Grecian wisdom, accompanied with a corresponding dread of the unknown dangers to be apprehended from philosophical innovations. Little was he aware that in turning the attention of men from the history of opinions and systems to the observation and study of nature, Bacon was laying the foundation of a bulwark against atheism, more stable and impregnable than the united labors of the ancients

[2]   Even the former interpretation is not agreeable (as appears manifestly from the context) to Bacon's idea. The prejudices which he has here more particularly in view are those which take their rise from a bias in the mind to imagine a greater *equality* and *uniformity* in nature than really exists. As an instance of this, he mentions the universal assumption among the ancient astronomers that all the celestial motions are performed in orbits perfectly circular—an assumption which a few years before Bacon wrote had been completely disproved by Kepler. To this he adds some other examples from physics and chemistry, after which he introduces the general reflection animadverted on by Cudworth. The whole passage concludes with these words: "So differing a harmony there is between the spirit of man and the spirit of nature."—(*Bacon, The Advancement of Learning.*)

The criticism may appear minute, but I cannot forbear to mention as a proof of the carelessness with which Cudworth had read Bacon that the prejudice supposed by the former to belong to the class of *idola specus* is expressly quoted by the latter as an example of the *idola tribus.*—See Book v. *De Augment. Scient.* chap. iv.

were able to rear—a bulwark which derives additional strength from every new accession to the stock of human knowledge.[3]

Whether Bacon's contempt for the final causes of the Aristotelians has not carried him to an extreme in recommending the *total* exclusion of them from Physics is a very different question and a question of much importance in the theory of the inductive logic. My own opinion is that his views on this point, if considered as applicable to the *present* state of experimental science, are extremely limited and erroneous. Perhaps, at the time when he wrote, such an exclusion may have appeared necessary, as the only effectual antidote against the errors which then infected every branch of philosophy; but granting this to be true, no good reason can be given for continuing the same language, at a period when the proper object of physics is too well understood to render it possible for the investigation of final causes to lead astray the most fanciful theorist. What harm can be apprehended from remarking those proofs of design which fall under the view of the physical

[3]   "The excellent work of Newton will prove an impregnable bulwark against the assaults of atheists."—Cotesii *Praef. in Edit. Secund. Principiorum.*

In the above vindication of Bacon, I have abstained from any appeal to the instances in which he has himself forcibly and eloquently expressed the same sentiments here ascribed to him; because I conceive that an author's real opinions are to be most indisputably judged of from the *general* spirit and tendency of his writings. The following passage, however, is too precious a document to be omitted on the present occasion. It is, indeed, one of the most hackneyed quotations in our language; but it forms on that very account the more striking a contrast to the voluminous and now neglected erudition displayed by Cudworth in defense of the same argument.

"I had rather believe all the fables in the Legend, and the Talmud, and the Alcoran, than that this universal frame is without a mind! It is true that a little philosophy inclineth man's mind to atheism; but depth in philosophy bringeth men's minds about to religion; for while the mind of man looketh upon second causes scattered, it may sometimes rest in them and go no farther; but when it beholdeth the chain of them confederate and linked together, it must needs fly to Providence and Deity: nay, even that school which is most accused of atheism, doth most demonstrate religion; that is, the school of Leucippus, and Democritus, and Epicurus; for it is a thousand times more credible, that four mutable elements and one immutable fifth essence, duly and eternally placed, need no God, than that an army of infinite small portions, or seeds unplaced, should have produced this order and beauty without a divine marshal."—Bacon's *Essays.* See also *De Aug. Scient.* L. I.

inquirer in the course of his studies? Or, if it should be thought foreign to *his* province to speak of *design,* he may at least be permitted to remark what *ends* are really accomplished by particular *means,* and what *advantages* result from the general laws by which the phenomena of nature are regulated. In doing this, he only states a *fact,* and if it be illogical to go further, he may leave the inference to the moralist or the divine.

In consequence, however, of the vague and commonplace declamation against final causes, sanctioned (as has been absurdly supposed) by those detached expressions of Bacon, which have suggested the foregoing reflections, it has for many years past become fashionable to omit the consideration of them entirely as inconsistent with the acknowledged rules of sound philosophizing; a caution (it may be remarked by the way) which is most scrupulously observed by those writers who are the most forward to censure every apparent *anomaly* or *disorder* in the economy of the universe. The effect of this has been to divest the study of nature of its most attractive charms and to sacrifice to a false idea of logical rigor all the moral impressions and pleasures which physical knowledge is fitted to yield.[4]

Nor is it merely in a *moral view* that the consideration of *uses* is interesting. There are some parts of nature in which it is necessary to complete the *physical theory;* nay, there are instances, in which it has proved a powerful, and perhaps indispensable, organ of *physical discovery*. That Bacon should not have been aware of this will not appear surprising when it is recollected that the chief facts which justify the observation have been brought to light since his time.

[4]   "If a traveler," says the great Mr. Boyle, "being in some ill-inhabited eastern country, should come to a large and fair building, such as one of the most stately of those they call caravanzeras, though he would esteem and be delighted with the magnificence of the structure, and the commodiousness of the apartments, yet supposing it to have been erected but for the honor or the pleasure of the founder, he would commend so stately a fabric, without thanking him for it; but, if he were satisfied that this commodious building was designed by the founder as a receptacle for passengers, who were freely to have the use of the many conveniences the apartments afforded, he would then think himself obliged not only to praise the magnificence, but with gratitude to acknowledge the bounty and the philanthropy of so munificent a benefactor."—Boyle's *Works,* vol. iv, p. 517, folio edition.

Of these *facts* the most remarkable are furnished by the science of anatomy. To understand the structure of an animal body, it is necessary not only to examine the *conformation* of the parts but to consider their *functions,* or in other words, to consider their *ends* and *uses:* nor indeed does the most accurate knowledge of the former, till perfected by the discovery of the latter, afford satisfaction to an inquisitive and scientific mind. Every anatomist accordingly, whatever his metaphysical creed may be, proceeds in his researches upon the maxim that no organ exists without its appropriate destination; and although he may often fail in his attempts to ascertain what this destination is, he never carries his skepticism so far as for a moment to doubt of the general principle. I am inclined to think that it is in this way the most important steps in physiology have been gained; the curiosity being constantly kept alive by some new problem in the animal machine, and at the same time checked in its wanderings by an irresistible conviction that nothing is made in vain. The memorable account given by Mr. Boyle of the circumstances which led to the discovery of the circulation of the blood is but one of the many testimonies which might be quoted in confirmation of this opinion.

"I remember that when I asked our famous Harvey, in the only discourse I had with him (which was but a little while before he died) what were the things which induced him to think of a circulation of the blood? He answered me, that when he took notice that the valves in the veins of so many parts of the body were so placed that they gave free passage to the blood toward the heart, but opposed the passage of the venal blood the contrary way, he was invited to think, that so provident a cause as nature had not placed so many valves without design; and no design seemed more probable than that, since the blood could not well, because of the interposing valves, be sent by the veins to the limbs, it should be sent through the arteries and return through the veins, whose valves did not oppose its course that way."[5]

[5]   Boyle's *Works*, vol. iv., p. 539, folio edition—See *Outlines of Moral Philosophy*, §§282, *seq.* (*Infra*, vol. vi.).

The reasoning here ascribed to Harvey seems now so very natural and obvious that some have been disposed to question his claim to the high rank commonly assigned to him among the improvers of science. The late

This perception of design and contrivance is more peculiarly impressive when we contemplate those instances in the animal economy in which the same effect is produced in *different* combinations of circumstances by *different* means, when we compare, for example, the circulation of the blood in the foetus with that in the body of the animal after it is born. On such an occasion, how is it possible to withhold the assent from the ingenious reflection of [our Scottish] Baxter!—"Art and means are designedly multiplied, that we might not take it for the effects of chance; and, in some cases, the method itself is different, that we might see it is not the effect of surd necessity."[6]

Dr. William Hunter has said that after the discovery of the valves in the veins, which Harvey learned, while in Italy, from his master Fabricius ab Aquapendente, the remaining step might easily have been made by any person of common abilities. "This discovery," he observes, "set Harvey to work upon the *use* of the heart and vascular system in animals; and, in the course of some years, he was so happy as to discover and to prove beyond all possibility of doubt the circulation of the blood." He afterward expresses his astonishment that this discovery should have been left for Harvey, adding that "Providence meant to reserve it for *him*, and would not let men *see what was before them, nor understand what they read.*"—Hunter's *Introductory Lectures*, p. 42, *et seq.*

Whatever opinion be formed on this point, Dr. Hunter's remarks are valuable as an additional proof of the regard paid by anatomists to *Final Causes*, in the study of physiology.

See also Haller; *Elementa Physiologiae*, vol. i., p. 204.

6   *Inquiry into the Nature of the Human Soul*, vol. i., p. 136, 3d ed.

The following passage from an old English divine may be of use for the further illustration of this argument. I quote it with the greater confidence as I find that the most eminent and original physiologist of the present age (M. Cuvier) has been led, by his enlightened researches concerning the laws of the animal economy, into a train of thinking strikingly similar.

"Man is always mending and altering his works, but nature observes the same tenor, because her works are so perfect that there is no place for amendments, nothing that can be reprehended. The most sagacious men in so many ages have not been able to find any flaw in these divinely contrived and formed machines: no blot or error in this great volume of the world, as if anything had been an imperfect essay at the first; nothing that can be altered for the better; nothing but if it were altered would be marred. This could not have been had man's body been the work of chance and not counsel and Providence. Why should there be constantly the same parts? Why should they retain constantly the same places? Nothing so contrary as constancy and chance. Should I see a man throw the same number a thousand times together upon but three dice, could you persuade me that this

The study of comparative anatomy leads at every step so directly and so manifestly to the same conclusion that even those physiologists who had nothing in view but the advancement of their own science unanimously agree in recommending the dissection of animals of different kinds as the most effectual of all helps for ascertaining the *functions* of the various organs in the human frame—tacitly assuming as an incontrovertible truth that in proportion to the variety of means by which the same effect is accomplished, the presumption increases that this effect was an *end* in the contemplation of the artist. "The intention of nature," says one author, "in the formation of the different parts, can nowhere be so well learned as from comparative anatomy; that is, if we would understand physiology, and reason on the functions of the animal economy, we must see how the same end is brought about in other species.—We must contemplate the part or organ in *different* animals, its shape, position, and connection with the other parts, and observe what thence arises. If we find *one common*

---

were accidental and that there was no necessary cause for it? How much more incredible then is it that constancy in such a variety, such a multiplicity of parts, should be the result of chance? Neither yet can these works be the effects of necessity of fate, for then there would be the same constancy observed in the smaller as well as in the larger parts and vessels; whereas *there* we see nature doth as it were sport itself, the minute ramifications of all the vessels, veins, arteries, and nerves, infinitely varying in individuals of the same species so that they are not in any two alike."—Ray's *Wisdom of God in the Creation.*

"Nature," says Cuvier, "while confining herself strictly within those limits which the conditions necessary for existence prescribed to her, has yielded to her spontaneous fecundity wherever these conditions did not limit her operations; and without ever passing beyond the small number of combinations that can be realized in the essential modifications of the important organs, she seems to have given full scope to her fancy, in filling up the subordinate parts. With respect to these, it is not inquired whether an individual form, whether a particular arrangement, be necessary; it seems often not to have been asked, whether it be even useful in order to reduce it to practice, it is sufficient that it be possible, that it destroy not the harmony of the whole. Accordingly, as we recede from the principal organs and approach to those of less importance, the varieties in structure and appearance become more numerous; and when we arrive at the surface of the body, where the parts the least essential, and whose injuries are the least momentous, are necessarily placed, the number of varieties is so great, that the conjoined labors of naturalists have not yet been able to give us an adequate idea of them."— *Leçons d'anatomie comparée.*

effect constantly produced, though in a very different way, we may safely conclude that this is the *use* or *function* of the part.— This reasoning can never betray us if we are but sure of the facts."[7]

The celebrated Albinus expresses himself to the same purpose in his preface to Harvey's *Exercitatio de Motu Cordis.* "We ought to dissect animals in which the parts whose functions we seek are the same with, or at least similar to, those of man; whence we may be permitted to form a judgment of the organs of the human body without fear of error. Other animals moreover, if they in any respect resemble man, are fitted to supply some information."

If Bacon had lived to read such testimonies as these in favor of the investigation of final causes, or had witnessed the discoveries to which it has led in the study of the animal economy, he would I doubt not have readily admitted that it was not altogether uninteresting and unprofitable, even to the *physical* inquirer. Such, however, is the influence of an illustrious name that in direct opposition to the evidence of historical facts, the assertion of the complete *sterility* of all these speculations is, to the present day, repeated, with undiminished confidence, by writers of unquestionable learning and talents. In one of the most noted physiological works which have lately appeared on the Continent, Bacon's apophthegm is cited more than once with unqualified approbation, although the author candidly owns that it is difficult for the most *reserved* philosopher always to keep it steadily in view in the course of his inquiries.[8]

The prejudice against final causes so generally avowed by the most eminent philosophers of France during the eighteenth century was first introduced into that country by Descartes. It must not, however, be imagined that in the mind of this great man it arose from any bias toward atheism. On the contrary, he himself tells us that his objection to the research of *uses* or *ends* was

---

[7]   *Letter,* by an anonymous correspondent, prefixed to Monro's *Comparative Anatomy* (London, 1744).

[8]   "I regard, with the great Bacon, the philosophy of final causes as sterile, but I confess it is very difficult for the most guarded philosopher to keep perfectly clear of it in the course of his explanations."—*Cabanis. Rapports du physique et du moral de l'homme.* Par M. le Senateur Cabanis. Vol. i., p. 352 (Paris, 1805).

founded entirely on the presumptuous confidence which it seemed to argue in the powers of human reason, as if it were conceivable that the limited faculties of man could penetrate into the counsels of Divine Wisdom. Of the existence of God he conceived that a demonstrative proof was afforded by the idea we are able to form of a Being infinitely perfect and necessarily existing; and it has with some probability been conjectured that it was his partiality to this new argument of his own which led him to reject the reasonings of his predecessors in support of the same conclusion.[9]

To this objection of Descartes, an elaborate, and in my opinion a most satisfactory reply, is to be found in the works of Mr. Boyle. The principal scope of his essay may be collected from the following short extract.

"Suppose that a countryman being in a clear day brought into the garden of some famous mathematician, should see there one of those curious gnomonic instruments that show at once the place of the sun in the zodiac, his declination from the equator, the day of the month, the length of the day, etc., etc. It would indeed be presumption in him, being unacquainted both with the mathematical disciplines, and the several intentions of the artist to pretend or think himself able to discover *all the ends* for which so curious and elaborate a piece was framed; but when he sees it furnished with a style, with horary lines and numbers, and in short, with all the requisites of a sundial, and manifestly perceives the

9   "We will not seek reasons of natural things from the end which God or nature proposed to himself in their creation (i.e., final causes), for we ought not to presume so far as to think that we are sharers in the counsels of Deity. . ."—(*Principia*, pars i. §28.) "Considering this more attentively, the first thing that occurs to me is the reflection that I must not be surprised if I am not always capable of comprehending the reasons why God acts as he does; nor must I doubt of his existence because I find, perhaps, that there are several other things besides the present respecting which I understand neither why nor how they were created by him; for knowing already that my nature is extremely weak and limited and that the nature of God on the other hand is immense, incomprehensible, and infinite, I have no longer any difficulty in discerning that there is an infinity of things in his power, whose causes transcend the grasp of my mind, and this consideration alone is sufficient to convince me that the whole class of final causes is of no avail in physical [or natural] things, for it appears to me that I cannot, without exposing myself to the charge of temerity, seek to discover the [impenetrable] ends of Deity."—*Descartes* (Eng. Tr.), *Meditatio Quarta.*

shadow to mark from time to time the hour of the day, it would be no more a presumption than an error to him to conclude, that (whatever other uses the instrument was fit or was designed for) it is a sundial that was meant to show the hour of the day."[10]

With this opinion of Boyle that of Newton so entirely coincided that (according to Maclaurin) he thought the consideration of final causes *essential* to true philosophy and was accustomed to congratulate himself on the effect of his writings in reviving an attention to them, after the attempt of Descartes to discard them from physics. On this occasion, Maclaurin has remarked, "that of all sort of causes, final causes are the most clearly placed in our view—and that it is difficult to comprehend why it should be thought arrogant to attend to the design and contrivance that is so evidently displayed in nature and obvious to all men—to maintain, for instance, that the eye was made for seeing, though we may not be able either to account mechanically for the refraction of light in its coats, or to explain how the image is propagated from the retina to the mind.[11] It is Newton's own language, however, which alone can do justice to his sentiments on the present subject.

"The main business of natural philosophy is to argue from phenomena, without feigning hypotheses, and to deduce causes from effects until we come to the very first cause, which certainly is not mechanical; and not only to unfold the mechanism of the world, but chiefly to resolve these and such like questions: *Whence is it,*

10   In the same essay, Mr. Boyle has offered some very judicious strictures on the abuses to which the research of final causes is liable when incautiously and presumptuously pursued. An abstract of these, accompanied with a few illustrations from later writers, might form an interesting chapter in a treatise of inductive logic.

The subject has been since prosecuted with considerable ingenuity by Le Sage of Geneva, who has even attempted (and not altogether without success) to lay down logical rules for the investigation of *ends.* To this study, which he was anxious to form into a separate science, he gave a very ill chosen name of *Teléologie*, a name, if I am not mistaken, first suggested by Wolfius. For some valuable fragments of his intended work with respect to it, see the *Account of His Life and Writings* by his friend M. Prevost (Geneva, 1805).

11   *Account of Newton's Philosophical Discoveries*, Book i., chap. ii.

that nature does nothing in vain[12] *and whence arises all that order and beauty which we see in the world?—How came the bodies of animals to be contrived with so much art, and for what ends were their several parts? Was the eye contrived without skill in optics and the ear without knowledge of sounds?"*[13]

In multiplying these quotations, I am well aware that authorities are not arguments; but when a prejudice to which authority alone has given currency is to be combated, what other refutation is likely to be effectual?

After all, it were to be wished that the scholastic phrase *final cause* could without affectation be dropped from our philosophical vocabulary, and some more unexceptionable mode of speaking substituted instead of it. In this elementary work I have not presumed to lay aside entirely a form of expression consecrated in the writings of Newton, and of his most eminent followers; but I am fully sensible of its impropriety and am not without hopes that I may contribute something to encourage the gradual disuse of it by the indiscriminate employment of the words *ends* and *uses* to convey the same idea. Little more, perhaps, than the general adoption of one or other of these terms is necessary to bring candid and reflecting minds to a uniformity of language as well as of sentiment on the point in question.

It was before observed with respect to anatomists that all of them without exception, whether professedly friendly or hostile to the inquisition of final causes, concur in availing themselves of its guidance in their physiological researches. A similar remark will be found to apply to other classes of scientific inquirers. Whatever their speculative opinions may be, the moment their curiosity is fairly engaged in the pursuit of truth, either physical or moral, they involuntarily, and often perhaps unconsciously, submit their understandings to a logic borrowed neither from the schools of Aristotle nor of Bacon. The ethical system (for example) of those ancient philosophers who held that virtue consists in following

12   Newton here refers to the axiom of the Aristotelic philosophy that *"Nature (or God) does nothing in vain."—Ed.*
13   Newton's *Optics*, query 28.

nature, not only involves a recognition of final causes, but represents the study of them in as far as regards the ends and destination of our own being as the great business and duty of life.[14] The system, too, of those physicians who profess to follow nature in the treatment of diseases, by watching and aiding her medicative powers, assumes the same doctrine as its fundamental principle. A still more remarkable illustration, however, of the influence which this species of evidence has over the belief, even when we are the least aware of its connection with metaphysical conclusions, occurs in the history of the French Economical System. Of the comprehensive and elevated views which at first suggested it, the title of *Physiocratie*, by which it was early distinguished, affords a strong presumptive proof; and the same thing is more fully demonstrated by the frequent recurrence made in it to the physical and moral laws of nature as the unerring standard which the legislator should keep in view in all his positive institutions.[15] I do not speak at present of the justness of these opinions. I wish only to remark that in the statement of them given by their original authors it is taken for granted as a truth self-evident and indisputable, not merely that benevolent design is manifested in all the physical and moral arrangements connected with this globe but that the study of these arrangements is indispensably necessary to lay a solid foundation for political science.

The same principles appear to have led Mr. Smith into that train of thinking which gave birth to his inquiries concerning national wealth. "Man," he observes in one of his oldest manuscripts now extant, "is generally considered by statesmen and projectors

14   "Study of things, the causes and the ends;
       Whence is our being, and to what it tends.
             Persius (Drummond) [*Sat.* iii. v. 66, *seq.*]

      "But what do I seek? to learn perfectly what nature is, and to follow
      it."   Epictetus [*Man.* c. 46]
15   "Those laws together constitute what is called *the law of nature*. All men and all human powers should be submitted to the control of those sovereign laws instituted by the Supreme Being. They are immutable, irrefragable, and the best possible, and consequently, the basis of the most perfect government and the fundamental rule of all positive laws; for positive laws are only enactments for maintaining the natural order which is evidently the most advantageous to the human race."—Quesnay.

as the materials of a sort of political mechanics. Projectors disturb nature in the course of her operations in human affairs, and it requires no more than to let her alone, and give her fair play in the pursuit of her own designs." And in another passage: "Little else is requisite to carry a state to the highest degree of opulence from the lowest barbarism, but peace, easy taxes, and a tolerable administration of justice, all the rest being brought about by the natural course of things. All governments which thwart this natural course, which force things into another channel, or which endeavor to arrest the progress of society at a particular point are unnatural, and to support themselves are obliged to be oppressive and tyrannical."[16] Various other passages of a similar import might be quoted, both from his *Wealth of Nations,* and from his *Theory of Moral Sentiments.*

This doctrine of Smith and Quesnay, which tends to simplify the theory of legislation, by exploding the policy of those complicated checks and restraints which swell the municipal codes of most nations, has now, I believe, become the prevailing creed of thinking men all over Europe, and, as commonly happens to prevailing creeds, has been pushed by many of its partisans far beyond the views and intentions of its original authors. Such, too, is the effect of fashion on the one hand and of obnoxious phrases on the other that it has found some of its most zealous abettors and propagators among writers who would without a moment's hesitation have rejected as puerile and superstitious any reference to *final causes* in a philosophical discussion.

Danger of Confounding Final with Physical Causes in the Philosophy of the Human Mind

Having said so much upon the research of final causes in *physics, properly so called,* I shall subjoin a few remarks on its application to the philosophy of the human mind—a science in which the just rules of investigation are as yet far from being generally understood. Of this no stronger proof can be produced than

16   *Biographical Memoirs of Smith, Robertson, and Reid,* p. 100. [*Infra,* vol. ix.]

the confusion between final and efficient causes, which perpetually recurs in the writings of our latest and most eminent moralists.
The same confusion, as I have already observed, prevailed in the
physical reasonings of the Aristotelians, but since the time of Bacon
has been so completely corrected that in the wildest theories of
modern naturalists hardly a vestige of it is to be traced.

To the logical error just mentioned it is owing that so many
false accounts have been given of the principles of human conduct
or of the motives by which men are stimulated to action. When
the general laws of our internal frame are attentively examined,
they will be found to have for their object the happiness and improvement both of the individual and of society. This is their final
cause, or the end for which we may presume they were destined
by our Maker. But in such cases it seldom happens that while
Man is obeying the *active impulses* of his nature, he has an idea
of the ultimate ends which he is promoting, or is able to calculate
the remote effects of the movements which he impresses on the
little wheels around him. These *active impulses,* therefore, may in
one sense be considered as the *efficient causes* of his conduct, inasmuch as they are the means employed to determine him to particular pursuits and habits, and as they operate (in the *first* instance, at least) without any reflection on his part on the purposes
to which they are subservient. Philosophers, however, have in
every age been extremely apt to conclude when they had discovered the salutary tendency of any active principle that it was from
a sense or foreknowledge of this tendency that the principle derived its origin. Hence have arisen the theories which attempt to
account for all our actions from self-love, and also those which
would resolve the whole of morality either into political views of
general expediency or into an enlightened regard to our own best
interests.

I do not know of any author who has been so completely aware
of this common error as Mr. Smith. In examining the principles
conected with our moral constitution, he always treats separately
of their *final causes* and of the *mechanism* (as he calls it) by which
nature accomplishes the effect; and he has even been at pains to
point out to his successors the great importance of attending to

the distinction between these two speculations. "In every part of the universe, we observe means adjusted with the nicest artifice to the ends which they are intended to produce; and in the mechanism of a plant or animal body, admire how everything is contrived for advancing the two great purposes of nature, the support of the individual, and the propagation of the species. But in these, and in all such objects, we still distinguish the efficient from the final cause of their several motions and organizations. The digestion of the food, the circulation of the blood, and the secretion of the several juices which are drawn from it are operations all of them necessary for the great purposes of animal life; yet we never endeavor to account for them from those purposes as from their efficient causes, nor imagine that the blood circulates, or the food digests, of its own accord, and with a view or intention to the purposes of circulation or digestion. The wheels of the watch are all admirably adapted to the end for which it was made, the pointing of the hour. All their various motions conspire in the nicest manner to produce this effect. If they were endowed with a desire and intention to produce it, they could not do it better. Yet, we never ascribe any such intention or desire to them, but to the watchmaker, and we know that they are put into motion by a spring, which intends the effect it produces as little as they do. But though, in accounting for the operations of bodies, we never fail to distinguish, in this manner, the efficient from the final cause, in accounting for those of the mind, we are apt to confound these two different things with one another. When, by natural principles, we are led to advance those ends which a refined and enlightened reason would recommend to us, we are very apt to impute to that reason, as to their efficient cause, the sentiments and actions by which we advance those ends, and to imagine that to be the wisdom of man, which, in reality, is the wisdom of God. Upon a superficial view, this cause seems sufficient to produce the effects which are ascribed to it; and the system of human nature seems to be more simple and agreeable when all its different operations are in this manner deduced from a single principle."[17]

These remarks apply with peculiar force to a theory of morals

17   *Theory of Moral Sentiments*, vol. i., p. 216, *et seq.*, 6th ed.

which has made much noise in our own times—a theory which resolves the obligation of all the different virtues into a sense of their *utility*. At the time when Mr. Smith wrote, it had been recently brought into fashion by the ingenious and refined disquisitions of Mr. Hume; and there can be little doubt that the foregoing strictures were meant by the author as an indirect refutation of his friend's doctrines.

The same theory (which is of a very ancient date[18]) has been since revived by Mr. Godwin and by the late excellent Dr. Paley. Widely as these two different writers differ in the *source* whence they derive their rule of conduct and the *sanctions* by which they enforce its observance, they are perfectly agreed about its paramount authority over every other principle of action. "Whatever is *expedient*," says Dr. Paley, "is *right*. It is the utility of any moral rule alone which constitutes the obligation of it.[19]. . . But then, it must be expedient *on the whole*, at the long run, in all its effects, collateral and remote, as well as those which are immediate and direct, as it is obvious that in computing consequences it makes no difference in what way or at what distance they ensue."[20] Mr. Godwin has nowhere expressed himself on this fundamental question of practical ethics in terms more decided and unqualified.

The observations quoted from Mr. Smith on the proneness of the mind, in moral speculations, to confound together efficient and final causes, furnish a key to the chief difficulty by which the patrons of this specious but very dangerous system have been misled.

[18]   "*Utility itself, to a great extent, the mother of right and equity.*"— Horace, *Sat.*, I. iii. 93.

[19]   *Principles of Moral and Political Philosophy*, vol. i., p. 70, 5th ed.

[20]   *Ibid.*, p. 78.

In another part of his work, Dr. Paley explicitly asserts that *every* moral rule is liable to be superseded in particular cases on the ground of expediency. "Moral philosophy cannot pronounce that any rule of morality is so rigid as to bend to no exceptions, nor, on the other hand, can she comprise these exceptions within any previous description. She confesses that the obligation of every law depends upon its ultimate utility, that this utility having a finite and determinate value, situations may be feigned and consequently may possibly arise in which the general tendency is outweighed by the enormity of the particular mischief, and of course, where ultimate utility renders it as much an act of duty to break the rule, as it is on the other occasions to observe it."—vol. ii., p. 411.

Among the qualities connected with the different virtues, there is none more striking than their beneficial influence on social happiness, and accordingly, moralists of all descriptions when employed in enforcing particular duties, such as justice, veracity, temperance, and the various charities of private life, never fail to enlarge on the numerous blessings which follow in their train. The same observation may be applied to *self-interest,* inasmuch as the most effectual way of promoting it is universally acknowledged to be by a strict and habitual regard to the obligations of morality. In consequence of this *unity of design,* which is not less conspicuous in the moral than in the natural world, it is easy for a philosopher to give a plausible explanation of all our duties from *one* principle, because the general tendency of all of them is to determine us to the same course of life. It does not, however, follow from this, that it is from such a comprehensive survey of the consequences of human conduct that our ideas of right and wrong are derived, or that we are entitled, in particular cases, to form rules of action to ourselves, drawn from speculative conclusions concerning the *final causes* of our moral constitution. If it be true (as some theologians have presumed to assert) that benevolence is the sole principle of action in the deity, we must suppose that the duties of veracity and justice were enjoined by Him, *not* on account of their intrinsic rectitude, but of their utility. But still, with respect to man, these are sacred and indispensable laws—laws which he never transgresses, without incurring the penalties of self-condemnation and remorse. And indeed if, without the guidance of any internal monitor, he were left to infer the duties incumbent on him from a calculation and comparison of remote effects, we may venture to affirm that there would not be enough of virtue left in the world to hold society together.

To those who have been accustomed to reflect on the general analogy of the human constitution and on the admirable adaptation of its various parts to that scene in which we are destined to act, this last consideration will, independently of any examination of the fact, suggest a very strong presumption a priori against the doctrine to which the foregoing remarks relate. For is it at all consonant with the other arrangements so wisely calculated for human happiness to suppose that the conduct of such a fallible and shortsighted creature as man would be left to be regulated by no other principle than the private opinion of each individual concerning the *expediency* of his own actions, or in other words, by the conjectures which he might form on the good or evil resulting *on the whole* from an endless train of future contingencies? Were this the case, the opinions of mankind with respect to the rules of morality would be as various as their judgments about the probable issue of the most doubtful and difficult determinations in politics. Numberless cases might be fancied in which a person would not only *claim* merit but actually *possess* it in consequence of actions which are generally regarded with indignation and abhorrence: for unless we admit such duties as justice, veracity, and gratitude to be immediately and imperatively sanctioned by the authority of reason and of conscience, it follows as a necessary inference that we are *bound* to violate them whenever by doing so we have a prospect of advancing any of the essential interests of society; or (which amounts to the same thing) that a good *end* is sufficient to sanctify whatever *means* may appear to us to be necessary for its accomplishment. Even men of the soundest and most penetrating understandings might frequently be led to the perpetration of enormities if they had no other light to guide them but what they derived from their own uncertain anticipations of futurity. And when we consider how small the number of such men is, in comparison of those whose judgments are perverted by the prejudices of education and their own selfish passions, it is easy to see what a scene of anarchy the world would become. Of this indeed we have too melancholy an experimental proof in the history of those individuals who have in practice adopted the rule of *general expediency* as their whole code of morality, a rule which the most execrable scourges of the human race have in all ages professed to follow and of which they have uniformly availed themselves as an apology for their deviations from the ordinary maxims of right and wrong.

Fortunately for mankind, the peace of society is not thus entrusted to accident, the great rules of a virtuous conduct being confessedly of such a nature as to be obvious to every sincere and well-disposed mind. And it is in a peculiar degree striking that while the *theory* of ethics involves some of the most abstruse questions which have ever employed the human faculties, the moral judgments and moral feelings of the most distant ages and nations with respect to all the most essential duties of life are one and the same.[21]

Of this theory of utility, so strongly recommended to some by the powerful genius of Hume, and to others by the well-merited popularity of Paley, the most satisfactory of all refutations is to be found in the work of Mr. Godwin. It is unnecessary to inquire how far the practical lessons he has inculcated are logically inferred from his fundamental principle; for although I apprehend much might be objected to these, even on his own hypotheses, yet, if such be the conclusions to which, in the judgment of so acute a reasoner, it *appeared* to lead with demonstrative evidence, nothing farther is requisite to illustrate the practical tendency of a system which, absolving men from the obligations imposed on them with so commanding an authority by the moral constitution of human nature, abandons every individual to the guidance of his own narrow views concerning the complicated interests of political society.[22]

[21]   "If we inquire after what is absolutely right, this is clear; if we seek what is most expedient, this is obscure. If we be of opinion, as indeed we ought to be, that nothing is expedient but what is right and honorable, we shall be in no doubt as to our duty."—Cicero, *Ep. ad Fam.*, iv. 2.

[22]   It is remarkable that Mr. Hume, by far the ablest advocate for the theory in question, has indirectly acknowledged its inconsistence with some of the most important facts which it professes to explain. "Though the *heart*," he observes in the 5th section of his *Inquiry concerning Morals*, "takes not part entirely with those general notions, nor regulates all its love and hatred by the universal abstract differences of vice and virtue, without regard to self, and the persons with whom we are more intimately connected; yet have these moral differences a considerable influence, and being sufficient at least for discourse, serve all the purposes in company, on the theater, and in the schools." On this passage, the following very curious note is to be found at the end of the volume, a note (by the way) which deserves to be added to the other proofs already given of the irresistible influence which the doctrine of final causes occasionally exercises over the most skeptical minds. "*It is wisely ordained by nature* that private connections should *commonly* prevail over universal views and considerations; otherwise our affections and actions would be dissipated and lost for want of a proper limited object." Does not this remark imply an acknowledgment, first, that the principle of

One very obvious consideration seems to have entirely escaped the notice of this, as well as of many other late inquirers: that, in ethical researches, not less than in those which relate to the material universe, the business of the philosopher is limited to the analytical investigation of general laws from the observed phenomena; and that if, in any instance, his conclusions should be found inconsistent with acknowledged facts, the former must necessarily be corrected or modified by the latter. On such occasions, the ultimate appeal must be always made to the moral sentiments and emotions of the human race. The representations, for example, which we read with so much delight in those poets of whatever age and country, who have most successfully touched the human heart—of the heroical sacrifices made to gratitude, to parental duty, to filial piety, to conjugal affection—are not amenable to the authority of any ethical theory, but are the most authentic records of the phenomena which it is the object of such theories to generalize. The sentiment of Publius Syrus—*The worst thing that can be said of a man is that he is ungrateful*—speaks a language which accords with every feeling of an unperverted mind; it speaks the language of nature, which it is the province of the moralist *not* to criticize but to listen to with reverence. By employing our reason to interpret and to obey this and the other moral suggestions of the heart, we may trust with confidence that we take the most effectual means in our power to augment the sum of human happiness, but the discovery of this connection between *virtue* and *utility* is the slow result of extensive and philosophical combinations, and it would soon cease to have a foundation in truth if men were to substitute their own conceptions of expediency instead of those rules of action which are inspired by the wisdom of God.

It must not be concluded from the foregoing observations that even in ethical inquiries the consideration of final causes is to be rejected. On the contrary, Mr. Smith himself, whose logical pre-

---

general expediency (the *sole* principle of virtuous conduct, according to Mr. Hume, in our most important transactions with our fellow creatures) would not contribute to the happiness of society, if men should *commonly* act upon it; and secondly, that some provision is made in our moral constitution, that we shall, in fact, be influenced by other motives in discharging the offices of private life?

cepts on this subject I have now been endeavoring to illustrate and enforce, has frequently indulged his curiosity in speculations about *uses* or *advantages* and seems plainly to have considered them as important objects of philosophical study, not less than *efficient* causes. The only caution to be observed is that the one may not be confounded with the other.

Between these two different researches, however, there is both in physics and ethics a very intimate connection. In various cases, the consideration of final causes had led to the discovery of some general law of nature; and in almost every case, the discovery of a general law clearly points out some wise and beneficent purposes to which it is subservient. Indeed, it is chiefly the prospect of such applications which renders the investigation of general laws interesting to the mind.

20

David Hume

MARRIAGE OF RELATIVES

HAD THE QUESTION of Henry's marriage with Catherine
been examined by the principles of sound philosophy, exempt
from superstition, it seemed not liable to much difficulty. The natural reason why marriage in certain degrees is prohibited by the
civil laws and condemned by the moral sentiments of all nations
is derived from men's care to preserve purity of manners, while
they reflect that if a commerce of love were authorized between
near relations, the frequent opportunities of intimate conversation,
especially during early youth, would introduce a universal dissoluteness and corruption. But as the customs of countries vary considerably, and open an intercourse more or less restrained between
different families or between the several members of the same family, we find that the moral precept, varying with its cause, is
susceptible without any inconvenience of very different latitude
in the several ages and nations of the world. The extreme delicacy
of the Greeks permitted no communication between persons of
different sexes, except where they lived under the same roof; and
even the apartments of a stepmother and her daughters were almost as much shut up against visits from the husband's sons as
against those from any stranger or more distant relation; hence in
that nation it was lawful for a man to marry not only his niece,

Reprinted from David Hume, *The History of England* (New York:
Harper & Brothers, 1879), III, 94–95. Title supplied. (It should be recalled that Catherine of Aragon had been married to Henry's deceased
brother, Arthur.—Ed.)

but his half-sister by the father—a liberty unknown to the Romans and other nations, where a more open intercourse was authorized between the sexes. Reasoning from this principle, it would appear that the ordinary commerce of life among great princes is so obstructed by ceremony and numerous attendants that no ill consequence would result among them from marrying a brother's widow, especially if the dispensation of the supreme priest be previously required in order to justify what may in common cases be condemned and to hinder the precedent from becoming too common and familiar. And as strong motives of public interest and tranquillity may frequently require such alliances between the foreign families, there is the less reason for extending toward them the full rigor of the rule which has place among individuals.

21

Francis Hutcheson

RELATIONSHIP AND MARRIAGE

THE NEARER DEGREES of consanguinity and affinity, Christians, and many heathen nations too have always looked upon as moral impediments of marriage. The natural reasons commonly alleged scarce seem to have force proportioned to the great infamy and the notions of impiety attending such marriages. The most abhorred kind is that between the ascending and descending degrees. Not only the inequality of years, but the natural reverence in these relations are very opposite to the equality produced by marriage. But greater inequalities of years sometimes do not make marriages either immoral, or even imprudent. And it is not every sort of reverence, due to higher merit or authority, or gratitude due for the greatest benefits, which would be inconsistent with this relation, though that of parents seems inconsistent. It is scarce accountable without some natural instinct of aversion to such mixtures, how they have been so universally abhorred. A monstrous practice received by one sect in Persia is no objection to this supposition, which is confirmed by the sentiments of all the world besides.

It is argued that brothers and sisters by living together from their infancy would fall too early into such passions and be less capable of resisting solicitation through their great intimacy were there not a severe prohibition making such commerce matter of

Reprinted from Francis Hutcheson, *A System of Moral Philosophy* (Glasgow and London, 1755), II, 170–73. Title supplied.

abhorrence. But it often happens that cousin-germans, and remoter relations are educated together in the same intimacy, and we see no dismal effects from the permission of intermarriages among them. And were these marriages with sisters lawful, one would think the early passions would do no more harm than they must frequently do on other occasions, where young people contract early acquaintance. If there be any natural aversion in this case too, as well as between parents and children, checking the general impulse, it seems not so strong, and we find that such marriages of brothers with sisters have been more received in heathen nations. There is more of equality in this relation; whereas the long habitual authority exercised by parents, and the reverence and subjection to which children are enured, may possibly without other principles restrain all these amorous inclinations so naturally requiring an equality.

Whatever natural causes there may be for the very general aversions to marriages among the nearer relations by consanguinity and even affinity, it is certain there have been such aversions in many nations little civilized, and where we can scarce imagine that either very artful considerations of general interest or very delicate sentiments of decency have occasioned them. And the abhorrence of such marriages was everywhere much higher than any reasons of expediency or prudence could have occasioned. Hence some ingenious men conclude that there has been some[1] early divine prohibition, the memory or tradition of which has been preserved among most nations, in some more distinctly, and in others less, as there was greater or less attention to the purity of manners.

There is one manifest and important reason of prudence why a wise legislator should prohibit such marriages, that were they not restrained and abhorred, the early opportunities would make them exceedingly frequent, and by this means the sacred bonds of affection would be too much confined, each family would be a little system by itself, detached from others; at least as to all the stronger bonds of affection. Whereas now, in consequence of the

---

1 This seems one of the best evidences for the Jewish tradition of the Praecepta Noachidarum.

prohibition and the general abhorrence ensuing upon it, or upon any other causes which may probably concur in this matter, multitudes of families are beautifully interwoven with each other in affection and interest, and friendly ties are much further diffused. There may be other reasons in nature not known to us, or not yet fully observed. A mixture of different families may be necessary to prevent a degeneracy of the human race; as some pretend that such intermixtures, or crossing the strain by cattle of a different breed, is necessary to prevent their degenerating, if we can decently make such comparisons.

VI. History and
Sociology

22

David Hume

OF SUPERSTITION AND ENTHUSIASM

THAT THE CORRUPTION of the best things produces the worst is grown into a maxim and is commonly proved, among other instances, by the pernicious effects of *superstition* and *enthusiasm*, the corruptions of true religion.

These two species of false religion, though both pernicious, are yet of a very different and even a contrary nature. The mind of man is subject to certain unaccountable terrors and apprehensions, proceeding either from the unhappy situation of private or public affairs, from ill health, from a gloomy and melancholy disposition, or from the concurrence of all these circumstances. In such a state of mind, infinite unknown evils are dreaded from unknown agents, and where real objects of terror are wanting, the soul, active to its own prejudice and fostering its predominant inclination, finds imaginary ones to whose power and malevolence it sets no limits. As these enemies are entirely invisible and unknown, the methods taken to appease them are equally unaccountable, and consist in ceremonies, observances, mortifications, sacrifices, presents, or in any practice, however absurd or frivolous, which either folly or knavery recommends to a blind and terrified credulity. Weakness, fear, melancholy, together with ignorance, are, therefore, the true sources of *superstition*.

Reprinted from David Hume, *Essays*, T. H. Green and T. H. Grose, eds. (London: Longmans Green, 1875), I, 144–50.

But the mind of man is also subject to an unaccountable elevation and presumption, arising from prosperous success, from luxuri-
ant health, from strong spirits, or from a bold and confident disposition. In such a state of mind, the imagination swells with great
but confused conceptions to which no sublunary beauties or enjoyments can correspond. Every thing mortal and perishable vanishes
as unworthy of attention. And a full range is given to the fancy in
the invisible regions or world of spirits where the soul is at liberty
to indulge itself in every imagination, which may best suit its
present taste and disposition. Hence arise raptures, transports, and
surprising flights of fancy; and confidence and presumption still
increasing, these raptures, being altogether unaccountable and
seeming quite beyond the reach of our ordinary faculties, are
attributed to the immediate inspiration of that Divine Being, who
is the object of devotion. In a little time, the inspired person comes
to regard himself as a distinguished favorite of the Divinity, and
when this frenzy once takes place, which is the summit of enthusiasm, every whimsy is consecrated: human reason and even morality are rejected as fallacious guides; and the fanatic madman
delivers himself over blindly and without reserve to the supposed
illapses of the spirit and to inspiration from above. Hope, pride,
presumption, a warm imagination, together with ignorance, are
therefore the true sources of *enthusiasm.*

These two species of false religion might afford occasion to
many speculations, but I shall confine myself at present to a few
reflections concerning their different influence on government and
society.

My first reflection is *that superstition is favorable to priestly
power and enthusiasm not less or rather more contrary to it than
sound reason and philosophy.* As superstition is founded on fear,
sorrow, and a depression of spirits, it represents the man to himself in such despicable colors that he appears unworthy, in his own
eyes, of approaching the divine presence and naturally has recourse
to any other person, whose sanctity of life, or perhaps impudence
and cunning, have made him be supposed more favored by the
Divinity. To him the superstitious entrust their devotions: to his
care they recommend their prayers, petitions, and sacrifices; and

by his means, they hope to render their addresses acceptable to their incensed Deity. Hence the origin of *priests*, who may justly be regarded as an invention of a timorous and abject superstition, which, ever diffident of itself, dares not offer up its own devotions, but ignorantly thinks to recommend itself to the Divinity by the mediation of his supposed friends and servants. As superstition is a considerable ingredient in almost all religions, even the most fanatical, there being nothing but philosophy able entirely to conquer these unaccountable terrors; hence it proceeds that in almost every sect of religion there are priests to be found, but the stronger mixture there is of superstition, the higher is the authority of the priesthood.

On the other hand, it may be observed that all enthusiasts have been free from the yoke of ecclesiastics and have expressed great independence in their devotion, with a contempt of forms, ceremonies, and traditions. The *Quakers* are the most egregious, though at the same time the most innocent enthusiasts that have yet been known, and are perhaps the only sect that have never admitted priests among them. The Independents, of all the *English* sectaries, approach nearest to the *Quakers* in fanaticism and in their freedom from priestly bondage. The *Presbyterians* follow after, at an equal distance in both particulars. In short this observation is founded in experience and will also appear to be founded in reason, if we consider that as enthusiasm arises from a presumptuous pride and confidence, it thinks itself sufficiently qualified to *approach* the Divinity without any human mediator. Its rapturous devotions are so fervent that it even imagines itself *actually* to *approach* him by the way of contemplation and inward converse; which makes it neglect all those outward ceremonies and observances to which the assistance of the priests appears so requisite in the eyes of their superstitious votaries. The fanatic consecrates himself and bestows on his own person a sacred character much superior to what forms and ceremonious institutions can confer on any other.

My *second* reflection with regard to these species of false religion is *that religions which partake of enthusiasm are on their first rise more furious and violent than those which partake of super-*

stition, but in a little time become more gentle and moderate. The
violence of this species of religion, when excited by novelty and
animated by opposition, appears from numberless instances; of the
Anabaptists in Germany, the *Camisards* in France, the *Levellers*
and the other fanatics in England, and the *Covenanters* in Scotland. Enthusiasm being founded on strong spirits and a presumptuous boldness of character, it naturally begets the most extreme
resolutions, especially after it rises to that height as to inspire the
deluded fanatic with the opinion of divine illuminations and with
a contempt for the common rules of reason, morality, and prudence.

It is thus enthusiasm produces the most cruel disorders in
human society, but its fury is like that of thunder and tempest,
which exhaust themselves in a little time and leave the air more
calm and pure than before. When the first fire of enthusiasm is
spent, men naturally, in all fanatical sects, sink into the greatest
remissness and coolness in sacred matters, there being no body
of men among them, endowed with sufficient authority, whose
interest is concerned to support the religious spirit: no rites, no
ceremonies, no holy observances, which may enter into the common train of life, and preserve the sacred principles from oblivion.
Superstition, on the contrary, steals in gradually and insensibly,
renders men tame and submissive, is acceptable to the magistrate,
and seems inoffensive to the people: until at last the priest, having
firmly established his authority, becomes the tyrant and disturber
of human society by his endless contentions, persecutions, and religious wars. How smoothly did the Romish church advance in her
acquisition of power? But into what dismal convulsions did she
throw all Europe in order to maintain it? On the other hand, our
sectaries, who were formerly such dangerous bigots, are now become very free reasoners; and the Quakers seem to approach
nearly the only regular body of Deists in the universe, the literati,
or the disciples of Confucius in China.[1]

My *third* observation on this head is *that superstition is an
enemy to civil liberty and enthusiasm a friend to it.* As superstition
groans under the dominion of priests, and enthusiasm is destructive

[1]   The Chinese Literati have no priests or ecclesiastical establishment.

of all ecclesiastical power, this sufficiently accounts for the present observation. Not to mention that enthusiasm, being the infirmity of bold and ambitious tempers, is naturally accompanied with a spirit of liberty; as superstition, on the contrary, renders men tame and abject and fits them for slavery. We learn from English history that during the civil wars the *Independents* and Deists, though the most opposite in their religious principles, yet were united in their political ones and were alike passionate for a commonwealth. And since the origin of Whig and Tory, the leaders of the Whigs have either been Deists or professed latitudinarians in their principles, that is, friends to toleration and indifferent to any particular sect of Christians; while the sectaries, who have all a strong tincture of enthusiasm, have always, without exception, concurred with that party in defense of civil liberty. The resemblance in their superstitions long united the high-church Tories and the Roman Catholics in support of prerogative and kingly power, though experience of the tolerating spirit of the Whigs seems of late to have reconciled the Catholics to that party.

The Molinists and *Jansenists* in *France* have a thousand unintelligible disputes, which are not worthy the reflection of a man of sense; but what principally distinguishes these two sects, and alone merits attention, is the different spirit of their religion. The Molinists conducted by the Jesuits are great friends to superstition, rigid observers of external forms and ceremonies, and devoted to the authority of the priests and to tradition. The Jansenists are enthusiasts and zealous promoters of the passionate devotion and of the inward life, little influenced by authority, and in a word, but half Catholics. The consequences are exactly conformable to the foregoing reasoning. The Jesuits are the tyrants of the people and the slaves of the court, and the Jansenists preserve alive the small sparks of the love of liberty, which are to be found in the French nation.

23

David Hume

REMARKS ON REFORM,
PURITANISM, AND LIBERTY

OF ALL THE EUROPEAN CHURCHES which shook off the yoke
of papal authority, no one proceeded with so much reason and
moderation as the Church of England—an advantage which had
been derived partly from the interposition of the civil magistrate in this innovation, partly from the gradual and slow steps by
which the Reformation was conducted in that kingdom. Rage and
animosity against the Catholic religion was as little indulged as
could be supposed in such a revolution; the fabric of the secular
hierarchy was maintained entire; the ancient liturgy was preserved
so far as was thought consistent with the new principles; many
ceremonies, become venerable from age and preceding use, were
retained; the splendor of the Romish worship, though removed,
had at least given place to order and decency; the distinctive habits
of the clergy, according to their different ranks, were continued;
no innovation was admitted merely from spite and opposition to
former usage; and the new religion, by mitigating the genius of
the ancient superstition and rendering it more compatible with the
peace and interests of society, had preserved itself in that happy
medium which wise men have always sought and which the people have so seldom been able to maintain.

Reprinted from David Hume, *History of England* (New York: Harper
& Bros., 1879), III, 526–31, 591–94; IV, 575–77; V, 203–4. Title
supplied.

But though such in general was the spirit of the Reformation in that country, many of the English reformers, being men of more warm complexions and more obstinate tempers endeavored to push matters to extremities against the Church of Rome and indulged themselves in the most violent contrariety and antipathy to all former practices. Among these, Hooper, who afterward suffered for his religion with such extraordinary constancy, was chiefly distinguished. This man was appointed, during the reign of Edward, to the see of Gloucester and made no scruple of accepting the episcopal office; but he refused to be consecrated in the episcopal habit, the cymar and rochet, which had formerly, he said, been abused by superstition, and which were thereby rendered unbecoming a true Christian. Cranmer and Ridley were surprised at this objection, which opposed the received practice and even the established laws, and though young Edward, desirous of promoting a man so celebrated for his eloquence, his zeal, and his morals, enjoined them to dispense with this ceremony, they were still determined to retain it. Hooper then embraced the resolution rather to refuse the bishopric than clothe himself in those hated garments; but it was deemed requisite that for the sake of the example he should not escape so easily. He was first confined to Cranmer's house, then thrown into prison until he should consent to be a bishop on the terms proposed; he was plied with conferences and reprimands and arguments; Bucer and Peter Martyr and the most celebrated foreign reformers were consulted on this important question; and a compromise, with great difficulty, was at last made that Hooper should not be obliged to wear commonly the obnoxious robes, but should agree to be consecrated in them and to use them during cathedral service—a condescension not a little extraordinary in a man of so inflexible a spirit as this reformer.

The same objection which had arisen with regard to the episcopal habit had been moved against the raiment of the inferior clergy, and the surplice, in particular, with the tippet and corner cap, was a great object of abhorrence to many of the popular zealots. In vain was it urged that particularly habits, as well as postures and ceremonies, having been constantly used by the clergy and employed in religious service, acquire a veneration in the eyes of the people, appear sacred in their apprehensions, excite their devotion, and contract a kind of mysterious virtue, which attaches the affections of men to the national and established worship; that, in order to produce this effect, a uniformity in these particulars is requisite and even a perseverance as far as possible in the former practice; and that the nation would be happy if, by retaining these inoffensive observances, the reformers could engage the people to renounce willingly what was absurd or pernicious in the ancient superstition. These arguments, which had influence with wise men, were the very reasons which engaged the violent Protestants to reject the habits. They pushed matters to a total opposition with the Church of Rome; every compliance, they said, was a symbolizing with Antichrist. And this spirit was carried so far by some reformers that, in a national remonstrance made afterward by the Church of Scotland against these habits, it was asked, "What has Christ Jesus to do with Belial? What has darkness to do with light? If surplices, corner caps, and tippets have been badges of idolaters in the very act of their idolatry, why should the preacher of Christian liberty and the open rebuker of all superstition partake with the dregs of the Romish beast? Yea, who is there that ought not rather to be afraid of taking in his hand or on his forehead the print and mark of that odious beast?" But this application was rejected by the English church.

There was only one instance in which the spirit of contradiction to the Romanists took place universally in England: the altar was removed from the wall, was placed in the middle of the church, and was thenceforth denominated the communion table. The reason why this innovation met with such general reception was that the nobility and gentry got thereby a pretense for making spoil of the plate, vestures, and rich ornaments which belonged to the altars.

These disputes, which had been started during the reign of Edward, were carried abroad by the Protestants who fled from the persecutions of Mary; and as the zeal of these men had received an increase from the furious cruelty of their enemies, they were generally inclined to carry their opposition to the utmost extremity against the practices of the Church of Rome. Their communication with Calvin and the other reformers who followed the discipline and worship of Geneva confirmed them in this obstinate reluctance; and though some of the refugees, particularly those who were established at Frankfort, still adhered to King Edward's liturgy, the prevailing spirit carried these confessors to seek a still farther reformation. On the accession of Elizabeth, they returned to their native country, and being regarded with general veneration on account of their zeal and past sufferings, they ventured to insist on the establishment of their projected model, nor did they want countenance from many considerable persons in the Queen's Council. But the princess herself, so far from being willing to despoil religion of the few ornaments and ceremonies which remained in it, was rather inclined to bring the public worship still nearer to the Romish ritual;[1] and she thought that the Reformation had already gone too far in shaking off those forms and observances which, without distracting men of more refined apprehensions, tend in a very innocent manner to allure and amuse and engage the vulgar. She took care to have a law for uniformity strictly enacted; she was empowered by the Parliament to add any new ceremonies which she thought proper, and though she was sparing in the exercise of this prerogative, she continued rigid in exacting an observance of the established laws, and in punishing all nonconformity. The zealots, therefore, who harbored a great antipathy to the episcopal order and to the whole liturgy were obliged in a great measure to conceal these sentiments, which would have been regarded as highly audacious and criminal, and they confined their avowed objections to the surplice, the confirmation of children,

1   *When Nowel, one of her chaplains, had spoken less reverently in a sermon preached before her of the sign of the cross she called aloud to him from her closet window, commanding him to retire from that ungodly digression and to return unto his text. And on the other side, when one of her divines had preached a sermon in defence of the real presense, she openly gave him thanks for his pains and piety. . . .* She would have absolutely forbidden the marriage of the clergy if Cecil had not interposed (Strype's *Life of Parker*, pp. 107, 108, 109). She was an enemy to sermons and usually said that she thought two or three preachers were sufficient for a whole county. It was probably for these reasons that one Doring told her to her face from the pulpit that she was like an untamed heifer that would not be ruled by God's people but obstructed his discipline (see *Life of Hooker*, prefixed to his works).

the sign of the cross in baptism, the ring in marriage, kneeling at
the sacrament, and bowing at the name of Jesus. So fruitless is it
for sovereigns to watch with a rigid care over orthodoxy and to
employ the sword in religious controversy that the work, perpetually renewed, is perpetually to begin; and a garb, a gesture, nay,
a metaphysical or grammatical distinction, when rendered important by the disputes of theologians and the zeal of the magistrate, is sufficient to destroy the unity of the church and even the
peace of society. These controversies had already excited such
ferment among the people that in some places they refused to frequent the churches where the habits and ceremonies were used,
would not salute the conforming clergy, and proceeded so far as
to revile them in the streets, to spit in their faces, and to use them
with all manner of contumely. And while the sovereign authority
checked these excesses, the flame was confined, not extinguished;
and burning fiercer from confinement, it burst out in the succeeding reigns to the destruction of the church and monarchy.

All enthusiasts, indulging themselves in rapturous flights, ecstasies, visions, inspirations, have a natural aversion to episcopal
authority, to ceremonies, rites, and forms, which they denominate
superstition, or beggarly elements, and which seem to restrain the
liberal effusions of their zeal and devotion; but there was another
set of opinions adopted by these innovators which rendered them
in a peculiar manner the object of Elizabeth's aversion. The same
bold and daring spirit which accompanied them in their addresses
to the divinity appeared in their political speculations, and the
principles of civil liberty, which, during some reigns, had been
little avowed in the nation and which were totally incompatible
with the present exorbitant prerogative had been strongly adopted
by this new sect. Scarcely any sovereign before Elizabeth, and
none after her, carried higher, both in speculation and in practice,
the authority of the crown; and the Puritans (so these sectaries
were called, on account of their pretending to a superior purity
of worship and discipline) could not recommend themselves
worse to her favor than by inculcating the doctrine of resisting or
restraining princes. From all these motives, the queen neglected
no opportunity of depressing those zealous innovators; and while

they were secretly countenanced by some of her most favorite ministers, Cecil, Leicester, Knolles, Bedford, Walsingham, she never was, to the end of her life reconciled to their principles and practices.

II

Peter Wentworth, a Puritan, who had signalized himself in former Parliaments by his free and undaunted spirit, opened this session [February 8, 1576] with a premeditated harangue, which drew on him the indignation of the House and gave great offense to the queen and the ministers. As it seems to contain a rude sketch of those principles of liberty which happily gained afterward the ascendant in England, it may not be improper to give, in a few words, the substance of it. He premised that the name of liberty is sweet, but the thing itself is precious beyond the most inestimable treasure, and that it behooved them to be careful, lest, contenting themselves with the sweetness of the name, they forego the substance and abandon what of all earthly possessions was of the highest value to the kingdom. He then proceeded to observe that freedom of speech in that House, a privilege so useful both to sovereign and subject, had been formerly infringed in many essential articles, and was at present exposed to the most imminent danger; that it was usual, when any subject of importance was handled, especially if it regarded religion, to surmise that these topics were disagreeable to the queen, and that the farther proceeding in them would draw down her indignation upon their temerity; that Solomon had justly affirmed the king's displeasure to be a messenger of death; and it was no wonder if men, even though urged by motives of conscience and duty, should be inclined to stop short when they found themselves exposed to so severe a penalty; that, by the employing of this argument, the House was incapacitated from serving their country, and even from serving the queen herself, whose ears, besieged by pernicious flatterers, were thereby rendered inaccessible to the most salutary truths; that it was a mockery to call an assembly a Parliament, yet deny it that privilege which was so essential to its being and with-

out which it must degenerate into an abject school of servility and
,dissimulation; that as the Parliament was the great guardian of the
laws, they ought to have liberty to discharge their trust, and to
maintain that authority whence even kings themselves derive
their being; that a king was constituted such by law, and though
he was not dependent on man, yet was he subordinate to God and
the law, and was obliged to make their prescriptions, not his own
will, the rule of his conduct; that even his commission, as God's
vicegerent, enforced, instead of loosening, this obligation, since he
was thereby invested with authority to execute on earth the will
of God, which is nothing but law and justice; that though these
surmises of displeasing the queen by their proceedings had im-
peached, in a very essential point, all freedom of speech, a privilege
granted them by a special law, yet was there a more express and
more dangerous invasion made on their liberties by frequent messages from the throne; that it had become a practice, when the
House was entering on any question, either ecclesiastical or civil,
to bring an order from the queen inhibiting them absolutely from
treating of such matters, and debarring them from all farther discussion of these momentous articles; that the prelates, emboldened
by her royal protection, had assumed a decisive power in all questions of religion, and required that every one should implicitly
submit his faith to their arbitrary determinations; that the love
which he bore his sovereign forbade him to be silent under such
abuses, or to sacrifice, on this important occasion, his duty to
servile flattery and complaisance; and that, as no earthly creature
was exempt from fault, so neither was the queen herself, but, in
imposing this servitude on her faithful Commons, she had committed a great and even dangerous fault against herself and the
whole commonwealth.

It is easy to observe from this speech that in this dawn of liberty the parliamentary style was still crude and unformed and that
the proper decorum of attacking ministers and counselors, without
interesting the honor of the crown or mentioning the person of the
sovereign, was not yet entirely established. The Commons expressed great displeasure at this unusual license: they sequestered
Wentworth from the House and committed him prisoner to the

sergeant-at-arms. They even ordered him to be examined by a committee, consisting of all those members who were also members of the privy council, and a report to be next day made to the House. This committee met in the star chamber, and wearing the aspect of that arbitrary court, summoned Wentworth to appear before them and answer for his behavior. But though the Commons had discovered so little delicacy or precaution in thus confounding their own authority with that of the star chamber, Wentworth better understood the principles of liberty and refused to give these counselors any account of his conduct in Parliament until he was satisfied that they acted, not as members of the privy council, but as a committee of the House. He justified his liberty of speech by pleading the rigor and hardship of the queen's messages, and notwithstanding that the committee showed him, by instances in other reigns, that the practice of sending such messages was not unprecedented, he would not agree to express any sorrow or repentance. The issue of the affair was that after a month's confinement the queen sent to the Commons, informing them that, from her special grace and favor, she had restored him to his liberty and to his place in the House. By this seeming lenity, she indirectly retained the power which she had assumed of imprisoning the members and obliging them to answer before her for their conduct in Parliament. And Sir Walter Mildmay endeavored to make the House sensible of her majesty's goodness in so gently remitting the indignation which she might justly conceive at the temerity of their member; but he informed them that they had not the liberty of speaking what and of whom they pleased and that indiscreet freedoms used in that House had, both in the present and foregoing ages, met with a proper chastisement. He warned them, therefore, not to abuse further the queen's clemency, lest she be constrained, contrary to her inclination, to turn an unsuccessful lenity into a necessary severity.

III

This Parliament [of 1621] is remarkable for being the epoch in which were first regularly formed, though without acquiring

these denominations, the parties of court and country—parties
which have ever since continued and which, while they often
threaten the total dissolution of the government, are the real cause
of its permanent life and vigor. In the ancient feudal constitution,
of which the English partook with other European nations, there
was a mixture not of authority and liberty, which we have since
enjoyed in this island and which now subsist uniformly together,
but of authority and anarchy, which perpetually shocked with each
other and which took place alternately, according as circumstances
were more or less favorable to either of them. A Parliament composed of barbarians, summoned from their fields and forests, un-
instructed by study, conversation, or travel; ignorant of their own
laws and history, and unacquainted with the situation of all foreign
nations; a Parliament called precariously by the king and dissolved
at his pleasure; sitting a few days, debating a few points prepared
for them, and whose members were impatient to return to their
own castles, where alone they were great, and to the chase, which
was their favorite amusement—such a Parliament was very little
fitted to enter into a discussion of all the questions of government
and to share, in a regular manner, the legal administration. The
name, the authority of the king alone appeared in the common
course of government; in extraordinary emergencies he assumed,
with still better reason, the sole direction. The imperfect and unformed laws left, in everything, a latitude of interpretation, and
when the ends pursued by the monarch were in general agreeable
to his subjects, little scruple or jealousy was entertained with
regard to the regularity of the means. During the reign of an able,
fortunate, or popular prince, no member of either House, much
less of the Lower, dared think of entering into a formed party in
opposition to the court, since the dissolution of the Parliament
must in a few days leave him unprotected to the vengeance of his
sovereign and to those stretches of prerogative which were then
so easily made in order to punish an obnoxious subject. During
an unpopular and weak reign, the current commonly ran so strong
against the monarch that none dared enlist themselves in the court
party; or if the prince was able to engage any considerable barons
on his side, the question was decided with arms in the field, not

by debates or arguments in a senate or assembly. And upon the whole, the chief circumstance which, during ancient times, retained the prince in any legal form of administration was that the sword, by the nature of the feudal tenures, remained still in the hands of his subjects; and this irregular and dangerous check had much more influence than the regular and methodical limits of the laws and constitution. As the nation could not be compelled, it was necessary that every public measure of consequence, particularly that of levying new taxes, should seem to be adopted by common consent and approbation.

The princes of the House of Tudor, partly by the vigor of their administration, partly by the concurrence of favorable circumstances, had been able to establish a more regular system of government; but they drew the constitution so near to despotism as diminished extremely the authority of the Parliament. The senate became, in a great degree, the organ of royal will and pleasure; opposition would have been regarded as a species of rebellion; and even religion, the most dangerous article in which innovations could be introduced, had admitted, in the course of a few years, four several alterations, from the authority alone of the sovereign. The Parliament was not then the road to honor and preferment; the talents of popular intrigue and eloquence were uncultivated and unknown, and though that assembly still preserved authority and retained the privilege of making laws and bestowing public money, the members acquired not, upon that account, either with prince or people, much more weight and consideration. What powers were necessary for conducting the machine of government, the king was accustomed of himself to assume. His own revenues supplied him with money sufficient for his ordinary expenses, and when extraordinary emergencies occurred, the prince needed not to solicit votes in Parliament, either for making laws or imposing taxes, both of which were now become requisite for public interest and preservation.

The security of individuals, so necessary to the liberty of popular councils, was totally unknown in that age. And as no despotic princes, scarcely even the Eastern tyrants, rule entirely without the concurrence of some assemblies, which supply both advice and authority, little but a mercenary force seems then to have been wanting toward the establishment of a simple monarchy in England. The militia, though more favorable to regal authority than the feudal institutions, was much inferior, in this respect, to disciplined armies; and if it did not preserve liberty to the people, it preserved at least the power, if ever the inclination should arise, of recovering it.

But so low, at the time, ran the inclination toward liberty that Elizabeth, the last of that arbitrary line, herself no less arbitrary, was yet the most renowned and most popular of all the sovereigns that had filled the throne of England. It was natural for James to take the government as he found it and to pursue her measures, which he heard so much applauded, nor did his penetration extend so far as to discover that neither his circumstances nor his character could support so extensive an authority. His narrow revenues and little frugality began now to render him dependent on his people, even in the ordinary course of administration; their increasing knowledge discovered to them that advantage which they had obtained and made them sensible of the inestimable value of civil liberty; and as he possessed too little dignity to command respect, and too much good nature to impress fear, a new spirit discovered itself every day in the Parliament; and a party, watchful of a free constitution, was regularly formed in the House of Commons.

But notwithstanding these advantages acquired to liberty, so extensive was royal authority, and so firmly established in all its parts, that it is probable the patriots of that age would have despaired of ever resisting it had they not been stimulated by religious motives, which inspire a courage unsurmountable by any human obstacle.

The same alliance which has ever prevailed between kingly power and ecclesiastical authority was now fully established in England, and while the prince assisted the clergy in suppressing schismatics and innovators, the clergy, in return, inculcated the doctrine of an unreserved submission and obedience to the civil magistrate. The genius of the Church of England, so kindly to monarchy, forwarded the confederacy; its submission to episcopal jurisdiction; its attachment to ceremonies, to order, and to a decent pomp and splendor of worship; and in a word, its affinity to the tame superstition of the Catholics rather than to the wild fanaticism of the Puritans.

On the other hand, opposition to the Church, and the persecutions under which they labored, were sufficient to throw the Puritans into the country party and to beget political principles little favorable to the high pretensions of the sovereign. The spirit, too, of enthusiasm, bold, daring, and uncontrolled, strongly disposed their minds to adopt republican tenets, and inclined them to arrogate, in their actions and conduct, the same liberty which they assumed in their rapturous flights and ecstasies. Ever since the first origin of that sect, through the whole reign of Elizabeth as well as of James, Puritanical principles had been understood in a double sense and expressed the opinions favorable both to political and to ecclesiastical liberty; and as the court, in order to discredit all parliamentary opposition, affixed the denomination of Puritans to its antagonists, the religious Puritans willingly adopted this idea, which was so advantageous to them and which confounded their cause with that of the patriots, or country party. Thus were the civil and ecclesiastical factions regularly formed; and the humor of the nation during that age running strongly toward fanatical extravagances, the spirit of civil liberty gradually revived from its lethargy, and by means of its religious associate, from which it reaped more advantage than honor, it secretly enlarged its dominion over the greater part of the kingdom.

IV

Whatever ridicule, to a philosophical mind, may be thrown on pious ceremonies, it must be confessed that during a very religious age no institutions can be more advantageous to the rude multitude and tend more to mollify that fierce and gloomy spirit of devotion to which they are subject. Even the English Church, though it had retained a share of popish ceremonies, may justly be thought too naked and unadorned, and still to approach too near the abstract and spiritual religion of the Puritans. Laud and his associates, by reviving a few primitive institutions of this nature, corrected the error of the first reformers and presented to the affrightened and astonished mind some sensible, exterior observance which might occupy it during its religious exercises and abate the violence of its disappointed efforts. The thought, no longer bent on that divine and mysterious essence so superior to the narrow capacities of mankind, was able, by means of the new model of devotion, to relax itself in the contemplation of pictures, postures, vestments, buildings; and all the fine arts which minister to religion thereby received additional encouragement. The primate, it is true, conducted this scheme, not with the enlarged sentiments and cool reflection of a legislator, but with the intemperate zeal of a sectary, and by overlooking the circumstances of the times, served rather to inflame that religious fury which he meant to repress. But this blemish is more to be regarded as a general imputation on the whole age than any particular failing of Laud's; and it is sufficient for his vindication to observe that his errors were the most excusable of all those which prevailed during that zealous period.

24

Adam Smith

HOW THE COMMERCE OF THE TOWNS CONTRIBUTED TO THE IMPROVEMENT OF THE COUNTRY

THE INCREASE AND RICHES of commercial and manufacturing towns contributed to the improvement and cultivation of the countries to which they belonged in three different ways.

First, by affording a great and ready market for the rude produce of the country, they gave encouragement to its cultivation and further improvement. This benefit was not even confined to the countries in which they were situated, but extended more or less to all those with which they had any dealings. To all of them they afforded a market for some part either of their rude or manufactured produce, and consequently, gave some encouragement to the industry and improvement of all. Their own country, however, on account of its neighborhood, necessarily derived the greatest benefit from this market. Its rude produce being charged with less carriage, the traders could pay the growers a better price for it, and yet afford it as cheap to the consumers as that of more distant countries.

Secondly, the wealth acquired by the inhabitants of cities was

Reprinted from Adam Smith, *The Wealth of Nations* (Edinburgh: Adam and Charles Black, 1863), pp. 181–85.

frequently employed in purchasing such lands as were to be sold, of which a great part would frequently be uncultivated. Merchants are commonly ambitious of becoming country gentlemen, and when they do, they are generally the best of all improvers. A merchant is accustomed to employ his money chiefly in profitable projects; whereas a mere country gentleman is accustomed to employ it chiefly in expense. The one often sees his money go from him and return to him again with a profit: the other, when once he parts with it, very seldom expects to see any more of it. Those different habits naturally affect their temper and disposition in every sort of business. The merchant is commonly a bold, a country gentleman a timid undertaker. The one is not afraid to lay out at once a large capital upon the improvement of his land, when he has a probable prospect of raising the value of it in proportion to the expense; the other, if he has any capital, which is not always the case, seldom ventures to employ it in this manner. If he improves at all, it is commonly not with a capital, but with what he can save out of his annual revenue. Whoever has had the fortune to live in a mercantile town situated in an unimproved country must have frequently observed how much more spirited the operations of merchants were in this way than those of mere country gentlemen. The habits, besides, of order, economy, and attention, to which mercantile business naturally forms a merchant, render him much fitter to execute, with profit and success, any project of improvement.

Thirdly, and lastly, commerce and manufactures gradually introduced order and good government, and with them, the liberty and security of individuals, among the inhabitants of the country, who had before lived almost in a continual state of war with their neighbors and of servile dependency upon their superiors. This, though it has been the least observed, is by far the most important of all their effects. Mr. Hume is the only writer who, so far as I know, has hitherto taken notice of it.

In a country which has neither foreign commerce, nor any of the finer manufactures, a great proprietor, having nothing for which he can exchange the great part of the produce of his lands which is over and above the maintenance of the cultivators, con-

sumes the whole in rustic hospitality at home. If this surplus produce is sufficient to maintain a hundred or a thousand men, he can
make use of it in no other way than by maintaining a hundred
or a thousand men. He is at all times, therefore, surrounded with
a multitude of retainers and dependents, who having no equivalent
to give in return for their maintenance, but being fed entirely by
his bounty, must obey him for the same reason that soldiers must
obey the prince who pays them. Before the extension of commerce
and manufactures in Europe, the hospitality of the rich and the
great, from the sovereign down to the smallest baron, exceeded
everything which in the present times we can easily form a notion
of. Westminster Hall was the dining room of William Rufus and
might frequently perhaps not be too large for his company. It was
reckoned a piece of magnificence in Thomas Becket, that he
strowed the floor of his hall with clean hay or rushes in the season,
in order that the knights and squires, who could not get seats,
might not spoil their fine clothes when they sat down on the floor
to eat their dinner. The great Earl of Warwick is said to have entertained every day at his different manors, thirty thousand people,
and though the number here may have been exaggerated, it must,
however, have been very great to admit of such exaggeration. A
hospitality nearly of the same kind was exercised not many years
ago in many different parts of the highlands of Scotland. It seems
to be common in all nations to whom commerce and manufactures
are little known. I have seen, says Doctor Pocock, an Arabian chief
dine in the streets of a town where he had come to sell his cattle,
and invite all passengers, even common beggars, to sit down with
him and partake of his banquet.

The occupiers of land were in every respect as dependent upon
the great proprietor as his retainers. Even such of them as were
not in a state of villanage were tenants at will who paid a rent
in no respect equivalent to the subsistence which the land afforded
them. A crown, half a crown, a sheep, a lamb, was some years ago
in the highlands of Scotland a common rent for lands which maintained a family. In some places it is so at this day; nor will money
at present purchase a greater quantity of commodities there than
in other places. In a country where the surplus produce of a large

estate must be consumed upon the estate itself, it will frequently be more convenient for the proprietor that part of it be consumed at a distance from his own house, provided they who consume it are as dependent upon him as either his retainers or his menial servants. He is thereby saved from the embarrassment of either too large a company or too large a family. A tenant at will, who possesses land sufficient to maintain his family for little more than a quit rent, is as dependent upon the proprietor as any servant or retainer whatever, and must obey him with as little reserve. Such a proprietor, as he feeds his servants and retainers at his own house, so he feeds his tenants at their houses. The subsistence of both is derived from his bounty and its continuance depends upon his good pleasure.

Upon the authority which the great proprietors necessarily had in such a state of things over their tenants and retainers was founded the power of the ancient barons. They necessarily became the judges in peace and the leaders in war of all who dwelt upon their estates. They could maintain order and execute the law within their respective demesnes, because each of them could there turn the whole force of all the inhabitants against the injustice of any one. No other person had sufficient authority to do this. The king, in particular, had not. In those ancient times he was little more than the great proprietor in his dominions, to whom, for the sake of common defense against their common enemies, the other great proprietors paid certain respects. To have enforced payment of a small debt within the lands of a great proprietor, where all the inhabitants were armed and accustomed to stand by one another, would have cost the king had he attempted it by his own authority almost the same effort as to extinguish a civil war. He was, therefore, obliged to abandon the administration of justice through the greater part of the country, to those who were capable of administering it; and for the same reason to leave the command of the country militia to those whom that militia would obey.

It is a mistake to imagine that those territorial jurisdictions took their origin from the feudal law. Not only the highest jurisdictions both civil and criminal, but the power of levying troops, of coining money, and even that of making by-laws for the government of their own people, were all rights possessed allodially by the great proprietors of land several centuries before even the name of the feudal law was known in Europe. The authority and jurisdiction of the Saxon lords in England appear to have been as great before the conquest as that of any of the Norman lords after it. But the feudal law is not supposed to have become the common law of England till after the conquest. That the most extensive authority and jurisdictions were possessed by the great lords in France allodially, long before the feudal law was introduced into that country, is a matter of fact that admits of no doubt. That authority and those jurisdictions all necessarily flowed from the state of property and manners just now described. Without remounting to the remote antiquities of either the French or English monarchies, we may find in much later times many proofs that such effects must always flow from such causes. It is not thirty years ago since Mr. Cameron of Lochiel, a gentleman of Lochabar in Scotland, without any legal warrant whatever, not being what was then called a lord of regality, nor even a tenant in chief, but a vassal of the Duke of Argyle, and without being so much as a justice of peace, used, notwithstanding, to exercise the highest criminal jurisdiction over his own people. He is said to have done so with great equity, though without any of the formalities of justice; and it is not improbable that the state of that part of the country at that time made it necessary for him to assume this authority in order to maintain the public peace. That gentleman, whose rent never exceeded five hundred pounds a year, carried, in 1745, eight hundred of his own people into the rebellion with him.

The introduction of the feudal law, so far from extending, may be regarded as an attempt to moderate the authority of the great allodial lords. It established a regular subordination, accompanied with a long train of services and duties, from the king down to the smallest proprietor. During the minority of the proprietor, the rent, together with the management of his lands, fell into the hands of his immediate superior, and consequently, those of all great proprietors into the hands of the king, who was charged with the maintenance and education of the pupil, and who, from his authority as guardian, was supposed to have a right of disposing of him in marriage, provided it was in a manner not unsuitable to his rank. But though this institution necessarily tended to strengthen the authority of the king and to weaken that of the great proprietors, it could not do either sufficiently for establishing order and good government among the inhabitants of the country, because it could not alter sufficiently that state of property and manners from which the disorders arose. The authority of government still continued to be, as before, too weak in the head and too strong in the inferior members, and the excessive strength of the inferior members was the cause of the weakness of the head. After the institution of feudal subordination, the king was as incapable of restraining the violence of the great lords as before. They still continued to make war according to their own discretion, almost continually upon one another, and very frequently upon the king; and the open country still continued to be a scene of violence, rapine, and disorder.

But what all the violence of the feudal institutions could never have effected, the silent and insensible operation of foreign commerce and manufactures gradually brought about. These gradually furnished the great proprietors with something for which they could exchange the whole surplus produce of their lands and which they could consume themselves without sharing it either with tenants or retainers. All for ourselves and nothing for other people seems, in every age of the world, to have been the vile maxim of the masters of mankind. As soon, therefore, as they could find a method of consuming the whole value of their rents themselves, they had no disposition to share them with any other persons. For a pair of diamond buckles perhaps, or for something as frivolous and useless, they exchanged the maintenance, or what is the same thing, the price of the maintenance of a thousand men for a year and with it the whole weight and authority which it could give them. The buckles, however, were to be all their own, and no other human creature was to have any share of them; whereas in the more ancient method of expense they must have shared with at least a thousand people. With the judges that were to determine the preference, this difference was perfectly decisive; and thus, for the gratification of the most childish, the meanest and the most sordid of all vanities, they gradually bartered their whole power and authority.

In a country where there is no foreign commerce, nor any of the finer manufactures, a man of ten thousand a year cannot well employ his revenue in any other way than in maintaining, perhaps, a thousand families, who are all of them necessarily at his command. In the present state of Europe, a man of ten thousand a year can spend his whole revenue, and he generally does so, without directly maintaining twenty people, or being able to command more than ten footmen not worth the commanding. Indirectly, perhaps, he maintains as great or even a greater number of people than he could have done by the ancient method of expense: for though the quantity of precious productions for which he exchanges his whole revenue be very small, the number of workmen employed in collecting and preparing it must necessarily have been very great. Its great price generally arises from the wages of their labor, and the profits of all their immediate employers. By paying that price he indirectly pays all those wages and profits, and thus indirectly contributes to the maintenance of all the workmen and their employers. He generally contributes, however, but a very small proportion to that of each; to very few perhaps a tenth, to many not a hundredth, and to some not a thousandth, nor even a ten thousandth part of their whole annual maintenance. Though he contributes, therefore, to the maintenance of them all, they are all more or less independent of him, because generally they can all be maintained without him.

When the great proprietors of land spend their rents in maintaining their tenants and retainers, each of them maintains entirely all his own tenants and all his own retainers. But when they spend them in maintaining tradesmen and artificers, they may, all of them taken together, perhaps, maintain as great, or, on account of the waste which attends rustic hospitality, a greater number of people than before. Each of them, however, taken singly, contributes often but a very small share to the maintenance of any individual of this greater number. Each tradesman or artificer derives his subsistence from the employment, not of one, but of a hundred or a thousand different customers. Though in some measure obliged to them all, therefore, he is not absolutely dependent upon any one of them.

The personal expense of the great proprietors having in this manner gradually increased, it was impossible that the number of their retainers should not as gradually diminish, till they were at last dismissed altogether. The same cause gradually led them to dismiss the unnecessary part of their tenants. Farms were enlarged, and the occupiers of land, notwithstanding the complaints of de-population, reduced to the number necessary for cultivating it, according to the imperfect state of cultivation and improvement in those times. By the removal of the unnecessary mouths and by exacting from the farmer the full value of the farm, a greater sur-plus, or what is the same thing, the price of a greater surplus, was obtained for the proprietor, which the merchants and manufac-turers soon furnished him with a method of spending upon his own person in the same manner as he had done the rest. The cause continuing to operate, he was desirous to raise his rents above what his lands, in the actual state of their improvement, could afford. His tenants could agree to this upon one condition only, that they should be secured in their possession, for such a term of years as might give them time to recover with profit whatever they should lay out in the further improvement of the land. The expensive vanity of the landlord made him willing to accept of this condition, and hence the origin of long leases.

Even a tenant at will, who pays the full value of the land, is not altogether dependent upon the landlord. The pecuniary ad-vantages which they receive from one another are mutual and equal, and such a tenant will expose neither his life nor his for-tune in the service of the proprietor. But if he has a lease for a long term of years, he is altogether independent; and his landlord must not expect from him even the most trifling service beyond what is either expressly stipulated in the lease, or imposed upon him by the common and known law of the country.

The tenants having in this manner become independent and the retainers being dismissed, the great proprietors were no longer capable of interrupting the regular execution of justice or of disturbing the peace of the country. Having sold their birthright, not like Esau for a mess of pottage in time of hunger and necessity, but in the wantonness of plenty, for trinkets and baubles, fitter to be the playthings of children than the serious pursuits of men, they became as insignificant as any substantial burgher or tradesman in a city. A regular government was established in the country as well as in the city, nobody having sufficient power to disturb its operations in the one, any more than in the other. . . .

A revolution of the greatest importance to the public happiness was in this manner brought about by two different orders of people, who had not the least intention to serve the public. To gratify the most childish vanity was the sole motive of the great proprietors. The merchants and artificers, much less ridiculous, acted merely from a view to their own interest, and in pursuit of their own pedlar principle of turning a penny wherever a penny was to be got. Neither of them had either knowledge or foresight of that great revolution which the folly of the one, and the industry of the other, was gradually bringing about.

It is thus that through the greater part of Europe the commerce and manufactures of cities, instead of being the effect, have been the cause and occasion of the improvement and cultivation of the country.

25

Adam Ferguson

OF THE POLITICAL ARTS

As THE COMMERCIAL ARTS originate in the necessities of
man's animal nature, the arts which may be termed political
originate in the wants and defects of instinctive society.

Animals, which are led by their instincts to form themselves
into troops or swarms and to combine their labors for subsistence,
accommodation, or safety, are likewise led, by the same power of
instinct, to some general polity or arrangement of parts for the
purpose of nature: an infant swarm of bees will follow the queen,
or mother of the hive, and wherever she settles will take their
abode. The human species also by the original instinct or destination of nature not only find themselves formed into troops or companies, but ranged also in a way to be directed or governed in
numbers together. The will of one is often a principle of action
to many. The parent leads his infant child. The courageous and
the able take an ascendant over the timorous and weak. And not
only in the family there is a subordination of personal quality of
sex and age; but in every troop or company some are qualified and
disposed to lead, others willing to be led. Inequalities of strength,
whether of mind or body, constitute a relation of dependence and
power, forming a species of government, which we may term instinctive, because it is prior to any concerted design or institution
on the part of those concerned.

Reprinted from Adam Ferguson, *Principles of Moral and Political Science* (Edinburgh, 1792), I, 256–65.

The courageous take a station in danger, under which the timid are fain to accept of protection. The wise point out the way to an end, which every one would gladly attain; and for the attainment of which persons of inferior ability submit to be governed by those of a stronger mind.

We must not, however, confound the effect of these inequalities in forming a species of actual government with any supposed right to command in one or obligation to obey in another. The first person you meet in the streets upon a difficulty that occurs in the way may win your confidence and incline you to receive his direction, but this does not amount to a right in him to command you, nor to an obligation on you to obey him. This right and obligation, as we shall have occasion to observe, is founded in convention alone and can be actually traced to this foundation, wherever such rights and obligations are really established.

Nor is it necessary, surely, in this place, to combat the arguments of those, who, in judging of political establishments, recur to the first suggestions of nature, as the model of what mankind are forever bound to retain. Men are destined to improve on their lot and on their first inventions and no more acquiesce in the first defective forms of society than they do in the first rudiments of other accommodation or in the first practice of any mechanical art.

We state the condition of rude society, as the material on which the genius of man is to work, not as a finished production, with which he is forever to remain contented. In this state we observe that there are, whether from nature or fortune, casual diversities in the state of the parties that produce a disparity of rank: that such disparity suggests the claims of prerogative to persons of one condition; inspires others with deference; or if prerogative be carried beyond certain limits, an alarm, on the subject of privileges, is taken by those over whom it is claimed.

If, in fixing the date of subordination, we take our accounts from ancient tradition and record alone, we must assume that in the rudest times it was known. For in every instance we read of transactions that imply the exaltation of particular persons above the ordinary level; we read of patricians or nobles who rose above the body of the people; and princes or kings who rose above the nobles and who were the heads or leaders of their several communities.

The first subjects of history are the wars of such leaders at the head of their followers, or the contests into which parties were engaged on the subject of their respective pretensions, whether prerogative or privilege.

Even, if we should suppose, as is probable, that the record of history, in such instances, is not correct, or does not reach far enough back, to make us acquainted with the earliest state of mankind; and that the condition of savage nations known in our own times, is better specimen of primeval society: yet, even amongst them, also, there is a distinction of persons, a leader and followers, a select council of the nation, and a body of the people; distinctions in which the foundations are actually laid for all the varieties of personal estimation and family distinction.

When disparities of rank are admitted among the parties which compose a society, what Tacitus relates of the ancient Germans may be safely assumed as so many laws of nature by which men are led before they have planned an establishment: that *in matters of small moment, the chiefs deliberate; but on great occasions all take a part; that royalty is attached to birth, and military command to valor.*

In the result of this natural or instinctive course of things, small states are inclined to democracy because a great proportion of the people is easily and frequently assembled. In states of greater extent, the nobles, or select class of the people, lay hold of the government because they have leisure to attend to it and are easily convened.

In societies of every description, as often as men have consulted and have occasion to act in a body, there is required some undivided authority, of which the first and simplest form is that which is conceived in the person of a king or a prince.

In arriving, therefore, even at the state of a principality, in some rude form, there does not appear any concerted design to establish a government. Nobility may take its rise from the distinction of personal qualities; from great ability and courage; from the luster of great actions; and from the influence of extensive possessions. What thus serves to distinguish a particular class or order of men from the multitude may serve also to distinguish an individual from his order or class; and a superiority thus obtained may be allowed to descend in the race. The offspring of heroes comes into the world with a luster borrowed from his progenitors. The child is taught to assume elevation as he advances in years, and his rank is acknowledged in the respect that is paid to his blood.

The distinction of royalty differs from that of nobility only in degree and is of the same origin. In the first admission of either, there probably was not any intention to form a constitution or give method and order to the affairs of state. Such distinctions, however, when once admitted, nevertheless operate to this effect, and before men had conceived the design of a political institution, or came under the supposed stipulation of magistrate and subject, they had already ranged themselves into different orders of which one is in a condition to govern and another in a state to obey.

So far then we may be inclined to think that the casual subordinations, not only of sex, age, and personal qualities, but those likewise of birth and fortune, may have preceded any formal intention to regulate the distribution of power.

But the forms which arise in this manner from instincts of nature, although they may serve for ages the purpose of political establishment, are however no more than a rude material on which the ingenuity of man is to be exercised. And his original lot in this as in other instances calls at first for his efforts to remove inconveniences which arise in it, rather than to improve the advantages of which it is susceptible, although in process of time, men have recourse to many institutions and conventions for both those purposes.

The defects of a rude society consist either in a want of order at home or in the want of security against invasions from abroad.

Disorders at home arise from the collision of private interests and passions, or from the interfering of private with public and common concerns. In the simplest society, even that of a family, parties may divide on the subject of personal considerations and the individual may apprehend an interest for himself apart from the common cause of his kindred.

Under such apprehensions, the effects, whether of natural affection, or brotherly love, or of family attachment may be prevented or greatly disturbed, and political institutions appear to have been at first suggested by the abuse to which society is exposed, in its casual state, whether of subordination or anarchy.

At one time, an institution is required to strengthen the hands of those who govern, against popular license, or private crimes. At another time, it is required to fix the limits of power or to guard against its abuse.

But, whether we thus assume the representations of tradition and early record in evidence of man's primeval state, or have recourse to the description of rude or unpolished hordes of our own times, we may conclude equally from either that the first object of concert or convention on the part of man is not to give society existence, but to perfect the society in which he finds himself already by nature placed; not to establish subordination, but to correct the abuse of a subordination already established; and that the material, on which the political genius of man is to work is not, as the poets have feigned, a scattered race in a state of individuality to be collected together into troops by the charms of music, or the lessons of philosophy. But a material much nearer the point to which the political art would carry it, a troop of men by mere instinct assembled together; placed in the subordinate relations of parent and child, of noble and plebeian, if not of rich and poor, or other adventitious, if not original distinction, which constitutes, in fact, a relation of power and dependence, by which a few are in condition to govern the many and a part has an ascendant over the whole.

The idea of men in any society, great or small, having ever assembled upon a foot of absolute equality, and without exclusion of any individual, to dispose of their government is altogether visionary and unknown in nature. Even where the inhabitants of the smallest district or village, with the most determined resolution to equalize the rights of men, have assembled, not to deliberate on national affairs, but to elect delegates for that purpose, half the people, under the distinction of sex, are excluded at once even from the right of election; a third of the remaining half under the distinction of nonage; still more under other accidental distinction; and where the remainder is not unanimous and must act by the majority, this governing part of the community may not exceed 18 per cent, or is under a fifth of the whole.

These exclusions are made upon the foot of a power in those who arrogate government, not upon a foot of consent in those who are subjected to it. Even the government of the majority, for which there could be no convention, unless the people were unanimous, proceeds upon a mere overbalance of power. Two may overrule one by the superiority of force, but this does not amount to a right in any one species of actual government whatever. Providence, indeed, has kindly determined that wherever there is society there should also be government of some kind or other to provide for the peace and cooperation of its members. The form of society, like other materials provided for human ingenuity to work upon, may be rude or defective and require the exercise of reason to remove its inconveniencies or to obtain the advantages of which it is susceptible. But the object of reason never can be to abolish the relation of power and dependence, for this nature has rendered impossible, but to guard against the abuses of power and procure to individuals equal security in their respective stations, however differing in point of acquired or original advantages.

We are not now inquiring what men ought to do, but what is the ordinary tract in which they proceed, and how far the exercises of their political situation is a part in that school of intellectual and moral improvement, in which they are destined to advance in knowledge, wisdom, and all the eligible habits of life. Mankind must be contented to act in the situations in which they find themselves placed, and except when urged by great occasions, seldom project and rarely at once obtain any great innovation. The party which has an advantage in the actual state of society endeavor to avail themselves of it; and the party that is aggrieved, strives to obtain relief. The effect is to preserve the establishment where parties are equally balanced, or to procure some change where either prevail. Even if the society should be led at any particular time by a single person of distinguished influence and authority, as in the examples of Lycurgus, Solon, or Romulus, to adopt at once a plan consisting of many regulations, still the effect could be no more than to define the condition in which parties should act, and in which they might find occasions no less trying and complicated than those in which they would have been otherwise engaged. A state governing itself upon the plan of Romulus might have found no less to do for its members than they themselves would have otherwise found in the condition of shepherds or robbers, the nursery from which this celebrated lawgiver is supposed to have collected the first members of that famous republic, which is supposed to have taken the first principles of political order from him.

The institutions ascribed to those celebrated lawgivers did not put an end to the political operations of state; they only placed the members of society in situations to act with advantage for the preservation and welfare of their country. Every new emergence required new measures for this purpose; and the law itself, however simple in a rude age, must have multiplied its clauses to keep pace with the growing affairs of a prosperous nation, and its application to questions of contested right, of criminal charge, or public arrangement, must have required continued attention on the part of the governed as well as the governing. Under the most accomplished institutions of government, it remained for the citizens, in every instance, to constitute and to wield the force of their community, whether for the suppression of disorders at home or the repulsion of injuries from abroad.

In whatever manner a constitution of government be obtained, whether upon the plan of a single person, or in the result of many successive institutions, its affairs must continue to exercise the faculties of those who are to be employed to conduct or to deliberate upon them, and to the extent of the numbers so employed, society itself is to be considered as a school in which men are to receive the instructions and perform the exercises of intelligence, of wisdom, and virtue. It is the soil on which human genius is destined to receive a principal part of its nourishment and to make the most vigorous shoots of which its nature is capable.

In this point of view, the attainment of a just political order otherwise so necessary to the welfare of mankind is to be considered also as an occasion on which the principal steps of man's progress are made, or in which a scene is opened that gives scope to his active disposition and is fitted, like other parts of his lot, to improve his faculties by rendering the exercise of them necessary to his preservation and well-being.

As the necessities of animal life might have been fewer than they are at present, or might have been entirely prevented; so the exigencies of civil society might have been supplied and regulated by mere instinct, as they are in the case of other animals, so as not to require any efforts of design or contrivance on the part of its members. Nature, however, has otherwise arranged the fortunes of man; and so disposed of his lot that, being provided with intellectual faculties, he ever meets with a suitable occasion by which they are called forth into use.

VII. The Range of Sociological Concern

Adam Ferguson

OF CONTRACT OR THE
PRINCIPLE OF
CONVENTIONAL OBLIGATION

A CONVENTION, or contract, is the mutual consent of parties to constitute, transfer, or reduce a right.

Where two or more persons therefore are consenting to the same or to mutual articles of agreement, they come respectively or mutually under the obligation of contract.

This obligation, in the case of mutual consent, is universally acknowledged, or universally pleaded, by those who exact the performance of a bargain: insomuch that even they who overlook every other foundation of right acknowledge compact as sufficient to support all the claims of justice in civil or political society.

The obligation of compact therefore must either be self-evident, or must be derived from some very obvious and self-evident principle. Mr. Hobbes denies the existence of any right prior to convention, but it must be owned that if in this his opinion bears hard upon human nature in denying the original rights of men he is exceedingly prompt to sustain the effect of convention in creating every right which men have occasion to plead in society, and his proceeding is to the following purpose.

The first requisite, according to him, in establishing any prin-

From Adam Ferguson, *Principles of Moral and Political Science* (London and Edinburgh, 1792), II, 214–25.

ciple of law with which men are bound to comply is: "That every man divest himself of the right he hath to all things by nature";[1] or, as he himself interprets, the supposed right of all men to all things, it being in effect, as he acknowledges, "no *better than if no man had a right to any thing*."[2] The first requisite in establishing a law of nature is that all men consent mutually that for the future there shall be such a thing as *right*; "but," continues he, "as this consent were utterly vain and of none effect, if this also were not a law of the same nature that every man is obliged to stand to and perform these convenants he maketh;"[3] it appears necessary to establish this obligation in general before the consent of parties can be supposed to establish it in any particular instance.

The breach or violation of covenants, according to this celebrated writer, is the *first species of injury*; but to a person who denies the previous existence of injury in the harm that may be done to the person of a man, it may be difficult to show how injury commences in this form and no other. If he deny that prior to convention there is any obligation to abstain from harm; if he admits that the violent may wound with his sword; that the insidious may ensnare with his cunning; why not that the faithless may, to procure an advantage to himself, betray the confidence he has been able to obtain?

To solve this problem, he has recourse to the following process of reasoning: *not to perform what is contracted for, being what all men call an injury,* he proves performance to be binding, *because non-performance is an absurdity in action, as self-contradiction is an absurdity in argument*: "For, as he which is driven to contradict an assertion by him before maintained, is said to be reduced to an absurdity, so he that through passion do or omit that which before he promised to do or not to omit is said to commit injustice, and there is in every breach of covenant a contradiction so called. He that violates a covenant, wills the doing and not doing of the same thing at the same time, which is a plain contradiction."[4]

---

1   *De corpore politico,* Part 1, chap. iii., sect. 1.
2   *Ibid.,* sect. 2.
3   *Ibid.,* chap. iii., sect. 1.
4   *Ibid.,* sect. 2.

Here it must be confessed the argument is distinctly stated; the obligation of contract, and with it, according to this author, all the positive rights of men, are made to rest on the merit of consistency, in preference to inconsistency or self-contradiction. It were irrational to say and unsay the same thing; therefore rational beings are bound in their actions to be consistent with their sayings, that is to say, *they are bound to observe their contracts.* To do otherwise would be to unsay in their actions, or in neglect of performance what they had previously said, in terms of a bargain or in expressions of consent.

Such reasoning but ill accounts for the indignation with which a breach of faith is universally considered by mankind. He who breaks faith may incur the charge of inconsistency it is true; but how different from the charge of *perfidy* or *treason.* The traitor next to the murderer is reckoned the most odious among criminals, and the argument now stated from Mr. Hobbes is the less fit to support the obligation of contract, or to account for the sentiments with which breach of faith is reprobated, that it would equally apply to evince an obligation where none is admitted, and to fix a criminal imputation where the passions relent, and where a person once inclined to the commission of a crime shrinks from guilt and returns to innocence.

Thus, upon the principle of consistency, as stated by this author, a person having once expressed an intention respecting a matter in which he himself alone is concerned, would be bound to fulfill his intention, whatever reason or consideration may have occurred to the contrary. If a person, for instance, has once proposed in his own mind, or mentioned in his talk an intention to carry his goods to market, he is no longer at liberty to withhold them. If he has threatened to kill his neighbor, his benefactor, or his parent, he is not at liberty to retract or to change his mind. In any supposed case of this sort, however, mankind would consider the threat as a crime, and the failure of performance, not as a breach of faith, but as the relenting of a mind which had yet some remains of ingenuity, a sense of innocence, and some disposition to atone for the guilt of having ever entertained so atrocious a purpose.

In this account of moral obligation collected from the ordinary sense of mankind, we find a clear apprehension of right and wrong prior to convention. We find an acknowledgment that convention itself may be wrong; the completion of it worse; and the breach of it right. As he who has engaged or bargained to commit a murder incurs a certain measure of guilt in the bargain he has made; this measure of guilt he would greatly augment by preserving consistency, or by proceeding to fulfill his bargain; and under such an unhappy engagement his duty manifestly is to become inconsistent and to decline the performance.

Some writers who have employed their ingenuity to a better purpose and who think more favorably of man's physical state than the last we have mentioned seem willing, nevertheless, to rest the obligations of men in society more upon convention than is necessary; and to reason from this topic of contract in cases to which the great injunction of natural law to abstain from harm is at least equally obvious and equally applicable.

Society itself is by such writers considered as the result of a bargain and the relative duties of men in society are traced up to a supposed original compact on the articles of which volumes have been written.[5] The intention of writers, in this form of their argument, is no doubt favorable to mankind, and the hypothesis of a conditional obligation is by them recurred to, merely in order that none of the parties in civil society may pretend a right to enjoy his peculiar advantage, without fulfilling also the condition to which he is peculiarly bound, or without contributing what is due from himself, in return for what he expects to receive from another. Thus, allegiance and protection being stated, as the reciprocal stipulations of magistrate and subject, the one is not to expect allegiance without administering protection nor the other to expect protection without the proper returns of allegiance and duty.

Were we to enumerate all the obligations of men in society, we should find many, no doubt, which arise from convention express or tacit; but it is far from being necessary or expedient to refer the whole to this title. The obligation to abstain from harm, and the right of every individual, to the utmost of his power to defend himself and his fellow creatures are prior to convention and are

5   Vide *Contrat social* of Rousseau.

indeed the foundation upon which conventional obligation itself is established.

Whoever has power may employ it in defending the innocent, and so far, the magistrate having the sword in his hand need not inquire whether the criminal that offends against the peace of his country has agreed to abstain from crimes or has agreed to submit to punishment. In repressing the crimes, and in giving examples to deter others from the commission of them, the magistrate does no more than what every other person, prior to convention, and to the extent of his power, is entitled to do.

But when the magistrate assumes to himself alone the prerogative of employing force for the repression of crimes; when he tells the injured that he must not attempt to do himself right, but must have recourse to the protection established by law; when he requires the subject to part with his substance to defray the expence of public service; when he assumes the right to positive command, in requiring the innocent to serve his country, as well as in requiring the injurious to abstain from harm; there, no doubt, he must be able to plead a special institution or convention, to which the people have agreed.

Laws and institutions in every community contain articles of agreement entered into by the parties with whom they originated and by their posterity who accede to them; but such agreements are all of them posterior to the existence of society and not the foundations upon which society was originally erected. The essential obligations of men in society are founded in what nature has done for them, not in what they themselves have agreed to perform, and such obligations can receive no conformation or sanction from the supposition of a contract which is merely fictitious or which did not exist.

The humane author of the treatise on crimes and punishments,[6] founding even the right to punish crimes on a supposed original compact and applying a well-known maxim of law that compacts are to be strictly interpreted, denies any right in the magistrate to inflict punishments more severe than are necessary to obtain the purpose for which parties contracted; that is, more severe than is

6   The Marquis Beccaria.

necessary to restrain crimes and to keep the peace of society. For
this being the object of parties in forming their compact, so far, he
argues, every person in society may be supposed to have acceded
to this contract, and no farther. This, however, is no more than a
circuitous way of asserting that the state or its magistrates have
no right to punish any crime further than is necessary for their own
defense or the defense of the cause entrusted to their charge; a
maxim that does not require consent to make it binding, but is implied in the first principle of natural law, which limits the means
of defense within the bounds of what is necessary for the preservation or recovery of a right.

If we must admit the supposition of an original compact, like a
bond of copartnery, constituting the foundation of society, and the
first charter of rights to its members; as there is no record of the
articles originally framed, these must now be inferred from the
principles of natural right; for we have no other source from which
to derive information of what men were likely to have stipulated
or agreed to perform in a period of which no vestige remains.

In the first treaty of peace by which men agreed to live in society together, we are told accordingly that they must have stipulated to abstain from harm. But whence this information? we may
ask. Not from the record of any such stipulation! Nay, but it may
be assumed from the manifest equity and reason of the supposed
article. This is first to allege that a person is bound to be just because he has bargained to be so, and next, to presume that he has
bargained to abstain from harm because it is just that he do so.

If we are to suppose, with Mr. Hobbes, or as is in some measure implied in his resting all the obligations of men in society
upon a supposed original compact, that there is no right and no obligation prior to convention, it will be difficult, surely, as the example of Mr. Hobbes himself will show, to find a foundation upon
which the obligation of contract itself may rest. If contract be the
sole foundation of right, all that is commonly said of an inherent
right in every person to defend himself, or of an obligation corresponding to this right on every person to abstain from harm,
must be renounced. The distinction, supposed between rights
original and adventitious, must be dropped. All the rights of men,

whether personal or real, are adventitious and begin with the consent of one man not to disturb the possession of another; and in short, no man is obliged, even in the latest hour of society, to abstain from harm, except so far as by some species of compact he has bound himself so to do.

Such consequences, however, are sufficiently absurd to justify our rejecting the principle on which they are founded and are probably far from the thoughts of many, who assume the social *compact*, as a *fiction of law*, upon which to rest their decisions in particular instances. To this principle, at any rate, we cannot have recourse in fixing the grounds of conventional obligation. That a compact may be binding, we must suppose some previous foundation upon which its obligation may rest, whether the consistency to which Mr. Hobbes refers, or the original right of every person to defend himself, to which we have so often referred in these disquisitions.

If the rule that forbids the commission of harm, or the principle of nature, on which is founded a right of defense, can be applied to the case of parties, so far pledging or accepting a *faith* which is pledged to them, as that, by the breach of this faith they may injure or be injured; it will follow that they ought to refrain from that injury, or may repel it, by obliging the party contracting to fulfill the terms of his contract.

By the law of nature, every party may defend his estate from every invasion that is made to impair it. Of the state which may be thus defended, men derive part from the hand of their Maker, which is accordingly to them matter of original right; part from their own act and deed, as in the case of occupancy or labor, already recited; and we may now subjoin that they derive part of their state also from the engagements in which others are bound to them; or from the faith that others have plighted.

The servant is secure in the engagement of a master to pay his wages; the master relies for his accommodation on the engagement of the servant to do his work. The landlord is rich in the engagement of tenants to pay his rents; the tenant bestows his labor and scatters his seed, trusting to the lease he has received from the landlord. Even the miser himself, who is disposed to hoard up his wealth, may not have a single penny or article of value in his possession. He is rich in the capacity merely of a creditor and in holding others obliged to pay the principal and interest, in which they are indebted by bond to him.

Such credit in one man toward another is a part of their social nature, and the person who is disposed to abuse his credit may wound or destroy by means of that instrument no less than by the arm of violence or the sword which he wields in his hand.

If it be admitted that men are by nature disposed mutually to give and to receive information; that where they have no special cause to distrust, they rely on the informations, assurances, or promises which they receive from others; and that great part in the conduct of every person is determined by informations or assurances so received. If the bewildered traveler in the dark turns confidently to the right, when he is told that there is a precipice on the left, it must evidently follow, that to mislead him, or to occasion his harm, by any misinformation, would be as criminal as to occation that harm by any other means.

Hence, we may conclude that a person being made to rely on the consent of another to constitute or to reduce a right is not bound to suffer by the other's breach of faith, but may proceed on the principle of self-defense to force the performance of a promise which makes a part of his state; and the principle upon which a person, who has come under any engagement, may be forced to fulfill that engagement is the same with that maxim, on which he may be forced to abstain from injury, or harm of any other kind, insomuch that the first principle of compulsory law, which is in appearance merely prohibitory, may branch into a variety of duties or obligations to do, or to omit to do, whatever may be a fit matter of stipulation between any two or more parties concerned.

To fail in the discharge of such duties is on many occasions at least termed *perfidy* or *breach of faith* and considered with a higher degree of abhorrence than even the injuries that are done by open force. This may, no doubt, proceed from circumstances peculiar to fraud and deceit. The traitor must have carried the mask of innocence to have obtained credit; he has stolen an advantage which he had not the courage openly to force. The contrast of fraud with the mask of innocence, which it wears, the cowardice which is imputed to the person who assumes that mask in order to wound, combine together in awakening the peculiar sentiment of indignation and hatred, with which perfidy or breach of faith is considered, and which, though they do not make any addition to what is at present the object of our discussion, namely, the right of every person to defend himself against such wrongs; yet they tend greatly to evince that the source of conventional obligation is much more deeply laid than the mere consistency of words and actions upon which it is founded by the philosopher now mentioned.

27

Thomas Reid

RIGHTS AND DUTIES

THE DIRECT INTENTION of Morals is to teach the duty of men: that of natural jurisprudence to teach the rights of men. Right and duty are things very different and have even a kind of opposition; yet they are so related that the one cannot even be conceived without the other, and he that understands the one must understand the other.

They have the same relation which credit has to debt. As all credit supposes an equivalent debt, so all right supposes a corresponding duty. There can be no credit in one party without an equivalent debt in another party; and there can be no right in one party without a corresponding duty in another party. The sum of credit shows the sum of debt; and the sum of men's rights shows, in like manner, the sum of their duty to one another.

The word *right* has a very different meaning, according as it is applied to actions or to persons. A right action is an action agreeable to our duty. But, when we speak of the *rights of men*, the word has a very different and a more artificial meaning. It is a term of art in law, and signifies all that a man may lawfully do, all that he may lawfully possess and use, and all that he may lawfully claim of any other person.

This comprehensive meaning of the word *right* and of the

Reprinted from Thomas Reid, *Essays on the Active Power of Man*, in *Works*, W. Hamilton, ed. (6th ed.; Edinburgh, 1863), II, pp. 643–44. Title supplied.

Latin word *jus*, which corresponds to it, though long adopted into common language, is too artificial to be the birth of common language. It is a term of art, contrived by civilians when the civil law became a profession.

The whole end and object of law is to protect the subjects in all that they may lawfully *do*, or *possess*, or *demand*. This threefold object of law, civilians have comprehended under the word *jus* or *right*, which they define, "a lawful claim to *do anything*, to *possess anything*, or to *demand some prestation from some other person*." The first of these may be called the right of *liberty*; the second that of *property*, which is also called a *real right*; the third is called *personal right*, because it respects some particular person or persons of whom the prestation may be demanded.

We can be at no loss to perceive the duties corresponding to the several kinds of rights. What I have a right to do, it is the duty of all men not to hinder me from doing. What is my property or real right, no man ought to take from me, or to molest me in the use and enjoyment of it. And what I have a right to demand of any man, it is his duty to perform. Between the right on the one hand, and the duty on the other, there is not only a necessary connection, but, in reality, they are only different expressions of the same meaning; just as it is the same thing to say, I am your debtor, and to say, you are my creditor, or as it is the same thing to say, I am your father, and to say, You are my son.

Thus we see that there is such a correspondence between the rights of men and the duties of men that the one points out the other, and a system of the one may be substituted for a system of the other.

But here an objection occurs. It may be said *that although every right implies a duty yet every duty does not imply a right*. Thus, it may be my duty to do a humane or kind office to a man who has no claim of right to it; and therefore a system of the rights of men, though it teach all the duties of strict justice, yet it leaves out all the duties of charity and humanity, without which the system of morals must be very lame.

In answer to this objection, it may be observed that as there is a strict notion of justice in which it is distinguished from humanity and charity, so there is a more extensive signification of it in which it includes those virtues. The ancient moralists, both Greek and Roman, under the cardinal virtue of justice, included beneficence, and in this extensive sense, it is often used in common language. The like may be said of right, which, in a sense not uncommon, is extended to every proper claim of humanity and charity, as well as to the claims of strict justice. But, as it is proper to distinguish these two kinds of claims by different names, writers in natural jurisprudence have given the name of *perfect* rights to the claims of strict justice and that of *imperfect* rights to the claims of charity and humanity. Thus, all the duties of humanity have imperfect rights corresponding to them, as those of strict justice have perfect rights.

Another objection may be *that there is still a class of duties to which no right, perfect or imperfect, corresponds.*

We are bound in duty to pay due respect, not only to what is truly the right of another, but to what, through ignorance or mistake, we believe to be his right. Thus, if my neighbor is possessed of a horse which he stole and to which he has no right, while I believe the horse to be really his and am ignorant of the theft, it is my duty to pay the same respect to this conceived right as if it were real. Here, then, is a moral obligation on one party without any corresponding right on the other.

To supply this defect in the system of rights, so as to make right and duty correspond in every instance, writers in jurisprudence have had recourse to something like what is called a fiction of law. They give the name of *right* to the claim which even the thief hath to the goods he has stolen, while the theft is unknown, and to all similar claims grounded on the ignorance or mistake of the parties concerned. And to distinguish this kind of right from genuine rights, perfect or imperfect, they call it an *external* right.

Thus it appears that although a system of the perfect rights of men, or the rights of strict justice, would be a lame substitute for a system of human duty, yet, when we add to it the imperfect and the external rights, it comprehends the whole duty we owe to our fellowmen.

28

Adam Smith

OF THE ORIGIN OF AMBITION
AND OF THE DISTINCTION
OF RANKS

It is because mankind are disposed to sympathize more entirely with our joy than with our sorrow that we make parade of our riches and conceal our poverty. Nothing is so mortifying as to be obliged to expose our distress to the view of the public and to feel that though our situation is open to the eyes of all mankind no mortal conceives for us the half of what we suffer. Nay, it is chiefly from this regard to the sentiments of mankind that we pursue riches and avoid poverty. For to what purpose is all the toil and bustle of this world? What is the end of avarice and ambition, of the pursuit of wealth, of power, and preeminence? Is it to supply the necessities of nature? The wages of the meanest laborer can supply them. We see that they afford him food and clothing, the comfort of a house, and of a family. If we examine his economy with rigor, we should find that he spends a great part of them upon conveniences, which may be regarded as superfluities, and that upon extraordinary occasions he can give something even to vanity and distinction. What then is the cause of our aversion to his situation, and why should those who have been educated in the higher ranks of life regard it as worse than death

Reprinted from Adam Smith, *The Theory of Moral Sentiments* (London and New York: G. Bell & Sons, 1892), pp. 70–83.

to be reduced to live, even without labor, upon the same simple fare with him, to dwell under the same lowly roof, and to be clothed in the same humble attire? Do they imagine that their stomach is better, or their sleep sounder, in a palace than in a cottage? The contrary has been so often observed and indeed is so very obvious, though it had never been observed, that there is nobody ignorant of it. From whence then arises that emulation which runs through all the different ranks of men and what are the advantages which we propose by that great purpose of human life which we call bettering our condition? To be observed, to be attended to, to be taken notice of with sympathy, complacency, and approbation, are all the advantages which we can propose to derive from it. It is the vanity, not the ease or the pleasure, which interests us. But vanity is always founded upon the belief of our being the object of attention and approbation. The rich man glories in his riches because he feels that they naturally draw upon him the attention of the world and that mankind are disposed to go along with him in all those agreeable emotions with which the advantages of his situation so readily inspire him. At the thought of this his heart seems to swell and dilate itself within him, and he is fonder of his wealth, upon this account, than for all the other advantages it procures him. The poor man, on the contrary, is ashamed of his poverty. He feels that it either places him out of the sight of mankind, or that if they take any notice of him they have, however, scarce any fellow-feeling with the misery and distress which he suffers. He is mortified upon both accounts; for though to be overlooked and to be disapproved of are things entirely different, yet as obscurity covers us from the daylight of honor and approbation, to feel that we are taken no notice of necessarily damps the most agreeable hope and disappoints the most ardent desire of human nature. The poor man goes out and comes in unheeded, and when in the midst of a crowd is in the same obscurity as if shut up in his own hovel. Those humble cares and painful attentions which occupy those in his situation afford no amusement to the dissipated and the gay. They turn away their eyes from him, or if the extremity of his distress forces them to look at him, it is only to spurn so disagreeable an object from among them. The fortunate and the proud wonder at the insolence of human wretchedness, that it should dare to present itself before them, and with the loathsome aspect of its misery presume to disturb the serenity of their happiness. The man of rank and distinction, on the contrary, is observed by all the world. Everybody is eager to look at him and to conceive, at least by sympathy, that joy and exultation with which his circumstances naturally inspire him. His actions are the objects of the public care. Scarce a word, scarce a gesture, can fall from him that is altogether neglected. In a great assembly he is the person upon whom all direct their eyes; it is upon him that their passions seem all to wait with expectation, in order to receive that movement and direction which he shall impress upon them; and if his behavior is not altogether absurd, he has every moment an opportunity of interesting mankind and of rendering himself the object of the observation and fellow-feeling of everybody about him. It is this, which, notwithstanding the restraint it imposes, notwithstanding the loss of liberty with which it is attended, renders greatness the object of envy, and compensates, in the opinion of mankind, all that toil, all that anxiety, all those mortifications, which must be undergone in the pursuit of it; and what is of yet more consequence, all that leisure, all that ease, that careless security, which are forfeited forever by the acquisition.

When we consider the condition of the great, in those delusive colors in which the imagination is apt to paint it, it seems to be almost the abstract idea of a perfect and happy state. It is the very state which, in all our waking dreams and idle reveries, we had sketched out to ourselves as the final object of all our desires. We feel, therefore, a peculiar sympathy with the satisfaction of those who are in it. We favor all their inclinations and forward all their wishes. What pity, we think, that any thing should spoil and corrupt so agreeable a situation! We could even wish them immortal, and it seems hard to us that death should at last put an end to such perfect enjoyment. It is cruel, we think, in nature to compel them from their exalted stations to that humble, but hospitable, home, which she has provided for all her children. Great king, live forever! is the compliment, which after the manner of eastern adulation, we should readily make them, if experience did not teach us its absurdity. Every calamity that befalls them, every injury that is done them, excites in the breast of the spectator ten times more compassion and resentment than he would have felt had the same things happened to other men. It is the misfortunes of kings only which afford the proper subjects for tragedy. They resemble, in this respect, the misfortunes of lovers. Those two situations are the chief which interest us upon the theater; because, in spite of all that reason and experience can tell us to the contrary, the prejudices of the imagination attach to these two states a happiness superior to any other. To disturb, or to put an end to, such perfect enjoyment, seems to be the most atrocious of all injuries. The traitor who conspires against the life of his monarch is thought a greater monster than any other murderer. All the innocent blood that was shed in the civil wars provoked less indignation than the death of Charles I. A stranger to human nature, who saw the indifference of men about the misery of their inferiors, and the regret and indignation which they feel for the misfortunes and sufferings of those above them, would be apt to imagine that pain must be more agonizing and the convulsions of death more terrible to persons of higher rank than to those of meaner stations.

Upon this disposition of mankind to go along with all the passions of the rich and the powerful, is founded the distinction of ranks and the order of society. Our obsequiousness to our superiors more frequently arises from our admiration for the advantages of their situation than from any private expectations of benefit from their goodwill. Their benefits can extend but to a few, but their fortunes interest almost everybody. We are eager to assist them in completing a system of happiness that approaches so near to perfection; and we desire to serve them for their own sake, without any other recompense but the vanity or the honor of obliging them. Neither is our deference to their inclinations founded chiefly, or altogether, upon a regard to the utility of such submission and to the order of society which is best supported by it. Even when the order of society seems to require that we should oppose them, we can hardly bring ourselves to do it. That kings are the servants of the people, to be obeyed, resisted, deposed, or punished, as the public conveniency may require, is the doctrine of reason and philosophy; but it is not the doctrine of nature. Nature would teach us to submit to them for their own sake, to tremble and bow down before their exalted station, to regard their smile as a reward sufficient to compensate any services, and to dread their displeasure, though no other evil were to follow from it, as the severest of all mortifications. To treat them in any respect as men, to reason and dispute with them upon ordinary occasions, requires such resolution that there are few men whose magnanimity can support them in it, unless they are likewise assisted by familiarity and acquaintance. The strongest motives, the most furious passions, fear, hatred, and resentment, are scarce sufficient to balance this natural disposition to respect them: and their conduct must, either justly or unjustly, have excited the highest degree of all those passions before the bulk of the people can be brought to oppose them with violence or to desire to see them either punished or deposed. Even when the people have been brought this length, they are apt to relent every moment and easily relapse into their habitual state of deference to those to whom they have been accustomed to look up as their natural superiors. They cannot stand the mortification of their monarch. Compassion soon takes the place of resentment, they forget all past provocations, their old principles of loyalty revive, and they run to reestablish the ruined authority of their old masters, with the same violence with which they had opposed it. The death of Charles I brought about the restoration of the royal family. Compassion for James II, when he was seized by the populace in making his escape on shipboard, had almost prevented the revolution, and made it go on more heavily than before.

Do the great seem insensible of the easy price at which they may acquire the public admiration; or do they seem to imagine that to them, as to other men, it must be the purchase either of sweat or of blood? By what important accomplishments is the young nobleman instructed to support the dignity of his rank and to render himself worthy of that superiority over his fellow citizens to which the virtue of his ancestors had raised them? Is it by knowledge, by industry, by patience, by self-denial, or by virtue

of any kind? As all his words, as all his motions are attended to,
he learns an habitual regard to every circumstance of ordinary
behavior and studies to perform all those small duties with the most
exact propriety. As he is conscious how much he is observed, and
how much mankind are disposed to favor all his inclinations, he
acts upon the most indifferent occasions with that freedom and
elevation which the thought of this naturally inspires. His air, his
manner, his deportment, all mark that elegant and graceful sense
of his own superiority which those who are born to inferior stations
can hardly ever arrive at. These are the arts by which he proposes
to make mankind more easily submit to his authority and to govern
their inclinations according to his own pleasure; and in this he is
seldom disappointed. These arts, supported by rank and preeminence, are upon ordinary occasions sufficient to govern the
world. Louis XIV, during the greater part of his reign, was regarded, not only in France, but over all Europe, as the most perfect model of a great prince. But what were the talents and virtues
by which he acquired this great reputation? Was it by the scrupulous and flexible justice of all his undertakings, by the immense
dangers and difficulties with which they were attended, or by
the unwearied and unrelenting application with which he pursued them? Was it by his extensive knowledge, by his exquisite
judgment, or by his heroic valor? It was by none of these qualities.
But he was, first of all, the most powerful prince in Europe, and
consequently held the highest rank among kings; and then, says
his historian, "he surpassed all his courtiers in the gracefulness
of his shape and the majestic beauty of his features. The sound of
his voice, noble and affecting, gained those hearts which his
presence intimidated. He had a step and a deportment which
could suit only him and his rank, and which would have been
ridiculous in any other person. The embarrassment which he
occasioned to those who spoke to him flattered that secret satisfaction with which he felt his own superiority. The old officer, who
was confounded, and faltered in asking him a favor, and not
being able to conclude his discourse, said to him, 'Sir, your majesty,
I hope, will believe that I do not tremble thus before your enemies,'
had no difficulty to obtain what he demanded." These frivolous

accomplishments, supported by his rank, and, no doubt too, by a degree of other talents and virtues, which seems, however, not to have been much above mediocrity, established this prince in the esteem of his own age and have drawn even from posterity a good deal of respect for his memory. Compared with these, in his own times, and in his own presence, no other virtue, it seems, appeared to have any merit. Knowledge, industry, valor, and beneficence trembled, were abashed, and lost all dignity, before them.

But it is not by accomplishments of this kind that the man of inferior rank must hope to distinguish himself. Politeness is so much the virtue of the great, that it will do little honor to anybody but themselves. The coxcomb who imitates their manner and affects to be eminent by the superior propriety of his ordinary behavior, is rewarded with a double share of contempt for his folly and presumption. Why should the man, whom nobody thinks it worth while to look at, be very anxious about the manner in which he holds up his head, or disposes of his arms, while he walks through a room? He is occupied surely with a very superfluous attention and with an attention too that marks a sense of his own importance, which no other mortal can go along with. The most perfect modesty and plainness, joined to as much negligence as is consistent with the respect due to the company, ought to be the chief characteristics of the behavior of a private man. If ever he hopes to distinguish himself, it must be by more important virtues. He must acquire dependents to balance the dependents of the great, and he has no other fund to pay them from but the labor of his body and the activity of his mind. He must cultivate these therefore: he must acquire superior knowledge in his profession and superior industry in the exercise of it. He must be patient in labor, resolute in danger, and firm in distress. These talents he must bring into public view, by the difficulty, importance, and, at the same time, good judgment of his understakings, and by the severe and unrelenting application with which he pursues them. Probity and prudence, generosity and frankness must characterize his behavior upon all ordinary occasions; and he must, at the same time, be forward to engage in all those situations, in which it requires the greatest talents and virtues to act with propriety, but in which the greatest applause is to be acquired by those who can acquit themselves with honor. With what impatience does the man of spirit and ambition, who is depressed by his situation, look round for some great opportunity to distinguish himself? No circumstances, which can afford this, appear to him undesirable. He even looks forward with satisfaction to the prospect of foreign war, or civil dissension, and with secret transport and delight, sees through all the confusion and bloodshed which attend them, the probability of those wished-for occasions presenting themselves in which he may draw upon himself the attention and admiration of mankind. The man of rank and distinction, on the contrary, whose whole glory consists in the propriety of his ordinary behavior, who is contented with the humble renown which this can afford him, and has no talents to acquire any other, is unwilling to embarass himself with what can be attended either with difficulty or distress. To figure at a ball is his great triumph, and to succeed in an intrigue of gallantry, his highest exploit. He has an aversion to all public confusions, not from the love of mankind, for the great never look upon their inferiors as their fellow creatures; nor yet from want of courage, for in that he is seldom defective; but from a consciousness that he possesses none of the virtues which are required in such situations and that the public attention will certainly be drawn away from him by others. He may be willing to expose himself to some little danger and to make a campaign when it happens to be the fashion, but he shudders with horror at the thought of any situation which demands the continual and long exertion of patience, industry, fortitude, and application of thought. These virtues are hardly ever to be met with in men who are born to those high stations. In all governments accordingly, even in monarchies, the highest offices are generally possessed, and the whole detail of the administration conducted, by men who were educated in the middle and inferior ranks of life, who have been carried forward by their own industry and abilities, though loaded with the jealousy, and opposed by the resentment, of all those who were born their superiors, and to whom the great, after having regarded them, first with contempt and afterwards with envy, are at last contented to truckle with the same abject meanness with which they desire that the rest of mankind should behave to themselves.

It is the loss of this easy empire over the affections of mankind which renders the fall from greatness so insupportable. When the family of the king of Macedon was led in triumph by Paulus Emilius, their misfortunes, it is said, made them divide, with their conqueror, the attention of the Roman people. The sight of the royal children, whose tender age rendered them insensible of their situation, struck the spectators, amid the public rejoicings and prosperity, with the tenderest sorrow and compassion. The king appeared next in the procession and seemed like one confounded and astonished, and bereft of all sentiment, by the greatness of his calamities. His friends and ministers followed after him. As they moved along, they often cast their eyes upon their fallen sovereign and always burst into tears at the sight; their whole behavior demonstrating that they thought not of their own misfortunes but were occupied entirely by the superior greatness of his. The generous Romans, on the contrary, beheld him with disdain and indignation, and regarded as unworthy of all compassion the man who could be so mean-spirited as to bear to live under such calamities. Yet what did those calamities amount to? According to the greater part of historians, he was to spend the remainder of his days, under the protection of a powerful and humane people, in a state which in itself should seem worthy of envy, a state of plenty, ease, leisure, and security, from which it was impossible for him, even by his own folly to fall. But he was no longer to be surrounded by that admiring mob of fools, flatterers, and dependents, who had formerly been accustomed to attend upon all his motions. He was no longer to be gazed upon by multitudes, nor to have it in his power to render himself the object of their respect, their gratitude, their love, their admiration. The passions of nations were no longer to mould themselves upon his inclinations. This was that insupportable calamity which bereaved the king of all sentiment, which made his friends forget their own misfortunes, and which the Roman magnanimity could scare conceive how any man could be so mean-spirited as to bear to survive.

"Love," says my Lord Rochefoucauld, "is commonly succeeded by ambition, but ambition is hardly ever succeeded by love." That passion, when once it has got entire possession of the breast, will admit neither a rival nor a successor. To those who have been accustomed to the possession, or even to the hope, of public admiration, all other pleasures sicken and decay. Of all the discarded statesmen who, for their own ease, have studied to get the better of ambition, and to despise those honors which they could no longer arrive at, how few have been able to succeed? The greater part have spent their time in the most listless and insipid indolence, chagrined at the thought of their own insignificancy, incapable of being interested in the occupations of private life, without enjoyment, except when they talked of their former greatness, and without satisfaction, except when they were employed in some vain project to recover it. Are you in earnest resolved never to barter your liberty for the lordly servitude of a court, but to live free, fearless, and independent? There seems to be one way to continue in that virtuous resolution; and perhaps but one. Never enter the place from whence so few have been able to return; never come within the circle of ambition; nor ever bring yourself into comparison with those masters of the earth who have already engrossed the attention of half mankind before you.

Of such mighty importance does it appear to be, in the imaginations of men, to stand in that situation which sets them most in the view of general sympathy and attention. And thus, place, that great object which divides the wives of aldermen, is the end of half the labors of human life; and is the cause of all the tumult and bustle, all the rapine and injustice, which avarice and ambition have introduced into this world. People of sense, it is said, indeed despise place, that is, they despise sitting at the head of the table and are indifferent who it is that is pointed out to the company by that frivolous circumstance, which the smallest advantage is capable of overbalancing. But rank, distinction, pre-eminince, no man despises, unless he is either raised very much above, or sunk very much below, the ordinary standard of human nature; unless he is either so confirmed in wisdom and real philosophy as to be satisfied that, while the propriety of his conduct renders him the just object of approbation, it is of little consequence though he be neither attended to nor approved of; or so habituated to the idea of his own meanness, so sunk in slothful and sottish indifference, as entirely to have forgot the desire, and almost the very wish, for superiority.

As to become the natural object of the joyous congratulations and sympathetic attentions of mankind is, in this manner, the circumstance which gives to prosperity all its dazzling splendor; so nothing darkens so much the gloom of adversity as to feel that our misfortunes are the objects, not of the fellow-feeling but of the contempt and aversion of our brethren. It is upon this account that the most dreadful calamities are not always those which it is most difficult to support. It is often more mortifying to appear in public under small disasters than under great misfortunes. The first excite no sympathy; but the second, though they may excite none that approaches to the anguish of the sufferer, call forth, however, a very lively compassion. The sentiments of the spectators are, in this last case, less wide of those of the sufferer, and their imperfect fellow-feeling lends him some assistance in supporting his misery. Before a gay assembly, a gentleman would be more mortified to appear covered with filth and rags than with blood and wounds. This last situation would interest their pity; the other would provoke their laughter. The judge who orders a criminal to be set in the pillory dishonors him more than if he had condemned him to the scaffold. The great prince, who, some years ago, caned a general officer at the head of his army disgraced him irrecoverably. The punishment would have been much less had he shot him through the body. By the laws of honor, to strike with a cane dishonors, to strike with a sword does not, for an obvious reason. Those slighter punishments, when inflicted on a gentleman, to whom dishonor is the greatest of all evils, come to be regarded among a humane and generous people as the most dreadful of any. With regard to persons of that rank, therefore, they are universally laid aside; and the law, while it takes their life upon many occasions, respects their honor upon almost all. To scourge a person of quality, or to set him in the pillory, upon account of any crime whatever, is a brutality of which no European government, except that of Russia, is capable.

A brave man is not rendered contemptible by being brought to the scaffold; he is, by being set in the pillory. His behavior in the one situation may gain him universal esteem and admiration. No behavior in the other can render him agreeable. The sympathy of the spectators supports him in the one case, and saves him from that shame, that consciousness, that his misery is felt by himself only, which is of all sentiments the most insupportable. There is no sympathy in the other; or, if there is any, it is not with his pain, which is a trifle, but with his consciousness of the want of sympathy with which this pain is attended. It is with his shame, not with his sorrow. Those who pity him blush and hang down their heads for him. He droops in the same manner, and feels himself irrecoverably degraded by the punishment, though not by the crime. The man, on the contrary, who dies with resolution, as he is naturally re-garded with the erect aspect of esteem and approbation, so he wears himself the same undaunted countenance; and, if the crime does not deprive him of the respect of others, the punishment never will. He has no suspicion that his situation is the object of contempt or derision to anybody and he can, with propriety, assume the air, not only of perfect serenity, but of triumph and exultation.

"Great dangers," says the Cardinal de Retz, "have their charms, because there is some glory to be got, even when we miscarry. But moderate dangers have nothing but what is horrible, because the loss of reputation always attends the want of success." His maxim has the same foundation with what we have been just now observing with regard to punishments.

Human virtue is superior to pain, to poverty, to danger, and to death; nor does it even require its utmost efforts to despise them. But to have its misery exposed to insult and derision, to be led in triumph, to be set up for the hand of scorn to point at, is a situation in which its constancy is much more apt to fail. Compared with the contempt of mankind, all other external evils are easily supported.

29

Adam Smith

THE THREE GREAT ORDERS
OF SOCIETY

THE WHOLE ANNUAL PRODUCE of the land and labor of
every country, or what comes to the same thing, the whole price
of that annual produce, naturally divides itself . . . into three parts
—the rent of land, the wages of labor, and the profits of stock—
and constitutes a revenue to three different orders of people—to
those who live by rent, to those who live by wages, and to those
who live by profit. These are the three great original and con-
stituent orders of every civilized society, from whose revenue that
of every other order is ultimately derived.

The interest of the first of those three great orders, it appears
from what has been just now said, is strictly and inseparably connected with the general interest of the society. Whatever either
promotes or obstructs the one necessarily promotes or obstructs
the other. When the public deliberates concerning any regulation
of commerce or police, the proprietors of land never can mislead
it, with a view to promote the interest of their own particular
order, at least, if they have any tolerable knowledge of that interest. They are, indeed, too often defective in this tolerable knowledge. They are the only one of the three orders whose revenue
costs them neither labor nor care, but comes to them, as it were,
of their own accord and independent of any plan or project of

Reprinted from Adam Smith, *The Wealth of Nations* (Edinburgh:
Adam and Charles Black, 1863), pp. 115–16. Title supplied.

their own. That indolence, which is the natural effect of the ease and security of their situation, renders them too often, not only ignorant, but incapable of that application of mind which is necessary in order to foresee and understand the consequences of any public regulation.

The interest of the second order, that of those who live by wages, is as strictly connected with the interest of the society as that of the first. The wages of the laborer . . . are never so high as when the demand for labor is continually rising, or when the quantity employed is every year increasing considerably. When this real wealth of the society becomes stationary, his wages are soon reduced to what is barely enough to enable him to bring up a family or to continue the race of laborers. When the society declines, they fall even below this. The order of proprietors may perhaps gain more by the prosperity of the society than that of laborers: but there is no order that suffers so cruelly from its decline. But though the interest of the laborer is strictly connected with that of the society, he is incapable either of comprehending that interest or of understanding its connection with his own. His condition leaves him no time to receive the necessary information, and his education and habits are commonly such as to render him unfit to judge even though he was fully informed. In the public deliberations, therefore, his voice is little heard and less regarded, except upon some particular occasions, when his clamor is animated, set on, and supported by his employers, not for his, but their own particular purposes.

His employers constitute the third order, that of those who live by profit. It is the stock that is employed for the sake of profit, which puts into motion the greater part of the useful labor of every society. The plans and projects of the employers of stock regulate and direct all the most important operations of labor, and profit is the end proposed by all those plans and projects. But the rate of profit does not, like rent and wages, rise with the prosperity, and fall with the declension, of the society. On the contrary, it is naturally low in rich, and high in poor countries, and it is always highest in the countries which are going fastest to ruin. The interest of this third order, therefore, has not the same connection with the general interest of the society as that of the other two. Merchants and master manufacturers are, in this order, the two classes of people who commonly employ the largest capitals, and who by their wealth draw to themselves the greatest share of public consideration. As during their whole lives they are engaged in plans and projects, they have frequently more acuteness of understanding than the greater part of country gentlemen. As their thoughts, however, are commonly exercised rather about the interest of their own particular branch of business than about that of the society, their judgment, even when given with the greatest candor (which it has not been upon every occasion), is much more to be depended upon with regard to the former of those two objects than with regard to the latter. Their superiority over the country gentlemen is not so much in their knowledge of the public interest as in their having a better knowledge of their own interest than he has of his. It is by this superior knowledge of their own interest that they have frequently imposed upon his generosity and persuaded him to give up both his own interest and that of the public, from a very simple but honest conviction that their interest, and not his, was the interest of the public. The interest of the dealers, however, in any particular branch of trade or manufactures is always in some respects different from, and even opposite to, that of the public. To widen the market and to narrow the competition is always the interest of the dealers. To widen the market may frequently be agreeable enough to the interest of the public; but to narrow the competition must always be against it and can serve only to enable the dealers, by raising their profits above what they naturally would be, to levy, for their own benefit, an absurd tax upon the rest of their fellow citizens. The proposal of any new law or regulation of commerce which comes from this order ought always to be listened to with great precaution and ought never to be adopted until after having been long and carefully examined, not only with the most scrupulous, but with the most suspicious attention. It comes from an order of men whose interest is never exactly the same with that of the public, who have generally an interest to deceive and even to oppress the public, and who accordingly have, upon many occasions, both deceived and oppressed it.

30

David Hume

OF THE POPULOUSNESS OF
ANCIENT NATIONS

It is to be remarked that all kinds of numbers are uncertain in ancient manuscripts and have been subject to much greater corruptions than any other part of the text, and that for an obvious reason. Any alteration in other places commonly affects the sense or grammar and is more readily perceived by the reader and transcriber.

Few enumerations of inhabitants have been made of any tract of country by any ancient author of good authority, so as to afford us a large enough view for comparison.

It is probable that there was formerly a good foundation for the number of citizens assigned to any free city; because they entered for a share in the government, and there were exact registers kept of them. But as the number of slaves is seldom mentioned, this leaves us in as great uncertainty as ever, with regard to the populousness even of single cities.

The first page of Thucydides is, in my opinion, the commencement of real history. All preceding narrations are so intermixed with fable, that philosophers ought to abandon them, in a great measure, to the embellishment of poets and orators.[1]

With regard to remote times, the numbers of people assigned

Reprinted from David Hume, *Essays*, T. H. Green and T. H. Grose, eds. (London: Longmans Green, 1875), II, pp. 414–417.

[1]   In general, there is more candor and sincerity in ancient historians, but less exactness and care, than in the moderns. Our speculative factions, especially those of religion, throw such an illusion over our minds that men

are often ridiculous and lose all credit and authority. The free citizens of Sybaris, able to bear arms, and actually drawn out in battle, were 300,000. They encountered at Siagra with 100,000 citizens of Crotona, another Greek city contiguous to them and were defeated. This is Diodorus *Siculus's*[2] account and is very seriously insisted on by that historian.[3] Strabo also mentions the same number of Sybarites.

Diodorus Siculus,[4] enumerating the inhabitants of Agrigentum, when it was destroyed by the *Carthaginians,* says that they amounted to 20,000 citizens, 200,000 strangers, besides slaves, who, in so opulent a city as he represents it, would probably be, at least, as numerous. We must remark that the women and the children are not included and that, therefore, upon the whole, this city must have contained near two millions of inhabitants.[5] And what was the reason of so immense an increase! They were industrious in cultivating the neighboring fields, not exceeding a small English county, and they traded with their wine and oil to Africa, which at that time produced none of these commodities.

Ptolemy, says Theocritus,[6] commands 33,333 cities. I suppose the singularity of the number was the reason of assigning it. Diodorus Siculus[7] assigns three millions of inhabitants to *Egypt,* a small number: but then he makes the number of cities amount to 18,000, an evident contradiction.

He says[8] the people were formerly seven millions. Thus remote times are always most envied and admired.

---

seem to regard impartiality to their adversaries and to heretics as a vice or weakness: But the commonness of books, by means of printing, has obliged modern historians to be more careful in avoiding contradictions and incongruities. Diodorus Siculus is a good writer, but it is with pain I see his narration contradict, in so many particulars, the two most authentic pieces of all Greek history, to wit, Xenophon's expedition, and Demosthenes's orations. Plutarch and Appian seem scarce ever to have read Cicero's epistles.

2   Lib. xii. 9.
3   Lib. vi. 26.
4   Lib. xiii. 90.
5   Diogenes *Laertius* (*in vita Empedoclis*) says, that Agrigentum contained only 800,000 inhabitants.
6   Idyll. 17.
7   Lib. i. 18.
8   Id. ibid.

That Xerxes's army was extremely numerous, I can readily believe; both from the great extent of his empire and from the practice among the eastern nations of encumbering their camp with a superfluous multitude: But will any rational man cite Herodotus's wonderful narrations as an authority? There is something very rational, I own, in Lysias's[9] argument upon this subject. Had not Xerxes's army been incredibly numerous, says he, he had never made a bridge over the Hellespont: it had been much easier to have transported his men over so short a passage with the numerous shipping of which he was master.

Polybius[10] says, that the Romans, between the first and second Punic wars, being threatened with an invasion from the Gauls, mustered all their own forces and those of their allies and found them amount to seven hundred thousand men able to bear arms: a great number surely, and which, when joined to the slaves, is probably not less, if not rather more, than that extent of country affords at present.[11] The enumeration too seems to have been made with some exactness, and Polybius gives us the detail of the particulars. But might not the number be magnified, in order to encourage the people?

Diodorus Siculus[12] makes the same enumeration amount to near a million. These variations are suspicious. He plainly too supposes that Italy in his time was not so populous: another suspicious circumstance. For who can believe that the inhabitants of that country diminished from the time of the first Punic war to that of the *triumvirates?*

Julius Caesar, according to Appian,[13] encountered four millions of Gauls, killed one million, and made another million prisoners.[14] Supposing the number of the enemy's army and that of the slain

9   *Orat. funebris*, 193.
10   Lib. ii. 24.
11   The country that supplied this number, was not above a third of Italy, *viz.* the Pope's dominions, Tuscany, and a part of the kingdom of Naples: But perhaps in those early times there were very few slaves, except in Rome, or the great cities.
12   Lib. ii. 5.
13   Celtica, c. 2.
14   Plutarch (*in vita Caes.* 15) makes the number that *Caesar* fought with amount to three millions; Julian (*in* Caesaribus) to two.

could be exactly assigned, which never is possible; how could it be known how often the same man returned into the armies, or how distinguish the new from the old levied soldiers? No attention ought ever to be given to such loose, exaggerated calculations; especially where the author does not tell us the mediums, upon which the calculations were founded.

Paterculus[15] makes the number of Gauls killed by *Caesar* amount only to 400,000: a more probable account, and more easily reconciled to the history of these wars given by that conqueror himself in his *Commentaries*.[16] The most bloody of his battles were fought against the Helvetii and the Germans.

One would imagine that every circumstance of the life and actions of Dionysius the elder might be regarded as authentic, and free from all fabulous exaggeration; both because he lived at a time when letters flourished most in Greece and because his chief historian was Philistus, a man allowed to be of great genius and who was a courtier and minister of that prince. But can we admit that he had a standing army of 100,000 foot, 10,000 horse; and a fleet of 400 gallies?[17] These, we may observe, were mercenary forces, and subsisted upon pay, like our armies in Europe. For the citizens were all disarmed; and when Dion afterward invaded Sicily, and called on his countrymen to vindicate their liberty, he was obliged to bring arms along with him, which he distributed among those who joined him.[18] In a state where agriculture alone flourishes, there may be many inhabitants; and if these be all armed and disciplined, a great force may be called out upon occasion: but great bodies of mercenary troops can never be maintained, without either great trade and numerous manufactures, or extensive dominions. The United Provinces never were masters of such a force by sea and land as that which is said to belong to

[15]   Lib. ii. cap. 47.

[16]   *Pliny*, lib. vii. cap. 25, says, that *Caesar* used to boast, that there had fallen in battle against him one million one hundred and ninety-two thousand men, besides those who perished in the civil wars. It is not probable, that that conqueror could ever pretend to be so exact in his computation. But allowing the fact, it is likely, that the *Helvetii, Germans,* and *Britons,* whom he slaughtered, would amount to near a half of the number.

[17]   *Diod. Sic.* lib. ii. 5.

[18]   Plutarch *in vita* Dionys, 25.

Dionysius; yet they possess as large a territory, perfectly well cultivated, and have much more resources from their commerce and
industry. *Diodorus Siculus* allows that even in his time the army
of Dionysius appeared incredible, that is, as I interpret it, was
entirely a fiction, and the opinion arose from the exaggerated flattery of the courtiers, and perhaps from the vanity and policy of
the tyrant himself.

31

Henry Home, Lord Kames

A GREAT CITY CONSIDERED
IN PHYSICAL, MORAL,
AND POLITICAL VIEWS

IN ALL AGES an opinion has been prevalent that a great city is a great evil, and that a capital may be too great for the state, as a head may be for the body. Considering, however, the very shallow reasons that have been given for this opinion, it should seem to be but slightly founded. There are several ordinances limiting the extent of Paris, and prohibiting new buildings beyond the prescribed bounds; the first of which is by Henry II *anno* 1549. These ordinances have been renewed from time to time, down to 1672, in which year there is an edict of Louis XIV to the same purpose. The reasons assigned are: "First, that by enlarging the city, the air would be rendered unwholesome. Second, that cleaning the streets would prove a great additional labor. Third, that adding to the number of inhabitants would raise the price of provisions, of labor, and of manufactures. Fourth, that ground would be covered with buildings instead of corn, which might hazard a scarcity. Fifth, that the country would be depopulated by the desire that people have to resort to the capital. And, lastly, that the difficulty of governing such numbers would be an encouragement to robbery and murder."

Reprinted from Henry Home, Lord Kames, *Sketches of the History of Man* (Edinburgh, 1813), II, 338–52.

In these reasons, the limiting the extent of the city and the limiting the number of inhabitants are jumbled together, as if they were the same. The only reasons that regard the former are the second and fourth, and these, at best, are trifling. The first reason urged against enlarging the city is a solid reason for enlarging it, supposing the numbers to be limited; for crowding is an infallible means to render the air unwholesome. Paris, with the same number of inhabitants that were in the days of the fourth Henry, occupies thrice the space, much to the health as well as comfort of the inhabitants. Had the ordinances mentioned been made effectual, the houses in Paris must all have been built story above story, ascending to the sky like the tower of Babel. Before the great fire *anno* 1666, the plague was frequent in London; but by widening the streets and enlarging the houses, there has not since been known in that great city any contagious distemper that deserves the name of a plague. The third, fifth, and last reasons conclude against permitting any addition to the number of inhabitants, but conclude nothing against enlarging the town. In a word, the measure adopted in these ordinances has little or no tendency to correct the evils complained of, and infallibly would inflame the chief of them. The measure that ought to have been adopted is to limit the number of inhabitants, not the extent of the town.

Queen Elizabeth of England, copying the French ordinances, issued a proclamation *anno* 1602 prohibiting any new buildings within three miles of London. The preamble is in the following words: "That foreseeing the great and manifold inconveniences and mischiefs which daily grow, and are likely to increase, in the city and suburbs of London, by confluence of people to inhabit the same; not only by reason that such multitudes can hardly be governed, to serve God and obey her Majesty, without constituting an addition of new officers, and enlarging their authority; but also can hardly be provided of food and other necessaries at a reasonable price; and finally, that as such multitudes of people, many of them poor, who must live by begging or worse means, are heaped up together, and in a sort smothered with many children and servants in one house or small tenement; it must needs follow, if any plague or other universal sickness come amongst them, that it would presently spread through the whole city and confines, and also into all parts of the realm."

There appears as little accuracy in this proclamation as in the French ordinances. The same error is observable in both, which is the limiting the extent of the city, instead of limiting the number of inhabitants. True it is indeed that the regulation would have a better effect in London than in Paris. As stone is in plenty about Paris, houses there may be carried to a great height, and are actually so carried in the old town: but there being no stone about London, the houses formerly were built of timber, now of brick, materials too frail for a lofty edifice.

Proceeding to particulars, the first objection, which is the expense of governing a great multitude, concludes against the number of inhabitants, not against the extent of the city. At the same time, the objection is at best doubtful in point of fact. Though vices abound in a great city, requiring the strictest attention of the magistrate; yet with a well-regulated police, it appears less expensive to govern 600,000 in one city than the same number in ten different cities. The second objection, viz., the high price of provisions, strikes only against numbers, not extent. Beside, whatever might have been the case in the days of Elizabeth when agriculture and internal commerce were in their infancy, there are at present not many towns in England where a temperate man may live cheaper than in London. The hazard of contagious distempers, which is the third objection, is an invincible argument against limiting the extent of a great town. It is mentioned above that from the year 1666, when the streets were widened and the houses enlarged, London has never been once visited by the plague. If the proclamation had taken effect, the houses must have been so crowded upon each other, and the streets so contracted, as to have occasioned plagues still more frequently than before the year 1666.

The Queen's immediate successors were not more clear-sighted than she had been. In the year 1624, King James issued a proclamation against building in London upon new foundations. Charles I issued two proclamations to the same purpose, one in the year 1625 and one in the year 1630.

The progress of political knowledge has unfolded many bad effects of a great city, more weighty than any urged in these proclamations. The first I shall mention is that people born and bred in a great city are commonly weak and effeminate. Vegetius,[1] observing that men bred to husbandry make the best soldiers, adds what follows. "But sometimes there is a necessity for arming the townspeople and calling them out to service. When this is the case, it ought to be the first care to enure them to labor, to march them up and down the country, to make them carry heavy burdens, and to harden them against the weather. Their food should be coarse and scanty, and they should be habituated to sleep alternately in their tents and in the open air. Then is the time to instruct them in the exercise of their arms. If the expedition is a distant one, they should be chiefly employed in the stations of posts or expresses, and removed as much as possible from the dangerous allurements that abound in large cities; that thus they may be invigorated both in mind and body." The luxury of a great city descends from the highest to the lowest, infecting all ranks of men; and there is little opportunity in it for such exercise as to render the body vigorous and robust.

The foregoing is a physical objection against a great city; the next regards morality. Virtue is exerted chiefly in restraint: vice, in giving freedom to desire. Moderation and self-command form a character the most susceptible of virtue: superfluity of animal spirits and love of pleasure form a character the most liable to vice. Low vices, pilfering, for example, or lying, draw few or no imitators; but vices that indicate a soul above restraint produce many admirers. Where a man boldly struggles against unlawful restraint, he is justly applauded and imitated; and the vulgar are not apt to distinguish nicely between lawful and unlawful restraint: the boldness is visible and they pierce no deeper. It is the unruly boy, full of animal spirits, who at public school is admired and imitated, not the virtuous and modest. Vices accordingly that show spirit are extremely infectious; virtue very little. Hence the corruption of a great city, which increases more and more in proportion to the number of inhabitants. But it is sufficient barely to

[1]   *De re militari*, lib. 1. cap. 3.

mention that objection, because it has been formerly insisted on.

The following bad effects are more of a political nature. A great town is a professed enemy to the free circulation of money. The current coin is accumulated in the capital, and distant provinces must sink into idleness; for without ready money neither arts nor manufactures can flourish. Thus we find less and less activity, in proportion commonly to the distance from the capital; and an absolute torpor in the extremities. The city of Milan affords a good proof of this observation. The money that the Emperor of Germany draws from it in taxes is carried to Vienna; not a farthing left but what is barely sufficient to defray the expense of government. Manufactures and commerce have gradually declined in proportion to the scarcity of money, and that city which the last century contained 300,000 inhabitants cannot now muster 90,000.[2] It may be observed beside that as horses in a great city must be provided with provender from a distance, the country is robbed of its dung, which goes to the rich fields round the city. But as manure laid upon poor land is of more advantage to the farmer than upon what is already highly improved, the depriving distant parts of manure is a loss to the nation in general. Nor is this all: the dung of an extensive city, the bulk of it at least, is so remote from the fields to which it must be carried that the expense of carriage swallows up the profit.

Another bad effect of accumulating money in the capital is that it raises the price of labor. The temptation of high wages in the capital robs the country of its best hands. And as they who resort to the capital are commonly young people, who remove as soon as they are fit for work, distant provinces are burdened with their maintenance without reaping any benefit by their labor.

But of all, the most deplorable effect of a great city is the pre-

2   Is not the following inference from these premises well founded, that it would be a ruinous measure to add Bengal to the British dominions? In what manner would the territorial revenues and other taxes be remitted to London? If in hard coin, that country would in time be drained of money, its manufactures would be annihilated, and depopulation ensue. If remitted in commodities, the public would be cheated, and little be added to the revenue. A land tax laid on as in Britain would be preferable in every respect; for it would be paid by the East India Company as proprietors of Bengal without deduction of a farthing.

venting of population, by shortening the lives of its inhabitants. Does a capital swell in proportion to the numbers that are drained from the country? Far from it. The air of a populous city is infected by multitudes crowded together; and people there seldom make out the usual time of life. With respect to London in particular, the fact cannot be dissembled. The burials in that immense city greatly exceed the births: the difference some affirm to be no less than ten thousand yearly; by the most moderate computation, not under seven or eight thousand. As London is far from being on the decline, that number must be supplied by the country; and the annual supply amounts probably to a greater number than were needed annually for recruiting our armies and navies in the late war with France. If so, London is a greater enemy to population than a bloody war would be, supposing it even to be perpetual. What an enormous tax is Britain thus subjected to for supporting her capital! The rearing and educating yearly for London 7,000 or 8,000 persons require an immense sum.

In Paris, if the bills of mortality can be relied on, the births and burials are nearly equal, being each of them about 19,000 yearly; and according to that computation, Paris should need no recruits from the country. But in that city, the bills of mortality cannot be depended on for burials. It is there universally the practice of high and low to have their infants nursed in the country until they be three years of age, and consequently those who die before that age are not enlisted. What proportion these bear to the whole is uncertain. But a guess may be made from such as die in London before the age of three, which are computed to be one half of the whole that die. Now, giving the utmost allowance for the healthiness of the country above that of a town, children from Paris that die in the country before the age of three cannot be brought so low as a third of those who die. On the other hand, the London bills of mortality are less to be depended on for births than for burials. None are enlisted but infants baptized by clergymen of the English church; and the numerous children of papists, dissenters, and other sectaries are left out of the account. Upon the whole, the difference between the births and burials in Paris and in London is much less than it appears to be on comparing the bills of mortality of these two cities.

At the same time, giving full allowance for children who are not brought into the London bills of mortality, there is the highest probability that a greater number of children are born in Paris than in London; and consequently that the former requires fewer recruits from the country than the latter. In Paris, domestic servants are encouraged to marry: they are observed to be more settled than when bachelors, and more attentive to their duty. In London, such marriages are discouraged, as rendering a servant more attentive to his own family than to that of his master. But a servant attentive to his own family will not for his own sake neglect that of his master. At any rate, is he not more to be depended on than a servant who continues single? What can be expected of idle and pampered bachelors but debauchery and every sort of corruption? Nothing restrains them from absolute profligacy but the eye of the master; who for that reason is their aversion, not their love. If the poor laws be named the folio of corruption, bachelor servants in London may well be considered as a large appendix. And this attracts the eye to the poor laws, which indeed make the chief difference between Paris and London, with respect to the present point. In Paris, certain funds are established for the poor, the yearly produce of which admits but a limited number. As that fund is always preoccupied, the low people who are not on the list have little or no prospect of bread, but from their own industry; and to the industrious, marriage is in a great measure necessary. In London, a parish is taxed in proportion to the number of its poor; and every person who is pleased to be idle is entitled to maintenance. Most things thrive by encouragement, and idleness above all. Certainty of maintenance renders the low people in England idle and profligate, especially in London, where luxury prevails, and infects every rank. So insolent are the London poor that scarce one of them will condescend to eat brown bread. There are accordingly in London a much greater number of idle and profligate wretches than in Paris, or in any other town, in proportion to the number of inhabitants. These wretches, in Doctor Swift's style,

never think of posterity, because posterity never thinks of them:
men who hunt after pleasure and live from day to day have no
notion of submitting to the burden of a family. These causes produce a greater number of children in Paris than in London; though
probably they differ not much in populousness.

I shall add but one other objection to a great city, which is not
slight. An overgrown capital, far above a rival, has, by numbers
and riches, a distressing influence in public affairs. The populace
are ductile, and easily misled by ambitious and designing magistrates. Nor are there wanting critical times, in which such magistrates, acquiring artificial influence, may have power to disturb
the public peace. That an overgrown capital may prove dangerous
to sovereignty has more than once been experienced both in Paris
and London.

It would give one the spleen to hear the French and English
zealously disputing about the extent of their capitals, as if the
prosperity of their country depended on that circumstance. To me
it appears like one glorying in the king's evil, or in any contagious
distemper. Much better employed would they be in contriving
means for lessening these cities. There is not a political measure
that would tend more to aggrandize the kingdom of France, or of
Britain, than to split its capital into several great towns. My plan
would be to confine the inhabitants of London to 100,000, composed of the King and his household, supreme courts of justice,
government boards, prime nobility and gentry, with necessary
shopkeepers, artists, and other dependents. Let the rest of the inhabitants be distributed into nine towns properly situated, some
for internal commerce, some for foreign. Such a plan would dif-
fuse life and vigor through every corner of the island.

To execute such a plan would, I acknowledge, require great
penetration and much perseverance. I shall suggest what occurs
at present. The first step must be to mark proper spots for the
nine towns, the most advantageous for trade or for manufactures.
If any of these spots be occupied already with small towns, so
much the better. The next step is a capitation tax on the inhabitants of London; the sum levied to be appropriated for encourag-
ing the new towns. One encouragement would have a good effect,

which is a premium to every man who builds in any of these towns, more or less, in proportion to the size of the house. This tax would banish from London every manufacture but of the most lucrative kind. When by this means the inhabitants of London are reduced to a number not much above 100,000, the near prospect of being relieved from the tax will make householders active to banish all above that number; and to prevent a renewal of the tax, a greater number will never again be permitted. It would require much political skill to proportion the sums to be levied and distributed, so as to have their proper effect, without overburdening the capital on the one hand, or giving too great encouragement for building on the other, which might tempt people to build for the premium merely, without any further view. Much will depend on an advantageous situation: houses built there will always find inhabitants.

The two great cities of London and Westminster are extremely ill fitted for local union. The latter, the seat of government and of the noblesse, infects the former with luxury and with love of show. The former, the seat of commerce, infects the latter with love of gain. The mixture of these opposite passions is productive of every groveling vice.

VIII. The Anthropological Impulse

Henry Home, Lord Kames

THE DEVELOPMENT OF
RELIGIOUS BELIEF

As no other science can vie with theology, either in dignity or importance, it justly claims to be a favorite study with every person endued with true taste and solid judgment. From the time that writing was invented, natural religion has employed pens without number, and yet in no language is there found a connected history of it. The present work will only admit a slight sketch, which I shall glory in, however imperfect, if it excite any one of superior talents to undertake a complete history.

That there exist beings, one or many, powerful above the human race is a proposition universally admitted as true in all ages and among all nations. I boldly call it universal, notwithstanding what is reported of some gross savages; for reports that contradict what is acknowledged to be general among men require more able vouchers than a few illiterate voyagers. Among many savage tribes, there are no words but for objects of external sense: Is it surprising that such people are incapable to express their religious perceptions, or any perception of internal sense? And from their silence can it be fairly presumed, that they have no such perception? The conviction that men have of superior powers in every country

Reprinted from Henry Home, Lord Kames, *Sketches of the History of Man* (Edinburgh, 1813), III, 251–59, 269–90 (from the sketch entitled "Principles and Progress of Theology," III, 251–450). Title supplied.

where there are words to express it is so well vouched that in fair reasoning it ought to be taken for granted among the few tribes where language is deficient. Even the grossest idolatry affords evidence of that conviction. No nation can be so brutish as to worship a stock or a stone, merely as such: the visible object is always imagined to be connected with some invisible power; and the worship paid to the former is as representing the latter or as in some manner connected with it. Every family among the ancient Lithuanians entertained a real serpent as a household god; and the same practice is at present universal among the Negroes in the kingdom of Whidah: it is not the serpent that is worshiped, but some deity imagined to reside in it. The ancient Egyptians were not idiots, to pay divine honors to a bull or a cat, as such: the divine honors were paid to a deity, as residing in these animals. The sun is to man a familiar object: since it is frequently obscured by clouds, and totally eclipsed during night, a savage naturally conceives it to be a great fire, sometimes flaming bright, sometimes obscured, and sometimes extinguished. Whence then sun worship, once universal among savages? Plainly from the same cause: it is not properly the sun that is worshiped, but a deity who is supposed to dwell in that luminary.

Taking it then for granted, that our conviction of superior powers has been long universal, the important question is from what cause it proceeds. A conviction so universal and so permanent cannot proceed from chance; but must have a cause operating constantly and invariably upon all men in all ages. Philosophers, who believe the world to be eternal and self-existent, and imagine it to be the only deity, though without intelligence, endeavor to account for our conviction of superior powers from the terror that thunder and other elementary convulsions raise in savages; and thence conclude that such belief is no evidence of a deity. Thus Lucretius,

> What man can boast that firm undaunted soul,
> That hears, unmov'd, when thunder shakes the pole;
> Nor shrinks with fear of an offended pow'r,
> When lightnings flash, and storms and tempests roar?

And Petronius Arbiter,

> When dread convulsions rock'd the lab'ring earth,
> And livid clouds first gave the thunder birth,
> Instinctive fear within the human breast
> The first ideas of a God impress'd.

It will readily be yielded to these gentlemen that savages, grossly ignorant of causes and effects, are apt to take fright at every unusual appearance and to think that some malignant being is the cause. And if they mean only that the first perception of deity among savages is occasioned by fear, I heartily subscribe to their opinion. But if they mean that such perceptions proceed from fear solely without having any other cause, I wish to be informed from what source is derived the belief we have of benevolent deities. Fear cannot be the source, and it will be seen anon that though malevolent deities were first recognized among savages, yet that in the progress of society the existence of benevolent deities was universally believed. The fact is certain, and therefore fear is not the sole cause of our believing the existence of superior beings.

It is beside to me evident that the belief even of malevolent deities, once universal among all the tribes of men, cannot be accounted for from fear solely. I observe, first, that there are many men, to whom an eclipse, an earthquake, and even thunder, are unknown: Egypt, in particular, though the country of superstition, is little or not at all acquainted with the two latter; and in Peru, though its government was a theocracy, thunder is not known. Nor do such appearances strike terror into every one who is acquainted with them. The universality of the belief must then have some cause more universal than fear. I observe next that if the belief were founded solely on fear, it would die away gradually as men improve in the knowledge of causes and effects: instruct a savage that thunder, an eclipse, an earthquake, proceed from natural causes and are not threatenings of an incensed deity; his fear of malevolent beings will vanish; and with it his belief in them, if founded solely on fear. Yet the direct contrary is true: in proportion as the human understanding ripens, our conviction of superior powers, or of a Deity, turns more and more firm and authoritative. . . .

Philosophers of more enlarged views and of deeper penetration may be inclined to think that the operations of nature and the government of this world, which loudly proclaim a Deity, may be sufficient to account for the universal belief of superior powers. And to give due weight to the argument, I shall relate a conversation between a Greenlander and a Danish missionary, mentioned by Crantz in his *History of Greenland*. "It is true," says the Greenlander, "we were ignorant Heathens, and knew little of a God, till you came. But you must not imagine, that no Greenlander thinks about these things. A kajak, with all its tackle and implements, cannot exist but by the labor of man; and one who does not understand it would spoil it. But the meanest bird requires more skill than the best kajak; and no man can make a bird. There is still more skill required to make a man: By whom then was he made? He proceeded from his parents, and they from their parents. But some must have been the first parents: Whence did they proceed? Common report says that they grew out of the earth: If so, why do not men still grow out of the earth? And from whence came the earth itself, the sun, the moon, the stars? Certainly there must be some being who made all these things, a being more wise than the wisest man." The reasoning here from effects to their causes is stated with great precision; and were all men equally penetrating with the Greenlander, such reasoning might perhaps be sufficient to account for the conviction of a Deity, universally spread among savages. But such penetration is a rare quality among savages; and yet the conviction of superior powers is universal, not excepting even the grossest savages, who are altogether incapable of reasoning like our Greenland philosopher. Natural history has made so rapid a progress of late years, and the finger of God is so visible to us in the various operations of nature, that we do not readily conceive how even savages can be ignorant: but it is a common fallacy in reasoning to judge of others by what we feel in ourselves. And to give juster notions of the condition of savages, I take liberty to introduce the Wogultzoi, a people in Siberia, exhibiting a striking picture of savages in their natural state. That people were baptized at the command of Prince Gagarin, governor of the province; and Laurent Lange, in his relation of a journey from Petersburgh to Peking *anno* 1715, gives the following account of their conversion. "I had curiosity," says he, "to question them about their worship before they embraced Christianity. They said that they had an idol hung upon a tree, before which they prostrated themselves, raising their eyes to heaven and howling with a loud voice. They could not explain what they meant by howling; but only, that every man howled in his own fashion. Being interrogated whether, in raising their eyes to heaven, they knew that a god is there, who sees all the actions, and even the thoughts of men; they answered simply that heaven is too far above them to know whether a god be there or not; and that they had no care but to provide meat and drink. Another question being put whether they had not more satisfaction in worshiping the living God than they formerly had in the darkness of idolatry; they answered, We see no great difference, and we do not break our heads about such matters." Judge how little capable such ignorant savages are to reason from effects to their causes and to trace a Deity from the operations of nature. It may be added with great certainty, that could they be made in any degree to conceive such reasoning, yet so weak and obscure would their conviction be as to rest there without moving them to any sort of worship, which, however, among savages goes hand in hand with the conviction of superior powers.

If fear be a cause altogether insufficient for our conviction of a Deity universal among all tribes, and if reasoning from effects to their causes can have no influence upon ignorant savages, What other cause is there to be laid hold of? One still remains, and imagination cannot figure another: to make this conviction universal, the image of the Deity must be stamped upon the mind of every human being, the ignorant equally with the knowing: nothing less is sufficient. And the original perception we have of Deity must proceed from an internal sense, which may be termed the *sense of Deity. . .*

The sense of Deity, like many other delicate senses, is in savages so faint and obscure as easily to be biased from truth. Among them, the belief of many superior beings is universal. And two causes join to produce that belief. The first is that being accustomed to a plurality of visible objects, men, mountains, trees, cattle, and such like, they are naturally led to imagine a like plurality in things not visible; and from that slight bias, slight indeed but natural, is partly derived the system of Polytheism, universal among savages. The other is that savages know little of the connection between causes and effects and still less of the order and government of the world: every event that is not familiar appears to them singular and extraordinary; and if such event exceed human power, it is without hesitation ascribed to a superior being. But as it occurs not to a savage, nor to any person who is not a philosopher that the many various events exceeding human power and seemingly unconnected may all proceed from the same cause; they are readily ascribed to different beings. Pliny ascribes Polytheism to the consciousness men have of their imbecility: "Our powers are confined within narrow bounds: we do not readily conceive powers in the Deity much more extensive: and we supply by number what is wanting in power." Polytheism, thus founded, is the first stage in the progress of theology, for it is embraced by the rudest savages, who have neither capacity nor inclination to pierce deeper into the nature of things.

This stage is distinguishable from others by a belief that all superior beings are malevolent. Man, by nature weak and helpless, is prone to fear, dreading every new object and every unusual event. Savages, having no protection against storms, tempests, nor other external accidents, and having no pleasures but in gratifying hunger, thirst, and animal love, have much to fear and little to hope. In that disconsolate condition, they attribute the bulk of their distresses to invisible beings, who in their opinion must be malevolent. This seems to have been the opinion of the Greeks in the days of Solon; as appears in a conversation between him and Crœsus, King of Lydia, mentioned in Herodotus in the first book of his history. "Crœsus," said Solon, "you ask me about human affairs; and I answer as one who thinks that all the gods are envious and disturbers of mankind." The Negroes on the coast of Guinea dread their deities as tyrants and oppressors: having no conception of a good deity, they attribute the few blessings they receive to the soil, to the rivers, to the trees, and to the plants. The Lithuanians continued pagans down to the fourteenth century, and worshiped in gloomy woods, where their deities were held to reside. Their worship probably was prompted by fear, which is allied to gloominess. The people of Kamchatka acknowledge to this day many malevolent deities, having little or no notion of a good deity. They believe the air, the water, the mountains, and the woods to be inhabited by malevolent spirits, whom they fear and worship. The savages of Guiana ascribe to the devil even their most common diseases; nor do they ever think of another remedy but to apply to a sorcerer to drive him away. Such Negroes as believe in the devil, paint his images white. Beside the Esquimaux, there are many tribes in the extensive country of Labrador, who believe the Deity to be malevolent and worship him out of fear. When they eat, they throw a piece of flesh into the fire as an offering to him; and when they go to sea in a canoe, they throw something on the shore to render him propitious. Sometimes, in a capricious fit, they go out with guns and hatchets to kill him; and on their return boast that they have done so.

Conviction of superior beings, who, like men, are of a mixed nature, sometimes doing good, sometimes mischief, constitutes the second stage. This came to be the system of theology in Greece. The introduction of writing among the Greeks, while they were little better than savages, produced a compound of character and maners that has not a parallel in any other nation. They were acute in science, skillful in fine arts, extremely deficient in morals, gross beyond conception in theology, and superstitious to a degree of folly; a strange jumble of exquisite sense and absurd nonsense. They held their gods to resemble men in their external figure, and to be corporeal. In the twenty-first book of the *Iliad,* Minerva with a huge stone beats Mars to the ground, whose monstrous body covered seven broad acres. As corporeal beings, they were supposed to require the nourishment of meat, drink, and sleep. Homer mentions more than once the inviting of gods to a feast: and Pausanias reports that in the temple of Bacchus at Athens there were figures of clay, representing a feast given by Amphyc-

tion to Bacchus and other deities. The inhabitants of the island
Java are not so gross in their conceptions as to think that the gods
eat the offerings presented to them; but it is their opinion that a
deity brings his mouth near the offering, sucks out all its savor,
and leaves it tasteless like water. The Grecian gods, as described
by Homer, dress, bathe, and anoint like mortals. Venus, after being
detected by her husband in the embraces of Mars, retires to
Paphos,

> Where to the power an hundred altars rise,
> And breathing odors scent the balmy skies;
> Concealed she bathes in consecrated bowers,
> The Graces ungents shed, ambrosial showers,
> Ungents that charm the gods! She last assumes
> Her wonderous robes; and full the goddess blooms.
>
> *Odyssey*, Book VIII

Juno's dress is most poetically described, *Iliad*, Book XIV. It
was also universally believed that the gods were fond of women
and had many children by them. The ancient Germans thought
more sensibly that the gods were too high to resemble men in any
degree, or to be confined within the walls of a temple. The Greeks
seem to have thought that the gods did not much exceed themselves in knowledge. When Agesilaus journeyed with his private
retinue, he usually lodged in a temple; making the gods witnesses,
says Plutarch, of his most secret actions. The Greeks thought that
a god, like a man, might know what passed within his own house;
without knowing anything passing at a distance. "If it be true,"
says Aristotle (*Rhetoric*, Book II), "that even the gods do not know
everything, there is little reason to expect great knowledge among
men." Agamemnon in Eschylus, putting off his traveling habit, and
dressing himself in splendid purple, is afraid of being seen and
envied by some jealous god. We learn from Seneca that people
strove for the seat next to the image of the deity, that their prayers
might be the better heard. But what we have chiefly to remark
upon this head is that the Grecian gods were, like men, held
capable of doing both good and ill. Jupiter, their highest deity,
was a ravisher of women and a notorious adulterer. In the second
book of the *Iliad*, he sends a lying dream to deceive Agamemnon.

Mars seduces Venus by bribes to commit adultery. In the Rhesus of Euripedes, Minerva, disguised like Venus, deceives Paris by a gross lie. The groundwork of the tragedy of Xuthus is a lying oracle, declaring Ion, son of Apollo and Creusa, to be the son of Xuthus. Orestes in Euripedes, having slain his mother Clytemnestra, excuses himself as having been misled by Apollo to commit the crime. "Ah!" says he, "had I consulted the ghost of my father, he would have dissuaded me from a crime that has proved my ruin, without doing him any good." He concludes with observing that he having acted by Apollo's command, Apollo is the only criminal. In a tragedy of Sophocles, Minerva makes no difficulty to cheat Ajax, promising to be his friend, while underhand she is serving Ulysses, his bitter enemy. Mercury, in revenge for the murder of his son Myrtilus, entails curses on Pelops the murderer and on all his race.

In general the gods, everywhere in Greek tragedies, are partial, unjust, tyrannical, and revengeful: the Greeks accordingly have no reserve in abusing their gods. In the tragedy of Prometheus, Jupiter, without the least ceremony, is accused of being an usurper. Eschylus proclaims publicly on the stage that Jupiter, a jealous, cruel, and implacable tyrant, had overturned everything in heaven and that the other gods were reduced to be his slaves. In the *Iliad*, Book XII, Menelaus addresses Jupiter in the following words: "O Father Jove! in wisdom, they say, thou excellest both men and gods. Yet all these ills proceed from thee; for the wicked thou dost aid in war. Thou art a friend to the Trojans, whose souls delight in force, who are never glutted with blood."

The gods were often treated with a sort of contemptuous familiarity and employed in very low offices. Nothing is more common than to introduce them as actors in Greek tragedies, frequently for trivial purposes: Apollo comes upon the stage most courteously to acquaint the audience with the subject of the play. Why is this not urged by our critics, as classical authority against the rule of Horace, "Nor let a god in person stand displayed. Unless the laboring plot deserve his aid?" Homer makes very useful servants of his gods. Minerva, in particular, is a faithful attendant upon Ulysses. She acts the herald and calls the chiefs to council. She marks the place where a great stone fell that was thrown by Ulysses. She assists Ulysses to hide his treasure in a cave and helps him to wrestle with the beggar. Ulysses being tossed with cares in bed, she descends from heaven to make him fall asleep. This last might possibly be squeezed into an allegory, if Minerva were not frequently introduced where there is no place for an allegory. Jupiter, Book XVII of the *Iliad,* is introduced comforting the steeds of Achilles for the death of Patroclus. Creusa keeps it a profound secret from her husband that she had a child by Apollo. It was held as little honorable in Greece to commit fornication with a god as with a man. It appears from Cicero that when Greek philosophers began to reason about the deity, their notions were wonderfully crude. One of the hardest morsels to digest in Plato's philosophy was a doctrine that God is incorporeal, which by many was thought absurd, for that, without a body, he could not have senses, nor prudence, nor pleasure.

The religious creed of the Romans seems to have been little less impure than that of the Greeks. It was a ceremony of theirs, in besieging a town, to evocate the tutelar deity and to tempt him by a reward to betray his friends and votaries. In that ceremony, the name of the tutelar deity was thought of importance; and for that reason, the tutelar deity of Rome was a profound secret. Appian of Alexandria, in his book of the Parthian war, reports that Anthony, reduced to extremity by the Parthians, lifted up his eyes to heaven, and besought the gods, that if any of them were jealous of his former happiness, they would pour their vengeance upon his head alone and suffer his army to escape. The story of Paris and the three goddesses gives no favorable impression, either of the morals or religion of the Romans' Juno. . . . Juno, not satisfied with wreaking her malice against the honest shepherd [Paris] declares war against his whole nation. Not even Aeneas, though a fugitive in foreign lands, escapes her fury. Their great god Jupiter is introduced on the stage by Plautus, to deceive Alcmena and to lie with her in the shape of her husband. Nay, it was the opinion of the Romans that this play made much for the honor of Jupiter; for in times of national troubles and calamities, it was commonly acted to appease his anger; a pregnant instance of the gross conceptions of that warlike people in morality, as well as in religion.

A division of invisible beings into benevolent and malevolent, without any mixture of these qualities, makes the third stage. The talents and feelings of men refine gradually under good government: social amusements begin to make a figure: benevolence is highly regarded; and some men are found without gall. [Men] having thus acquired a notion of pure benevolence, and finding it exemplified in some eminent persons, it was an easy step in the progress of theological opinions to bestow the same character upon some superior beings. This led men to distinguish their gods into two kinds, essentially different, one entirely benevolent, another entirely malevolent; and the difference between good and ill, which are diametrically opposite, favored that distinction. Fortunate events out of the common course of nature were accordingly ascribed to benevolent deities, and unfortunate events of that kind to malevolent. In the time of Pliny the elder, malevolent deities were worshiped at Rome. He mentions a temple dedicated to *Bad Fortune,* another to the disease termed a *Fever.* The Lacedemonians worshiped *Death* and *Fear;* and the people of Cadiz *Poverty* and *Old Age;* in order to deprecate their wrath. Such gods were by the Romans termed *Averrunci,* as putting away evil.

Conviction of one supreme benevolent Deity, and of inferior deities, some benevolent, some malevolent, is the fourth stage. Such conviction, which gains ground in proportion as morality ripens, arises from a remarkable difference between gratitude and fear. [I being] willing to show my gratitude for some kindness proceeding from an unknown hand, several persons occur to my conjectures; but I always fix at last upon one person as the most likely. Fear is of an opposite nature: it expands itself upon every suspicious person and blackens them all. Thus, upon providential good fortune above the power of man, we naturally rest upon one benevolent Deity as the cause, and to him we confine our gratitude and veneration. When on the other hand we are struck with an uncommon calamity, everything that possibly may be the cause raises terror. Hence the propensity in savages to multiply objects of fear, but to confine their gratitude and veneration to a single object. Gratitude and veneration, at the same time, are of such a nature as to raise a high opinion of the person who is their object; and when a single invisible being is understood to pour out blessings with a liberal hand, good men, inflamed with gratitude, put no bounds to the power and benevolence of that being. And thus one supreme benevolent Deity comes to be recognized among the more enlightened savages. With respect to malevolent deities, as they are supposed to be numerous, and there is no natural impulse for elevating one above another; they are all of them held to be of an inferior rank, subordinate to the supreme Deity.

Unity in the Supreme Being hath, among philosophers, a more solid foundation, namely, unity of design and of order in the creation and government of this world. At the same time, the passion of gratitude, which leads even savages to the attribute of unity in the Supreme Being, prepares the mind for relishing the proof of that unity, founded on the unity of his works.

The belief of one supreme benevolent Deity, and of subordinate deities benevolent and malevolent, is and has been more universal than any other religious creed. I confine myself to a few instances, for a complete enumeration would be endless. The different savage tribes in Dutch Guiana agree pretty much in their articles of faith. They hold the existence of one supreme Deity, whose chief attribute is benevolence, and to him they ascribe every good that happens. But as it is against his nature to do ill, they believe in subordinate malevolent beings, like our devil, who occasion thunder, hurricanes, earthquakes, and who are the authors of death, diseases, and of every misfortune. To these devils, termed in their language *Yowahoos*, they direct every supplication in order to avert their malevolence, while the supreme Deity is entirely neglected: so much more powerful among savages is fear than gratitude. The North American savages have all of them a notion of a supreme Deity, creator, and governor of the world; and of inferior deities, some good, some ill. These are supposed to have bodies and to live much as men do, but without being subjected to any distress. The same creed prevails among the Negroes of Benin and Congo, among the people of New Zealand,

among the inhabitants of Java, of Madagascar, of the Molucca
Islands, and of the Caribbee Islands. The Chingulese, a tribe in
the island of Ceylon, acknowledge one God creator of the universe,
with subordinate deities who act as his deputies: agriculture is the
peculiar province of one, navigation of another. The creed of the
Tonquinese is nearly the same. The inhabitants of Otaheité,
termed *King George's Island*, believe in one supreme Deity, and
in inferior deities without end, who preside over particular parts
of the creation. They pay no adoration to the supreme Deity, thinking him too far elevated above his creatures to concern himself
with what they do. They believe the stars to be children of the
sun and moon, and an eclipse to be the time of copulation. The
Naudowessies are the farthest remote from our colonies of any
of the North Americans whom we are in any degree acquainted
with. They acknowledge one Supreme Being or giver of life, to
whom they look up as the source of good, and from whom no
evil can proceed. They acknowledge also a bad spirit of great
power, by whom all the evils that befall mankind are inflicted.
To him they pray in their distresses, begging that he will either
avert their troubles or mitigate them. They acknowledge beside
good spirits of an inferior degree, who in their particular depart-
ments contribute to the happiness of mortals. But they seem to
have no notion of a spirit divested of matter. They believe their
gods to be of the human form, but of a nature more excellent than
man. They believe in a future state and that their employments
will be similar to what they are engaged in here, but without
labor or fatigue; in short, that they shall live forever in regions
of plenty and enjoy in a higher degree every gratification they
delight in here. According to Arnobius, certain Roman deities
presided over the various operations of men. Venus presided over
carnal copulation; Puta assisted at pruning trees; and Peta in
requesting benefits; Nemestrinus was god of the woods, Nodutus
ripened corn, and Terensis helped to thrash it; Vibilia assisted
travelers; orphans were under the care of Orbona, and dying
persons, of Naenia; Ossilago hardened the bones of infants; and
Mellonia protected bees and bestowed sweetness on their honey.
The inhabitants of the island of Formosa recognize two supreme

deities in company; the one a male, god of the men, the other a female, goddess of the women. The bulk of their inferior deities are the souls of upright men, who are constantly doing good, and the souls of wicked men, who are constantly doing ill. The inland Negroes acknowledge one Supreme Being, creator of all things, attributing to him infinite power, infinite knowledge, and ubiquity. They believe that the dead are converted into spirits, termed by them *Iananini*, or protectors, being appointed to guard their parents and relations. The ancient Goths and several other northern nations acknowledged one Supreme Being, and at the same time worshiped three subordinate deities; Thor, reputed the same with Jupiter; Oden, or Woden, the same with Mars; and Friga, the same with Venus. Socrates, taking the cup of poison from the executioner, held it up toward heaven, and pouring out some of it as an oblation to the supreme Deity, pronounced the following prayer: "I implore the immortal God that my translation hence may be happy." Then turning to Crito, said, "O Crito! I owe a cock to Esculapius, pay it." From this incident we find that Socrates, soaring above his countrymen, had attained to the belief of a supreme benevolent Deity. But in that dark age of religion, such purity is not to be expected from Socrates himself as to have rejected subordinate deities, even of the mercenary kind.

Different offices being assigned to the gods, as above mentioned, proper names followed of course. And when a god was ascertained by a name, the busy mind would naturally proceed to trace his genealogy.

As unity in the Deity was not an established doctrine in the countries where the Christian religion was first promulgated, Christianity could not fail to prevail over Paganism, for improvements in the mental faculties lead by sure steps, though slow, to one God.

The fifth stage is the belief of one supreme benevolent Deity, as in that immediately foregoing, with many inferior benevolent deities, and one only who is malevolent. As men improve in natural knowledge and become skillful in tracing causes from effects, they find much less malice and ill design than was imagined: humanity at last prevails, which with improved knowledge banishes the suspicion of ill design in every case where an event can be explained without it. In a word, a settled opinion of good prevailing in the world produced conviction among some nations, less ignorant than their neighbors and less brutal, that there is but one malevolent subordinate deity, and good subordinate deities without number. The ancient Persians acknowledged two principles; one all good and all powerful, named *Hormuz,* and by the Greeks corruptly *Oromazes*; the other evil, named *Ahariman,* and by the Greeks *Arimanes.* Some authors assert that the Persians held these two principles to be coeternal; others that Oromazes first subsisted alone, that he created both light and darkness, and that he created Arimanes out of darkness. That the latter was the opinion of the ancient Persions, appears from their Bible, termed the *Sadder,* which teaches that there is one God supreme over all, many good angels, and but one evil spirit. Plutarch acquaints us that Hormus and Ahariman, ever at variance, formed each of them creatures of their own stamp; that the former created good genii, such as goodness, truth, wisdom, justice; and that the latter created evil genii, such as infidelity, falsehood, oppression, theft. This system of theology, commonly termed the *Manichean System,* is said to be also the religious creed of Pegu, with the following addition, that the evil principle only is to be worshiped; which is abundantly probable, as fear is a predominant passion in barbarians. The people of Florida believe in a supreme benevolent Deity and a subordinate deity that is malevolent: neglecting the former, who they say, does no harm, they bend their whole attention to soften the latter, who they say, torments them day and night. The inhabitants of Darien acknowledge but one evil spirit, of whom they are desperately afraid. The Hottentots, mentioned by some writers as altogether destitute of religion, are on the contrary farther advanced toward its purity than some of their neighbors. Their creed is that there is a Supreme Being, who is goodness itself, of whom they have no occasion to stand in awe, as he is incapable by his nature to hurt them; that there is also a malevolent spirit, subordinate to the former, who must be served and worshiped in order to avert his malice. The Epicurean doctrine with respect to the gods in general, that being happy in themselves they extend not their providential care to men, differs not widely from what the Hottentot believes with respect to the Supreme Being.

Having traced the sense of deity, from its dawn in the grossest savages to its approaching maturity among enlightened nations, we proceed to the last stage of the progress, which makes the true system of theology; and that is conviction of a Supreme Being, boundless in every perfection, without subordinate deities, benevolent or malevolent. Savages learn early to trace the chain of causes and effects, with respect to ordinary events: they know that fasting produces hunger, that labor occasions weariness, that fire burns, that the sun and rain contribute to vegetation. But when they go beyound such familiar events, they lose sight of cause and effect: the changes of weather, of winds, of heat and cold, impress them with a notion of chance: earthquakes, hurricanes, storms of thunder and lightning, which fill them with terror, are ascribed to malignant beings of greater power than man. In the progress of knowledge light begins to break in upon them, they discover that such phenomena, however tremendous, come under the general law of cause and effect, and that there is no ground for ascribing them to malignant spirits. At the same time, our more refined senses ripen by degrees: social affections come to prevail and morality makes a deep impression. In maturity of sense and understanding, benevolence appears more and more; and beautiful final causes are discovered in many of nature's productions that formerly were thought useless, or perhaps hurtful, and the time may come, we have solid ground to hope that it will come, when doubts and difficulties about the government of Providence will all of them be cleared up, and every event be found conducive to the general good. Such views of Providence banish malevolent deities; and we settle at last in a most comfortable opinion; either that there are no such beings; or that, if they exist and are permitted to perpetrate any mischief, it is in order to produce greater good. Thus, through a long maze of errors, man arrives at true religion, acknowledging but one Being, supreme in power, intelligence, and benevolence, who created all other beings, to whom all other beings are subjected, and who directs every event to answer the best purposes. This system is true theology.

James Burnet, Lord Monboddo

EXAMPLES FROM ANCIENT AND MODERN HISTORY OF MEN LIVING IN THE BRUTISH STATE, WITHOUT ARTS OR CIVILITY

[MY NOTION of the original state of man] is very different from the notions commonly received and will no doubt appear incredible to those who have been taught that man is by nature a rational, as well as a social and political animal, and have read large volumes on the subject of the *law of nature* founded all upon the supposition that civil society, or the political life, is the *original* and *natural* state of man.... I will now proceed to show, from the history both of the ancient and modern world, that there have been found whole nations, not indeed altogether without arts or civility (for that is impossible, since, according to my hypothesis, they associated together only for the purpose of carrying on some joint work), but with so little of either, that we can be at no loss to suppose a prior state in which there were none at all.

And I will begin with instances furnished me by an ancient author, namely Diodorus Siculus, who was a traveler as well as an historian, and whose work, the greatest part of which is un-

Reprinted from James Burnet, Lord Monboddo, *Of the Origin and Progress of Language* (2d ed.; Edinburgh, 1774), I, 236–69.

happily lost, was the fruit of the labor of thirty years, which he
spent in collecting materials, and traveling into those countries that
he had occasion to mention in his history.[1] I am the more inclined
to lay weight upon the facts recorded by him that his style is very
plain and simple, so that he appears to me to have spent that time
in preparing and digesting the *matter* of his history, which many
historians, ancient as well as modern, have spent in adorning their
style. In the beginning of his history, he says that men at first
lived dispersed and subsisted upon the natural productions of the
earth; that they had no use of speech and uttered only inarticulate
cries; but that having herded together, for fear, as he says, of the
wild beasts, they invented a language and imposed names upon
things.[2] This opinion of the original state of man he no doubt
formed from the study of many ancient books of history that are
now lost. But, besides this, he relates particular facts concerning
certain savage nations which lived, either in Africa, or upon the
opposite coast of the Indian Ocean, or that gulf of it which is
now called the Red Sea. Of these he had an opportunity of being
very well informed, by the curiosity of one of the Ptolemies,
king of Egypt, who . . . sent men whom he could trust, on purpose
to be informed concerning such nations; and besides, the passion
he had for hunting elephants led him to discover more of Africa
than I believe has been discovered in modern times.

The first instance I shall mention from Diodorus is of a nation,
if a herd of men may be called so, of . . . *fish eaters*, who lived near
the strait which joins the Indian Ocean to the Red Sea or Arabian
gulf, upon the Asiatic side. They went naked and lived entirely
by fishing, which they practised without any art, other than that
of making dikes or mounds of stones, to prevent the fish which had
come with the full tide into the hollows and gullies upon that
coast, from going out again with the ebbing tide and then catching them in those ponds as in a net[3] In this way they employed

1   Diodor. *Biblioth*. lib. I. *in initio*.
2   Lib. 1. cap. 8. edit. Wesseling.
3   This is precisely the way of fishing practised by the inhabitants of
New Holland, as described by Dampier in his Travels. This Dampier appears
to me to be one of the most accurate and judicious of our modern travelers,
so that, when we find him agreeing in his account of the customs of barbarous

themselves for four days, and the fifth day they all set out for the upland country, where there were certain springs of fresh water of which they drank, after having filled their bellies with fish. This journey, says our author, they performed just like a herd of cattle, making a great noise and uttering loud cries, but all inarticulate; and after having filled their bellies with water, so that they could hardly walk, they returned to their habitations upon the coast, and there passed a whole day incapable to do any thing, lying upon the ground, and hardly able to breathe through fullness; after which they returned to their only occupation, of fishing in the manner above described: and this was the round of their life. The women and children were common, belonging to the herd. They had no sense of what is just, honest, or decent, living entirely under the guidance of instinct and appetite. They had no arts, unless we give that name to their way of fishing above mentioned, and a certain method which they had of curing and preserving their fish, very particularly described by Diodorus. They used no weapons except stones and the sharp horns of goats, with which they killed the stronger fish. They had no use of fire, but roasted their fish upon the rocks by the heat of the sun. Neither do they appear to me to have had the faculty of speech; for, though our author does not expressly say so, yet I think it is his meaning, from the account he gives of their journey to the springs; and it is clear that they had nothing like religion or government.[4]

The next nation he mentions is that of the *Insensibles*, as he calls them. . . . Of these he says expressly, that they had not the use of speech, but made signs, like our dumb people, with their heads and hands. They lived, he says, promiscuously with other animals, and particularly with seals, which, he says, catch the fish in the same manner that these men did, who were also of the race of fish eaters; and he adds, that they lived with those other animals, and with one another, with great good faith, and in great peace and concord. The most extraordinary particular he tells concerning them is, that they never used water, nor any kind of liquid,

nations, with an ancient historian, whom I am persuaded he never read, nor perhaps ever heard of, we can hardly doubt of the truth of the fact.
4   Diod. lib. p. 106. Stephani.

not having so much as an idea of that sort of nourishment;[5] though even this, I think, is less incredible than what more than one modern traveler has told us of people in the South Sea that, when they had occasion to be long at sea, supplied the want of liquids by drinking sea water.

The next nation mentioned by Diodorus, that I shall take notice of, is one upon the African side, in that part of Ethiopia which is above Egypt. They were of a quite different race, being what he calls . . . *wood eaters;* for they subsisted entirely upon the woods, eating either the fruits of the trees, or when they could not get these, chewing the tender shoots, and young branches, as we see cattle do in this country. This way of living made them very nimble in climbing trees; and they leapt, says our author, with amazing agility, from one branch or tree to another, using both feet and hands; and, when they happened to fall, their bodies were so light that they received no hurt.[6] They too went naked, had no arms but sticks, like the orangoutangs, who are still to be found on the same continent, and their wives and children were in common. *Diod.*, p. 111.

Diodorus concludes his account of those savage African nations by telling us that in the southern part of that great peninsula there are races of men who, in the human form, live a life altogether brutal. P. 115.

Thus far Diodorus Siculus from whose account it is evident that there were in Africa and the opposite continent of Asia, in his time, herds of people that lived without any civil society, even

5   Diod. lib. 3. p. 108.
6   The wild girl [mentioned above] must have been of a race of people very like this mentioned by Diodorus: for she climbed trees like a squirrel, and leaped from one branch to another, upon all fours, with wonderful agility, as I was informed by the people of the village of Songé in Champaigne, where she was caught; and she still retained, when I saw her, a mark of the use of her hands as feet in leaping; for her thumbs were of an unusual breadth. When she happened to fall, too, she was so light and nimble that she received very little hurt. For the Abbess of the convent of Chalons (near to Songé), where she was confined for some time after she was taken, showed me a very high window from which she leapt into the street, without receiving much harm; and what she did receive, she imputed to the gross aliment they had given her, which she said had made her so much heavier than when she lived upon wild food.

the domestic society of man and wife, which is the first step toward forming a state or political society.

With Diodorus, in this account of the savageness and barbarity of the people of Africa, agrees Herodotus; a man of the greatest curiosity and diligence, and whose authority may be depended upon, when he relates a thing simply as an historical fact and not as a hearsay. He speaks of herds of people in this peninsula that coupled together promiscuously . . . like cattle, lib. 4. c. 180; and of men and women absolutely wild, lib. 4. c. 191; and, particularly of the Troglodytes he says that they fed upon serpents and other reptiles, were hunted like wild beasts by the Garamantes, and by way of language made a kind of murmuring inarticulate sound, which he compares to the cry of a bat, *ibid.*, c. 183. And it is not unlikely that it is the same kind of language that Mons. de la Condamine reports to have been spoken by a nation that he met with upon the banks of the river Amazons; for it was a muttering murmuring kind of noise, as he has described it, and which appeared to him to be formed by drawing in the breath; probably because it was a low and obscure sound, not unlike that which a man makes who is very hoarse by reason of a cold.[7]

As to modern authorities, I will begin with that of Leo Africanus, an African Moor of the sixteenth century, who, coming to Rome, did there abjure the Mahometan faith, and was baptized by the name of the pontiff who then filled the papal chair, Leo X. He had traveled much in the interior parts of Africa with caravans of merchants and appears to me to have known more of that country than any modern. He wrote a description of it in Arabic, which is translated into Latin, and published in nine books, containing a very accurate account, both of the men and manners, and natural curiosities of the country; and he agrees

---

7 There is a race of men yet to be found in that part of ancient Ethiopia that we call Abyssinia, whose language resembles still more that of the *Troglodytes*, as described by Herodotus; for it makes a hissing kind of noise, very fitly expressed by the Greek word τονζω (in Latin *strídeo*), which Herodotus applies to the language of the *Troglodytes*, and which I suppose resembles the sound made by a bat. Of these people in Ethiopia, Linnaeus, as I was informed by one of his scholars, had an account from two travelers who had been in that country at different times; and both agreed in this and several other particulars concerning those men. See *Linnaei Systema Naturae*, vol. 1. p. 33.

with Diodorus as to the savageness of some of the people of Africa, and particularly, he says that in the inward parts of the country, southward from Barbary, there are people that live a life entirely brutish, without government or policy, copulating promiscuously with their females, after the manner of the brutes.[8] And he mentions another nation, to whom he gives a name, calling them *Bornians*, who lived not far distant from the fountain of the river Niger. These people, says he, are without religion of any kind and have their women and children in common.[9]

The next modern author I shall mention is likewise a very diligent and accurate writer. It is Garcilasso de la Vega, who has written in Spanish the history of the Incas of Peru, of whose race he himself was.[10] According to his account of that country, when the first Inca began his conquests, or rather his taming or civilization of men (for he was a conqueror of that kind, such as the Egyptians report their Osiris to have been); it was inhabited, for the greater part, by men living in a state altogether brutish, without government, civility, or arts of any kind, and such of them as were in any degree civilized had a tradition preserved among them that they had been taught, as the subjects of the Incas were, by men who came from distant countries and imported among them the arts of life. And more particularly, he relates that in some parts

8   Lib. 7. *in initio.*
9   *Ibid.,* p. 656.
10   He was born, as he informs us, eight years after the Spanish conquest of Peru was completed. His mother was the grand-daughter, if I mistake not, of the Inca that preceded him who was dethroned and put to death by the Spaniards. He was brought up among his relations of the Inca race, till he was twenty years of age; and from his mother and her brothers, as he tells us, he received information of the facts which he relates in his history. He also employed his school fellows the Indians, after he had formed the design of writing it, to get him information from all parts of the country. His history, therefore, I think, may be credited as much as any that is only from tradition, which, however, this history was not altogether, for they had a kind of records by threads and knots. And indeed the facts he relates, and his manner of relating them, bear intrinsic marks of truth, at least, that no falsehood or fiction was intended. And, with respect to the principal facts, we may believe a tradition that went no farther back than four hundred years; about which time the first Inca, Manco Capac, began his reign; especially when it was preserved in the family of that prince, and we may believe carefully preserved, and the more carefully that they had no written records.

of Peru, which were afterwards civilized by the Incas, the people were under no kind of government, living together in herds or flocks, like so many cattle or sheep, and, like them, copulating promiscuously.[11] In other parts of the country they did not so much as live in herds, but dwelt in caves, and holes of rocks and mountains, in small numbers of two or three together, feeding upon herbs, grass, roots, and wild fruits, and copulating promiscuously.[12] And, in later times, under the fourth or fifth Inca, he mentions a people in the great province of Chirihuana, who lived altogether like beasts, wandering in the mountains and woods, without religion or worship of any kind and without any community or political government, unless when they associated to infest their neighbors, and make use of them for food; for the end of their wars was to eat their enemies. These people were so brutish, and the country of so difficult access, that the Inca gave over thoughts of conquering or civilizing them; and the Spaniards afterward attempted it, but without success, lib. 7. c. 17. He mentions also another people of the same province, that lived near the Cape of *Passau*, who, never having been conquered, or rather civilized, by the Incas, lived, even at the time the author wrote, in a state of the utmost savageness and barbarity having no religion at all and worshipping nothing either above or below them; inhabiting caves, and hollows of trees, without communication, friendship, or commerce, and hardly having language sufficient to understand one another.[13] One of the Incas, he says, coming with an army to subdue them, but despairing of being able to reclaim them from their brutish life, said to his people, "Come, let us return again, for these deserve not the honor of our dominion." Upon which the whole army faced about and returned home.[14] And these people were in that state of barbarity, or very little better, at the time the author wrote, for he says he himself saw some of them.[15] He further tells us, that one of the Incas found men that preyed on one another like wild beasts, attacking their fellow creatures for no

[11]   Lib. 1. c. 5 et 6.
[12]   Ibid., c. 7.
[13]   Lib. 1. c. 4 et 5.
[14]   Lib. 9. c. 8.
[15]   Lib. 9. c. 8.

other purpose than to eat them. These the Inca hunted on the mountains, and in the woods, like so many wild beasts.[16]

But the communication and intercourse that has been between the several parts of the old world on this side of the globe, and likewise between the old and the new world discovered by Columbus, during these last three hundred years, has made so great a change in the manners and way of living of men in those countries that it is not there we are now to look for people living in the natural state, but in another part of the world, as yet very imperfectly discovered, and with which we have had hitherto very little intercourse, I mean the countries in the South Sea and such parts of the Atlantic Ocean as have not been frequented by European ships. What I shall here set down of the wild people found in those countries is taken from a French collection of voyages to the South Sea, printed at Paris in the year 1756, in two volumes 4to. The author's name, as I am informed, is Labrosse.

Americus Vespucius, who made the discovery of the continent of America for the King of Spain, and gave his name to it, was afterward employed by the King of Portugal, in whose service he made a voyage in that great ocean which extends from Brazil eastward, towards the Cape of Good Hope, and in this voyage he discovered a great tract of country, which he calls a continent, where he found a people who, though living together in herds, had neither government, religion, nor arts, nor any property; and every one of them had as many wives as he pleased. Americus was among them seven and twenty days, which was long enough to have observed what he affirms of their manner of living. Vol. 1. p. 96 of *Labrosse's Collection*.

Jack *the Hermit*, a Dutch traveler, affirms, that the people of Terra del Fuego live entirely like brutes, without religion, or policy, or any the least regard to decency (vol. 1, p. 445). And the same is said of them by an English traveler, Sir John Narburgh (vol. 2 p. 33). They are besides cannibals, and have not the least idea of honesty or good faith in their dealings (vol. 1, p. 445).

Another Dutch traveler, one Roggeveen, came to an island in

[16]   Lib. 8. c. 3. See also c. 6 & 7 of the same book; where there are other accounts to the same purpose.

the South Sea, where he could not find out that the people had any kind of government, but some way or other they had got a religion, in which they were very zealous, and trusted to it for their defence, in place of arms, against the Europeans (vol. 2, p. 235).

Many people in those countries have been found without almost any of the arts of life, even the art of defending themselves, or attacking their enemies; for but few of them have been found that have the use of the bow and arrow. Most of them, like the Orangoutangs, use nothing but sticks and stones, and the last mentioned people, who had so much religion, used no arms at all. Sir Francis Drake discovered certain islands in the South Sea, to the north of the line, where he found inhabitants who had the nails of their fingers about an inch long, which he understood served them for offensive arms (vol. 1, p. 197). And Le Mere met with a people in New Guinea, who used their teeth as an offensive weapon, and bit like dogs (vol. 2, pp. 396 and 397). Among such a people, if there was any government or civil society, it must have been very imperfect and of late institution.

This is all so far as I have observed that has hitherto been discovered in the South Sea concerning the natural state of men there. But we have reason to expect from those countries, in a short time, much greater and more certain discoveries, such as I hope will improve and enlarge the knowledge of our own species as much as the natural history of other animals and of plants and minerals.

From the South Sea I will come back again to Africa, a country of very great extent, in which, if it were well searched, and the interior parts of it discovered, I am persuaded that all the several steps of the human progression might be traced, and perhaps all the varieties of the species discovered. I have already stated what I have learned both from ancient and modern authors, concerning barbarous nations inhabiting that country, and I will now communicate to the public a piece of intelligence from thence relating to our subject, which I received, since publishing the first edition of this volume, from a man whose veracity and exactness is well known to all those who are acquainted with him. And indeed, the simple, plain, and accurate manner in which he tells his story is sufficient to convince every one who hears him of the truth of it. His name is Peter Greenhill, doctor of physic, residing at present in the north of Scotland. He was sixteen years employed in the African trade, during ten of which he resided constantly in the country and learned the language of one of the nations on that coast. He says he was well informed of a nation inhabiting to the eastward of Cape Palmas whose language was so rude and imperfect that they were obliged to supply the defects of it by signs and gestures and therefore could not understand one another in the dark. He further says that he knew one Gregory, a captain of a ship, who was in use to trade for slaves in the river Gaboon, opposite to the Island of St. Thomas, where the Portuguese have a settlement; that he saw this Captain Gregory at Fort Cape Coast, upon his return from a voyage to this river, when he told him and several other gentlemen that there was a savage people inhabiting the inland country above the mouth of the river Gaboon, who did not live in society, had no use of language, and were hunted like wild beasts, by the more civilized nations in their neighborhood, taken and sold for slaves to the Europeans; that he and the rest of the company laughed at this story as altogether incredible, Upon which the captain said that he had two of them on board his ship, whom he would show to them; that he had got them from the natives at the mouth of the river, but as he was well acquainted with them and had gained their love by making them presents, they did not impose upon him, as they frequently did upon other Europeans, by selling them as slaves, but gave them in a present, telling him that they did not believe they were men but monkies, because they could not speak. The next day after this conversation, the doctor saw them. They were two girls about the age of eleven or twelve, of the human form in every respect, with the features, complexion, and woolly hair of the natives of the country, and the look and behavior of human creatures; that they got slaves of different nations to speak to them; but they understood nothing of what they said, nor did they speak to one another while the doctor saw them; and the captain told him that all the while they were on board his ship, which was three weeks, they did not, even in their intercourse with one another, utter one articulate sound, as far as he heard or could learn; that they are well known to the Portuguese, and called by them *Bouraas*, that is, beasts of burden; that, some days thereafter, Captain Gregory sold them, with other slaves, to the captain of a Dutch vessel. The doctor added that, for his part, after seeing them, he had not the least doubt of their being men, and he says the captain was of the same opinion; for he said that being asked by one of the natives at the mouth of the river Gaboon whether he believed them to be men, he told them he thought they were men as much as either of them was.

From the account given by this gentleman, we may see the progress of language among savages. First, we have a number of wild men not associated, or at least not living in so close an intercourse of society as is necessary for the invention of language, and therefore without the use of speech. And we may observe how surprisingly this story told by Dr. Greenhill agrees with the account above mentioned given by Herodotus, of the Troglodytes, inhabiting the same country of Africa, who were likewise hunted by the neighboring nations like so many beasts, and instead of speaking, made a noise like that of a bat. Nor it is to be wondered that the Negroes at the mouth of the river Gaboon, and the doctor himself and his companions, at first believed them to be monkies, not men, because they did not speak, proceeding upon the vulgar error that language is natural to man and that therefore whatever animal does not speak is not a man. But, among other things belonging to the men of that country, it is to be observed that they had woolly hair, which none of the monkey race, as far as I can learn, have. Next, we have a people that had learned a little articulation, but not so much as to communicate their thoughts to one another, without the help of the natural language of signs. The next step is to what may be called a language, very rude and imperfect indeed, but such as is sufficient for communication, with little or no help from action or gesture: of this kind is the language of the Hurons in North America and other barbarous languages, of which I shall speak in the sequel. And last of all comes the language of art, which is the subject of the second volume of this work.

Before I conclude this article of travels, I will quote one traveler more, very little known, but who reports an extraordinary fact concerning our species, which I will relate as a matter of curiosity, though it belong not to my subject, except in as far as it tends to give us more enlarged views of human nature, without which I am sensible that what I have said and shall further say of the natural state of man, will appear whimsical and ridiculous. The name of this traveler is Keoping, a Swede by birth, who, in the year 1647, went to the East Indies and there served on board a Dutch ship of force, belonging to the Dutch East-India Company, in quality of lieutenant. In sailing through those seas they had occasion to come upon the coast of an island in the gulf of Bengal, one of the Nicobar Islands,[18] where they saw men with tails like those of cats and which they moved in the same manner. They came in canoes alongside of the ship with an intention to trade with the Dutch and to give them parrots in exchange for iron, which they wanted very much. Several of them came aboard the ship, and many more would have come; but the Dutch were afraid of being overpowered by their numbers; and therefore they fired their great guns and frightened them away. The next day they sent ashore a boat with five men, but they not having returned the following night, the day after the captain sent a larger boat ashore with more hands, and two pieces of cannon. When they landed, the men with the tails came about them in great numbers: by firing their cannon they chased them away; but found only the bones of their companions, who had been devoured by the savages; and the boat in which they had landed they found taken to pieces and the iron of it carried away.

The author who relates this is, as I am well informed, an author of very good credit.[19] He writes in a simple plain manner, not like a

[18]   It is to be observed, that there are several islands of this name lying in a string at the north end of Sumatra. We are not, therefore, to imagine, that our Swedish traveler is convicted of a lie by other travelers, who have touched at some one of these islands and have not found men with tails.

[19]   The story is told in the sixth volume of Linnaeus's *Amoenitates academicae*, in an academical oration of one Hoppius, a scholar, as I suppose, of Linnaeus, who relates the story upon the credit of this Keoping, with several other circumstances besides those I have mentioned. As I knew nothing then of any other author who had spoken of men with tails, I thought the fact

man who intended to impose a lie upon the world, merely for the silly pleasure of making people stare; and if it be a lie (for it cannot be a mistake), it is the only lie in his book; for everything else that he has related of animals and vegetables has been found to be true. I am sensible, however, that those who believe that men are and always have been the same in all ages and nations of the world, and such as we see them in Europe will think this story quite incredible, but for my own part I am convinced that we have not yet discovered all the variety of nature, not even in our own species; and the most incredible thing, in my apprehension, that could be told, supposing there were no facts to contradict it, would be that all the men in the different parts of the earth were the same in size, figure, shape, and color. I am therefore disposed to believe, upon credible evidence, that there are still greater varieties in our species than what is mentioned by this traveler: For, that there are men with tails, such as the ancients gave to their satyrs, is a fact so well attested that I think it cannot be doubted.[20] But our Swedish traveler, so far as I know, is the only

---

extraordinary, and was not disposed to believe it, without knowing who this Keoping was, and what credit he deserved. I therefore wrote to Linnaeus, inquiring about him, and desiring to know where his book was to be found. . . .

I got the book from Stockholm. It is in the Swedish language, which I do not understand; but that passage of it having been translated to me by a Swedish gentleman, I found it to agree exactly with the story told by Hoppius. And the gentleman, who was very well acquainted with the book, confirmed what Linnaeus says, of its being written in a plain and simple style, bearing intrinsic marks of truth. . . .

20   See *Linnaei Systema Naturae*, vol. 1, p. 33, and Buffon's *Natural History*. Those who have not studied the variety of nature in animals, and particularly in man, the most various of all animals, will think this story of men with tails very ridiculous and will laugh at the credulity of the author for seeming to believe such stories; but the philosopher, who is more disposed to inquire than to laugh and deride will not reject it, at once, as a thing incredible, that there should be such a variety in our species, as well as in the simian tribe, which is so near of kin to us. That there have been individuals in Europe, with tails, is, I think, a fact incontestible. Mr. Maillet, the author of the description of Egypt, a man of great curiosity and observation, affirms, in a work that he calls *Telliamed*, that he himself saw several men of that kind, whom he names, and of whom he gives a particular account. And I could produce legal evidence by witnesses yet living of a man in Inverness, one Barber, a teacher of mathematics, who had a tail, about half a foot long;

one who speaks of tails of such length as those of the inhabitants of Nicobar.

That these animals were men, as they trafficked, and used the art of navigation, I think cannot be denied. It appears that they herded together and lived in some kind of society, but whether they had the use of language or not does not appear from our author's relation: And I should incline to think that they had not, and that in this respect they resembled the orangoutangs, though in other respects they appear to have been farther advanced in

---

which he carefully concealed during his life; but was discovered after his death, which happened about twenty years ago. Nor will any man, who knows the structure of the human body, and the nature of a tail, which is nothing else but an elongation of the rump-bone, be surprised that this should sometimes happen. . . .

I think it is at least probable . . . that there is a race or nation of men with tails. For as this variety has been found in women as well as men, if two of this kind should go together, I think it can hardly be doubted that the children would likewise have tails. The like happens in the case of men with six fingers, some of whose children have commonly that peculiarity, even when they match with women who have the ordinary number of fingers. (See the observations that Maupertuis has made upon this subject, in his Letters.) And if two *sexdigitaires*, as Maupertuis calls them, should go together, I think it cannot be doubted that the whole race would have that variety. If in this manner tails should be continued in the race, then there would be families, and at last nations of tailed men. And so it would be what I call a *variety of the species,* not of the individual only. And that it truly is so, I think is a fact sufficiently attested. One of those tailed men mentioned by Mr. Maillet was a black, whom he saw at Tripoli, and who informed him that he was from the island of Borneo in the East Indies, where he said the most of the men and women had tails. . . . Gemelli Carreri, in his *Travels,* relates, that, in Manila and the other Philippine Islands, there are Negroes to be seen with tails from four to five inches long, vol. 5, p. 68. Paris ed. 1719. Buffon, *Hist. natur.,* vol. 3, p. 401. And the same author says that he was told by certain Jesuits, men whom he could believe, that there was in the island of Mindora, near to Manila, a race of men called *Manghiens,* who had all tails, from four to five inches long, and that some of these men had been converted to the Catholic faith. *Ibid.,* vol. 5, p. 92. Buffon, *ubi supra.* And John Struys, in his *Travels,* relates that he himself saw in the island of Formosa a man with a tail more than a foot long all covered with red hair and very like the tail of an ox, and that this man told him, that all those in the southern part of this island had tails of the same kind. Struys' *Travels,* vol. 1, p. 101, printed at Rouen, 1719.—Buffon, *ubi supra,* p. 403.

That the reader may have in one view everything that I know upon this subject, I will mention some Etruscan vases, in which men were represented with long tails, like those of the inhabitants of Nicobar. See the collection of

the arts of life, for I do not think that any traveler has said that the orangoutangs practice navigation or commerce. They live, however, in society; act together in concert, particularly in attacking elephants; build huts, and no doubt practise other arts, both for sustenance and defense, So that they may be reckoned to be in the

the Count de Caylus, vol. 2, plates 23 and 29. Those vases are of very high antiquity, many of them older, it is believed, than the foundation of Rome. And, I think it is probable that the men with tails painted upon them were not creatures of the imagination (for from whence should such a fancy have come?) but creatures that then really existed as much as the animals that we see represented in Egyptian sculpture, such as the *cynocephali*, or dog-headed men or monkies (call them how you please), resembling the Egyptian god called by Virgil *latrator Anubis*, and such as the *sphinxes*, I mean the Egyptian Sphinxes, not the winged Sphinx of the Grecian poets. See what Dr. Tyson has collected upon this subject, in his appendix to the dissection of the orangoutang, pp. 38 and 56. If more ancient authorities, upon this subject, are wanted, we have that of Ptolemy in his geography, who speaks of the inhabitants of certain islands in his time, who had tails. And if we will connect ancient authorities with modern, we have that of Marco Paolo, the Venetian, who traveled in the East, in the twelfth century and relates that in the kingdom of Lambry there are men inhabiting the mountains who have tails as long as a palm. See Buffon, *ibid.*, p. 403. . . .

All these authorities notwithstanding, Mr. Buffon seems not to believe that there are any men with tails existing. We cannot, he says, believe entirely what Struys has said. He has exaggerated; he has copied Marco Paolo, and Gemelli Carreri, and Ptolemy, *ibid.*, p. 403. Mr. Buffon, however, appears to believe in another variety of our species, much more extraordinary, and such as, I believe, is not to be found in any other species of animal; I mean that of men with one leg very much bigger than the other, which, he says, is to be found in a nation somewhere in India; *ibid.*, p. 414; and this is not the effect of disease, but a peculiarity which they have from their birth.

Notwithstanding, therefore, the authority of Mr. Buffon on the other side, these facts, attested by so many different authors, ancient and modern, fully convince me of the existence of men with tails. If, however, the reader should still have any doubt, he must, I think, at least, allow the matter to be problematical, and like every other variety of our species, well deserving to be inquired into, unless, perhaps, he be of the number of those philosophers who set bounds to Omnipotence and pronounce decisively that man with such variations cannot exist. This dogmatical spirit has gone so far in the age in which we live that many will not believe that there is in our species the common variation of great and small, from the size of ten or eleven feet, to that of two or three. As to the first, Mr. Hawksworth, in the introduction to the late collection of voyages round the world, has fairly stated the evidence on both sides; by which I think it is proved, as much as a fact of that kind can well be, unless we shall set mere negative evidence against positive, that men of such a size are to be found in the southern parts of the south continent of America. And that there were once pygmies in Africa is positively averred

first stage of the human progression, being associated, and practicing certain arts of life; but not so far advanced as to have invented the great art of language; to which I think the inhabitants of Nicobar must have approached nearer (if they have not already found it out) as they are so much further advanced in other arts.

---

by a very diligent inquirer into the history of animals, I mean Aristotle. *Histor. animal.* lib. 8. c. 12. This Aristotle relates upon information which he thought could be depended upon. But one Nonnosus, who was sent ambassador to Ethiopia by the emperor Justinian, saw himself, in his travels to that country, very little men, whom he describes particularly. See *Photii Biblioth.* cod. 3. p. m. 7. And I have little doubt but that the Jockos or small orangoutangs are of this pygmy race of men.

The same spirit of unbelief in the variety of nature's works appears to have possessed some of the authors of antiquity, particularly Strabo, who rejects, as fabulous, what several authors, whom he names, had related of extraordinary varieties of our species that were to be seen in India; such as the . . . men with eyes in their breast; the . . . men with one leg. Lib. 15. p. m. 489. and lib. 2. p. 48. But even such stories we ought not rashly to reject, as absolutely incredible, especially such of them as agree with modern accounts. Now, Sir Walter Raleigh has told us that he was informed of a people in South America who had their eyes in their breasts; and an Esquimaux girl, who was taken prisoner by the French in Canada, after she had learned to speak French, related that she had seen a whole nation of men with but one leg. This story is told both by Charlevoix, in his account of Canada, and by the author of *Telliamed,* p. 254; who adds that the girl, after having been several times examined and reexamined, stood constantly to the truth of the story. In short, a modest inquirer into nature will set no other bound to the variety of her productions than that which Aristotle has set, in that famous maxim of his, adopted, I see, by Mr. Buffon. *Quicquid fieri potest, fit. Everything, that can exist, does exist;* and everything can exist that does not imply a contradiction. We ought, therefore, to listen to credible evidence concerning the existence of any animal, however strange, unless we can take upon us to pronounce decisively, that it is impossible by nature that such an animal should exist.

Bibliographical Note

THE MOST IMPORTANT ITEMS for understanding the Scottish moralists are of course their own works. A very useful bibliography of the main works of the eight men considered and presented in this volume is provided by Gladys Bryson, *Man and Society: The Scottish Inquiry of the Eighteenth Century* (Princeton, N. J.: Princeton University Press, 1945), at pp. 275–79. (Bryson's book itself is a reliable study of the Scots.) A much more extensive and painstaking bibliography of the works of the eight and of their contemporaries and successors in "Scottish philosophy" is offered by T. E. Jessop, *A Bibliography of David Hume and of Scottish Philosophy* (London: A. Brown and Sons, 1938). (Jessop also includes numerous secondary references.) I do not aspire to rival Jessop or even Bryson. Rather, the present paragraph is intended simply to aid the interested reader who has little or no familiarity with the Scottish moralists to become acquainted with their work and to get to the heart of it as soon as may be. In Hutcheson's case, his *A System of Moral Philosophy*, 2 vols.; (Glasgow and London, 1755), is a comprehensive exposition of his outlook. (Despite its publication date of 1755, however, it may not render Hutcheson's final views on all matters. See William R. Scott, *Francis Hutcheson* [Cambridge: The University Press, 1900], pp. 244–46.) Adam Smith's *The Theory of Moral Sentiments* (London: G. Bell and Sons, 1892) and *The Wealth of Nations* are of course indispensable. I have used and referred to J. R. McCulloch's edition of the latter work (Edinburgh: Charles and Adam Black, 1863), but the Modern Library edition, edited by E. Cannan (New York, 1937), is more widely available. Thomas Reid's *Works*, edited by W. Hamilton (2 vols.; Edinburgh, 1863), will yield something to the sociologist prepared to examine them carefully and read them selectively. Adam Ferguson is best represented by his *Principles of Moral and Political Science* (2 vols.; Edinburgh, 1792), a far better book on the whole, it appears to me, than his *Essay on the History of Civil*

Society (8th ed.; Philadelphia, 1819), which contains a number of fine passages but not much more. (His *History of the Progress and Termination of the Roman Republic* [5 vols.; Edinburgh, 1825], well known in its time, may be mentioned incidentally as indicating his strong historical interests.) Dugald Stewart's writings are brought together in his *Collected Works*, edited by W. Hamilton (10 vols.; Edinburgh: Constable and Co., 1854–58). (An eleventh volume of translations of quotations from foreign languages in the previous ten was published in 1860.) Stewart is likely to be sociologically relevant, if not inspired (though he sometimes transcends himself), almost anywhere. His titles or labels for things can be deceptive and it is accordingly the more necessary to study his volumes attentively. David Hume's *Treatise of Human Nature*, edited by T. H. Green and T. H. Grose (2 vols.; London: Longmans, Green, 1898), is the most difficult of his books but certainly rewarding. His *Essays*, edited by T. H. Green and T. H. Grose (2 vols.; London: Longmans, Green and Co., 1875), are not always profound, but they are nearly always shrewd and likely to be stimulating to a sociologist. His *History of England* (6 vols.; New York: Harper and Bros., 1879), is still astonishingly readable and often suggestive. Kames is well enough revealed in his *Essays on the Principles of Morality and Natural Religion* (Anon.) (Edinburgh, 1751) and in his *Sketches of the History of Man* (3 vols.; Edinburgh, 1813). Much of what is significant in Monboddo is afforded in the first volume of his *Of the Origin and Progress of Language* (2nd ed.; Edinburgh, 1774). Anyone concerned with the Scottish moralists would be unwise not to read with close attention Bernard Mandeville's *The Fable of the Bees*, edited by F. B. Kaye (2 vols.; Oxford: Clarendon Press, 1924).

Secondary materials are very considerable. I mention a strictly limited number of items that I have found in some way helpful. The Scottish social background is presented in Henry G. Graham's *The Social Life of Scotland in the Eighteenth Century* (London, A. and C. Black, Ltd., 1937). A sketch of modern Scottish history is afforded in George S. Pryde's *Scotland from 1603 to the Present Day* (London: T. Nelson and Sons, Ltd., 1962), which has a good selective bibliography. Biographical and critical studies bulk large. William R. Scott's biographical and critical *Francis Hutcheson* has already been mentioned. The same author's *Adam*

Smith as Student and Professor (Glasgow: Jackson, Son and Co., 1937), is detailed enough on Smith's early life to satisfy the most consuming curiosity. Charles R. Fay's *Adam Smith and the Scotland of his Day* (Cambridge: Cambridge University Press, 1956), is a scholar's notebook on its topic, and at some points quite interesting. John Rae's biography of Smith (originally, 1895) has recently been reprinted with a lengthy introduction by Jacob Viner, mainly designed "to identify errors, omissions, ambiguities, uncertainties in the information Rae presents." Thus Viner in his "Guide" to John Rae, *Life of Adam Smith* (New York: Augustus M. Kelley, Bookseller, 1965), p. 14. Two worthwhile studies of Ferguson are William C. Lehmann's *Adam Ferguson and the Beginnings of Modern Sociology* (New York: Columbia University Press, 1930), and David Kettler's *The Social and Political Thought of Adam Ferguson* (Columbus: Ohio State University Press, 1965). Still worth reading for its fine grasp of a number of essentials in the sociology of Smith and Ferguson is Hermann Huth's *Soziale und Individualistische Auffassung im Achtzehnten Jahrhundert, vornehmlich bei Adam Smith und Adam Ferguson* (Leipzig: Duncker and Humblot, 1907). For Hume, Ernest C. Mossner's *Life of David Hume* (Austin: University of Texas Press, 1954), is biographically valuable although not greatly revealing about his work—nor, in fairness, is it really intended to be the latter. A clear exposition of points often of much interest to the sociologist is afforded by John B. Stewart, *The Moral and Political Philosophy of David Hume* (New York: Columbia University Press, 1963). J. B. Black, *The Art of History: A Study of Four Great Historians of the Eighteenth Century* (London: Methuen and Co., 1926), has a very readable discussion of Hume as historian. Friedrich Meinecke, *Die Entstehung des Historismus* (2 vols.; Munich and Berlin: R. Oldenbourg, 1936), is valuable not only for its commentaries in volume one (pp. 209–47 and 281–88) on the work of Hume and Ferguson but throughout both its volumes for its brilliant treatment of the phenomenon, so important for the Scots, of unintended social outcomes of individual actions. Dugald Stewart's writing on his fellow Scots should be mentioned. In his *Collected Works*, edited by W. Hamilton (10 vols.; Edinburgh, 1854–58), I, 427–84, Stewart treats "the metaphysical philosophy of Scotland," not in an inordinately revealing, yet in an interesting fashion. Volume ten of the *Collected Works* (same edition), presents Stewart's bio-graphical memoirs of Adam Smith and Thomas Reid (as well as of the historian, William Robertson) and is prefixed by a long memoir of Stewart himself by John Veitch. Again among older books, Alexander F. Tytler's *Memoirs of the Life and Writings of Henry Home of Kames* (2nd ed., 3 vols.; Edinburgh, 1814), con-tains useful material. William Knight's *Lord Monboddo and Some of His Contemporaries* (London: J. Murray, 1900), consists mostly of correspondence, preceded by an informative introduction by Knight. One more set of sketches of our eight men is provided by Henry G. Graham's *Scottish Men of Letters in the Eighteenth Century* (London: A. and C. Black, 1901). Graham writes with a light touch, but he is discerning and sensible. Two other critical works may be referred to. Volume two of Leslie Stephen's *History of English Thought in the Eighteenth Century* (New York: Har-court, Brace and World, 1962) is of mixed quality. It has many able comments. But its rather depreciative view (II, 65), of Smith's *Theory of Moral Sentiments* seems to me untenable. Furthermore, while Hume undoubtedly had his limitations as a historian, it strikes me as equally beyond doubt that Stephen (II, 154–57) exaggerates them. And Stephen (II, 181–82) too readily dismisses Ferguson, possibly because he may not have looked beyond the *Essay on the History of Civil Society*. Finally, Henry T. Buckle remains stimulating on the subject of the Scots. His *History of Civilization in England* (New York: Hearst's International Library, 1913) vol. II, Part II, chap. 6 examines "the Scotch intellect during the eighteenth century." Buckle is particularly good on the method of economics.

Of men close to the circle of our eight, John Millar is one of the most interesting. Millar's life and work are resumed in a way significant for all the Scottish moralists by William C. Lehmann in *John Millar of Glasgow* (Cambridge: Cambridge University Press, 1960). (Lehmann reprints Millar's book on rank and others of the latter's writings.) James Slotkin's *Readings in Early Anthropology* (Chicago: Aldine, 1965), pp. 412–60, gives numerous quotations from "the Scotch School," including material from the works of Ferguson, Kames, Monboddo, Smith, and Dugald Stewart, and also from James Beattie, James Dunbar, John Millar, William Robertson, and Gilbert Stuart.